CATALOGUE OF GREEK COINS.

THE PTOLEMIES, KINGS OF EGYPT.

BY REGINALD STUART POOLE,
CORRESPONDENT OF THE INSTITUTE OF FRANCE.

WITH THIRTY-TWO PLATES.

1883.

Copyright © 2013 Read Books Ltd.
This book is copyright and may not be
reproduced or copied in any way without
the express permission of the publisher in writing

British Library Cataloguing-in-Publication Data
A catalogue record for this book is available from the
British Library

Reginald Stuart Poole

Reginald Stuart Poole was an English archaeologist, numismatist and orientalist. He was born on 27th January 1832, in London, England – the son of the Reverend Edward Poole, a well-known bibliophile. His parents became estranged during his early childhood however, and his mother, Sophia Lane Poole, took her sons to Egypt to live with her brother, the Orientalist, Edward William Lane.

During their seven-year residence in Cairo from 1842 to 1849, Lane Poole wrote *The Englishwoman in Egypt*, while her son was imbibing an early taste for Egyptian antiquities. He began his Egyptian studies with relish, examining private collections in Cairo and Alexandria, and twice travelling up the Nile. Before he was seventeen, Reginald had contributed a series of articles to the *Literary Gazette which were* republished in 1851 as '*Horae Aegyptiacae*', or, '*The Chronology of Ancient Egypt*'. In 1852, Reginald became an assistant with the British Museum, and was assigned to the department of coins and medals, of which in 1870, he became keeper. In that capacity he did work of the highest value, alike as a writer, teacher and administrator. In 1882 he was further responsible for founding the 'Egypt Exploration Fund', and in 1884 for starting the 'Society of English Medallists'. This latter society was founded with the hope of reviving the design and production of cast medals.

In his personal life, Reginald Stuart Poole married Eliza Christina Forlonge, daughter of William Forlone on 29th October, 1870. The couple had four children together.

Some of Poole's best work was done in his articles for the 9th edition of the *Encyclopædia Britannica*, on Egypt, Hieroglyphics and Numismatics; he also wrote for **Smith's** 'Dictionary of the Bible', and published volumes dealing with his special subjects. He was also the driving force in the production of British Museum catalogues of Greek coins, which still remain the standard reference set, and whose publication is the foundation-stone of modern Greek numismatics. In 1873 he published the first volume (on Italy), which was followed by three further volumes (Syria, 1878; Ptolemies, 1883; Roman Egypt, 1892).

Poole's principal contribution to Egyptology was his aforementioned founding of the 'Egypt Exploration Fund' (in 1882), in order to promote excavation and study of ancient Egypt. Poole devoted most of his spare time and energy to the fund, and was its honorary secretary (1882–5) and later its vice-president (1885–95). Many of his decisions are in retrospect considered misguided though, such as favouring Edouard Naville over the more meticulous archaeologist Flinders Petrie. His relations with the latter were for a time cool, after Petrie had blamed Poole for the fund's poor administration, which was largely owing to Poole's being seriously overworked.

In 1883, Poole was appointed by the Royal Academy as a lecturer on Greek, Egyptian and medallic art, a post which he held for the next two years. He was also awarded an honorary degree from Cambridge University in the same year. In 1889, he succeeded Sir Charles Newton as the Yates professor of archaeology at University College London. After this successful academic career, on 31st January 1893, he retired from the British Museum and in 1894, resigned his professorship because of failing health.

Reginald Stuat Poole died of heart disease, at his home at 2 Gledstanes Road, West Kensington, London, on 8th February 1895 – at the age of sixty-three.

PREFACE.

This volume of the Catalogue of Greek Coins describes the money of the Ptolemies. It forms part of the series devoted to the coinage of Alexander's successors, of which the Catalogue of the Coins of the Seleucidae has already appeared.

The difficulties of the production of this work have been very great; but they have been lightened by generous aid which is here gratefully acknowledged. M. Revillout, of the Egyptian Department in the Louvre, has afforded valuable information on disputed points of chronology, and M. J. P. Six, of Amsterdam, on the order of the coinage, while Mr. Head and Professor Gardner have assisted in the revision. To M. Feuardent, of Paris, the author's thanks are due for affording him the opportunity of examining and publishing rare coins, particularly from the collection of M. Demetrio, of Alexandria, whose liberality in the matter deserves especial acknowledgment.

REGINALD STUART POOLE.

BRITISH MUSEUM.
November, 1882.

CONTENTS.

	PAGE
PREFACE	v
LIST OF PLATES	xi

INTRODUCTION :—
§ 1. ARRANGEMENT.
    Principles of Classification xiii
    Ptolemy I. First Coinage, not here represented. Second, Attic. Third, Attic and Rhodian. Fourth, Rhodian. Gold stater of Cyrene. Local Coinage of Ptolemy. Monetary reform under Ptolemy as king. Phoenician standard finally adopted for gold and silver. Coins of Ptolemy as king. Discussion of earliest Ptolemaïc regal coins. Group with title king; mostly with Δ. Group with title Soter, of Phoenicia, struck under Ptolemy II. and III. Title Soter dates from 25th year of Ptolemy II. B.C. 261-0. Coins with Δ, partly of Philadelphus, his First Coinage; partly of Ptolemy I., his Sixth. Coins without Δ, Fifth Coinage of Ptolemy I. Coinage of Cyrenaïca discussed; of Ptolemy I. and II; Magas governor, king, a second time governor . . . - . xv
    Ptolemy II. First General Coinage. Monetary change in middle of reign. Cyprus, Second Coinage. Buckler as symbol. Phoenicia, First and Second Coinages. Title Soter. New copper coinage of Phoenicia and Egypt xxxii
    Ptolemy II. and Arsinoë II. with Ptolemy I. and Berenice I. Medallic issues of Philadelphus. Coins with four portraits. Later issues xxxviii
    Arsinoë II. Variety of types. Later issues . . xxxix

CONTENTS.

	PAGE
Ptolemy III. Cyprus, First Coinage ; Second. Phoenicia, First Coinage ; Second ; Third. Egypt, First Coinage ; Second. Cornucopiæ as symbol. Cyrenaïca	xlii
Berenice II. Import of title βασίλισσα. Cyrenaïca	xlv
Note on coins of Cyrene with inscription KOINON	xlvii
Ptolemy IV. Cyprus, Ordinary currency; Dionysiac silver. Phoenicia, First Coinage ; Second. Egypt.	xlix
Arsinoë III.	liii
Ptolemy V., Epiphanes. Cyprus, beginning of series of dated tetradrachms; their arrangement. Coins of Epiphanes, Cyprus ; Phoenicia ; Egypt ; Cyrenaïca. Types	liii
Ptolemy VI., Philometor. Regency of Cleopatra I., Cyprus; Egypt; Cyrenaïca. Classification of Cyprian currencies of Philometor and Physcon. Mint-letters ΓΑ used for Paphos and at Alexandria. Regency of Eulaeus and Lenaeus; Cyprus; Egypt. Usurpation of Antiochus IV.; Egypt. Joint reign of Philometor and Physcon, Cyprus ; Egypt ; Cyrenaïca. Sole reign of Philometor, Cyprus ; Phoenicia ; Egypt	lix
Ptolemy VI. and Ptolemy VII., Eupator	lxvi
Ptolemy VIII., Euergetes II. (Physcon), Cyrenaïca. Alexandrian mint. Sole reign after Philometor, Cyprus; Egypt. Coregency, Cyprus; Egypt	lxviii
Ptolemy VIII. and Ptolemy IX., Philopator II.	lxxii
Uncertain Coins of, and anterior to, the period of Ptolemy VI. and VIII. Uncertain of about time of Physcon. Coins of an Era	lxxiii
Ptolemy X., Soter II. (Lathyrus), Ptolemy XI., Alexander I., and Ptolemy (Apion) King of Cyprus. Cyprus, Lathyrus ; Alexander ; first periods ; Lathyrus, second reign. Egypt, Lathyrus; Alexander. Double dates of Cleopatra III. and Alexander. Cyrenaïca; Lathyrus, Apion	lxxvi
Ptolemy XIII., Neus Dionysus (Auletes)	lxxx

CONTENTS.

	PAGE
Ptolemy, King of Cyprus	lxxxi
Coins of Successors of Auletes. Cyprus, Cleopatra VII. ; Ptolemy XV. and Arsinoë IV? Egypt, Cleopatra VII.; Ptolemy XVI.	lxxxii
§ 2. MINTS :—	
Cyprus ; Phoenicia; Egypt ; Cyrenaica ; Asia Minor? and doubtful.	lxxxv
§ 3. WEIGHTS:—	
Gold and Silver; Copper	xc
TABLE I. STEMMA PTOLEMAEORUM	xciii
TABLE II. CHRONOLOGY	xciv
TABLE III. MINTS AND DATES	xcvi
Ptolemaeus I., Soter I.	1
Magas, Governor of Cyrenaica	11
Ptolemaeus I. and Ptolemaeus II.	13
Ptolemaeus II., Philadelphus	24
Magas, Governor	37
Magas, King	38
Magas, Governor, second time	38
Ptolemaeus II. and Arsinoë II. with Ptolemaeus I. and Berenice I.	40
Arsinoë II., Philadelphos	42
Ptolemaeus III., Euergetes I.	46
Berenice II., Euergetis	59
Berenice II. and Ptolemaeus III.	61
Ptolemaeus IV., Philopator I.	62
Arsinoë III., Philopator	67
Arsinoë III. and Ptolemaeus IV.	67
Ptolemaeus V., Epiphanes	68
Ptolemaeus VI., Philometor I.	78
Cleopatra I., Regent	78
Eulaeus and Lenaeus, Regents	80
Antiochus IV., Epiphanes	81
Ptolemaeus VIII., Euergetes II.	82
Ptolemaeus VI. and Ptolemaeus VIII.	82
Ptolemaeus VI., alone	83
Ptolemaeus VI. and Ptolemaeus VII., Eupator	87

CONTENTS.

	PAGE
Ptolemaeus VIII., Euergetes II.	88
Ptolemaeus VIII. with Cleopatra II. and III.	95
Ptolemaeus VIII. with Ptolemaeus IX., Philopator II.	96
Ptolemaeus VIII. ?	100
Coins dated by an uncertain Era	101
Ptolemaeus X., Soter II. :—	
With Cleopatra III.	104
Alone	108
Ptolemaeus XI., Alexander I.	110
With Cleopatra III.	112
Alone	113
Ptolemaeus X., last reign	114
Ptolemaeus (Apion) King of Cyrene ?	114
Ptolemaeus XIII., Neus Dionysus :—	
First Reign	115
Second Reign	116
Ptolemaeus, King of Cyprus	118
Ptolemaeus XV. and Arsinoë IV ?	121
Cleopatra VII., Philopator	122
Cleopatra VII. and Ptolemaeus XVI., Caesar	122
Ptolemaeus XVI.	124

INDEXES.

Index I., Geographical	125
Index II., Types	127
Index III., Symbols	130
Index IV., Kings and Governors	132
Table of Weights	134
Table of Measures	136

LIST OF PLATES.

- I. Ptolemaeus Soter as Governor.
- II. Ptolemaeus Soter.
- III. Ptolemaeus Soter and Ptolemaeus Philadelphus.
- IV. Ptolemaeus Philadelphus.
- V. Ptolemaeus Philadelphus.
- VI. Ptolemaeus Philadelphus, Magas.
- VII. Ptolemaeus Philadelphus and Family.
- VIII. Arsinoë Philadelphos.
- IX. Ptolemaeus Euergetes.
- X. Ptolemaeus Euergetes.
- XI. Ptolemaeus Euergetes.
- XII. Ptolemaeus Euergetes.
- XIII. Ptolemaeus Euergetes, Berenice II.
- XIV. Ptolemaeus Philopator.
- XV. Ptolemaeus Philopator, Arsinoë Philopator.
- XVI. Ptolemaeus Epiphanes.
- XVII. Ptolemaeus Epiphanes.
- XVIII. Ptolemaeus Epiphanes, Ptolemaeus Philometor, and Cleopatra I.
- XIX. Ptolemaeus Philometor.
- XX. Ptolemaeus Philometor.
- XXI. Ptolemaeus Euergetes II.
- XXII. Ptolemaeus Euergetes II.
- XXIII. Ptolemaeus Euergetes II. and Cleopatra II. and III.
- XXIV. Ptolemaeus Euergetes II., &c.
- XXV. Coins of an Era.
- XXVI. Ptolemaeus Soter II. and Cleopatra III.
- XXVII. Ptolemaeus Soter II., Ptolemaeus Alexander I.
- XXVIII. Ptolemaeus Alexander I. and Cleopatra III., Ptolemaeus Soter II., Ptolemaeus Apion.

XXIX. Ptolemaeus Neus Dionysus, Ptolemaeus King of Cyprus.
XXX. Ptolemaeus King of Cyprus, Cleopatra VII., Ptolemaeus Cæsar.
XXXI. Coins with portraits, not Egyptian currency, (1) Arsinoë, of Ephesus; (2) Berenice II., of Marathus; (3) Philopator I? of Marathus; (4) Neus Dionysus, of Ascalon; (5) Ptolemaeus XIV., of Ascalon; (6) Cleopatra VII., of Ascalon; (7) Cleopatra VII. and Antonius of Antioch.
XXXII. Coins (no. 1 excepted) not in the British Museum.

COINAGE OF THE PTOLEMIES.

INTRODUCTION.

I. ARRANGEMENT.

Difficulty of classification.
No series of coins struck by the successors of Alexander is more difficult to class than that of the Ptolemies, no one indeed so difficult except the less important issues of the Pergamene kings.

Chronological data.
The regular silver coinage presents the head of the first Ptolemy, and the name common to him and his descendants. The gold and exceptional silver money bears the portraits of Ptolemy I. and of other kings and queens, and sometimes their special titles, and the names of the queens; but the gold coins, as a class, are by no means struck in the lifetimes of the sovereigns whose portraits are seen on them. The copper money has almost always heads derived from mythology. There is no reckoning from an era, like that of the Seleucidae, save in the issue of a foreign dependency which does not illustrate the ordinary coinage. Most of the silver coins, indeed nearly all those of the later Ptolemies, are dated by the regnal years of the kings under whom they were struck, and it is upon their evidence that the chronological sequence of the whole coinage in all metals can be approximately determined.

The geographical indications are even less definite than the chronological. The mints of Cyprus and Phoenicia are certain, but those of Egypt, and most of those of the Cyrenaïca, can only be described as unattributed to mints, but falling within the territorial limits which the fabric and the provenance indicate. The money of Asia Minor occupies a middle place, a few mints being probably ascertained.

Geographical data.

It has thus been possible to arrange the coins in the Catalogue in historical order, usually in the succession of reigns, but sometimes under coinages covering several reigns, there being cases in which it is convenient or necessary to treat a coinage as a whole. These coinages are however exceptional, and may thus be specially treated.

Arrangement, historical under reigns, or coinages.

Farther, each series is divided into geographical groups. It is necessary here to explain the main principles of arrangement, which are not so obvious as those based on the succession of reigns.

Subdivisions, geographical under reigns, or coinages.

The main geographical groups of the Ptolemaïc coinage are those of (1) Cyprus, (2) Asia Minor, (3) Phoenicia, (4) Egypt, and (5) Cyrenaïca. The coinage of Cyprus, as the most complete in chronological indications, has been placed at the head. The group of Asia Minor is merely a temporary issue of the first and second Ptolemies, best placed after the mints of Cyprus. The important currency of Phoenicia, characterized by distinctive peculiarities of style and manner of issue, and second only to the Cyprian in historical indications, holds the next place. The Egyptian money, historically and artistically inferior, follows. The money of the

Geographical groups.

Cyprus.

Asia Minor.

Phoenicia.

Egypt.

Cyrenaica.

Deviations from order under Ptolemy I. and II.

Cyrenaïca has a very special character throughout, which marks it as the least connected with the sister currencies: it thus closes the order. With the first and second Ptolemies it is not possible to adhere strictly to this system. For instance, Ptolemy II. first coined for the whole empire, except the Cyrenaïca, a uniform currency. In the middle of his reign the Phoenician issues on a new system break this uniformity. Consequently they are placed after the general coinage, and before that of the Cyrenaïca.

The arrangement of the Catalogue is thus first historical, and secondly geographical. The grounds of the arrangement have now to be stated, under the historical divisions, the reader being referred to the section on *Mints* for the grounds of geographical identification.

Coins of Ptolemy I., Soter.

Ptolemy I. Periods of reign.

The rule of the first Ptolemy may be divided into five periods, the dates of which, like nearly all in this volume, are taken from Lepsius's *Königsbuch der Aegypter* (Syn. Taf. p. 9):—

			B.C.
1. Ptolemy,	Governor for Philip Aridaeus	. .	323–316
2. ,,	,, Alexander IV.	. .	316–311
3. ,,	Independent during Interregnum	.	311–305
4. ,,	King	.	305–284
(5. ,,	Ex-King	.	284–283 [?])

Six coinages.

Ptolemy seems to have struck no less than six coinages, besides unimportant local issues:—

	Types of silver.	Name.	Wt.
1.	of Alexander the Great.	Philip (Aridaeus).	Attic.
2.	,, Alex.IV.,rev.of Alex.Gr.	Alexander (IV.).	,,
3.	,, Alexander IV.	,,	Attic and Rhodian.
4.	,, ,,	,,	Rhodian.
5.	,, Ptolemaeus.	Ptolemaeus.	Phoenician.
6.	,, ,,	,,	,,

The First Coinage is of gold and silver on the Attic Standard.

First Coinage.
Ptolemy governor for Philip Aridaeus, B.C. 323–316.

As Ptolemy acknowledges Aridaeus as king in his hieroglyphic inscriptions, it is reasonable to suppose some of that sovereign's money to have been struck by the governor while ruling in his name. The coins of Aridaeus are found in Egypt. One of his gold staters may be attributed with probability to a mint of that country. (Usual types: ΔI, and thunderbolt in field of rev.). It is, however, at present impossible to separate the issues of Ptolemy during this period from those of the other generals. The whole coinage of Aridaeus is therefore classed under that of the kings of Macedon.

The coins which bear the name of Alexander IV., commonly called Alexander Aegus by modern writers, must cover the whole time from the end of the reign of Aridaeus until the accession of Ptolemy as king, the money bearing the name Ptolemy without the royal title being local and unimportant.

The Second Coinage, so far as we know of silver tetradrachms

Second Coinage.
(Pl. i. 1.)
Tetradrachms, rev. of Alex. the Great.
Attic standard.
Ptolemy governor for Alex. IV., 316–311.

only, undoubtedly stands next in order to the money of Philip Aridaeus. The weight is still Attic, and the types retain the reverse-type of Alexander the Great and Aridaeus, the seated Zeus Aëtophoros, with a new obverse-type, that of Alexander IV., the head of Alexander the Great with the horn of Ammon, clad in the elephant's skin and aegis. This obverse-type is thus similar to the well-known one of the second coinage of Lysimachus, in which the horned Alexander is bare-headed. The fabric of the coinage of Aridaeus, and that of Alexander the Great, struck during his reign and shortly after (Müller, Numismatique d'Alexandre le Grand, Classe IV.), is maintained. The thunderbolt, which is constant in the field of the reverse, may be regarded as Ptolemy's badge, as it occurs in combination with the eagle as the general reverse-type of regal Ptolemaïc coins, with the exception of limited groups, most of which are personally commemorative. It is thus evident that these coins form a first departure from the types of Alexander the Great and Aridaeus, and the true beginning of the Ptolemaïc coinage, introducing a new obverse-type and a constant special badge. The moneyer's letters OP, it may be noticed, are found in this currency (no. 1), and that of Alexander the Great. This

Struck in Egypt? coinage was probably issued in Egypt, at the first the most secure part of Ptolemy's dominions. The scantiness of the series would imply a short period of issue, as the greater quantity of that with the new reverse type of Alexander IV. would suggest a longer one. Moreover a remarkable monogram of a moneyer ⊕ is common to the larger group and to Alexander's money, and therefore we cannot widely separate the two.*

The Third and Fourth Coinages present in the silver money the same obverse-type as the Second, but the reverse bears a new type, the figure of the Macedonian Athena Alkis, with the eagle on the thunderbolt in the field, which was Ptolemy's badge. The fabric is less thick and consequently more spread than that of

---

* A remarkable coin procured in Egypt by the Rev. Greville J. Chester is of Phoenician weight, as if subsequent to the Fourth Coinage (p. xviii.), but while presenting the head of Alexander of the Third and Fourth Coinages, has the reverse of the Second, with however the Ptolemaïc eagle in the field, as in the Third and Fourth. It is perhaps of a local coinage in Phoenicia. (Pl. xxxii. 2.)

the Second Coinage. In type these coinages, the Third and Fourth, are the same: they are distinguished by their weight.

The Third Coinage shows a farther departure from the system before in use, by the adoption of the Rhodian standard for its drachms, whereas the tetradrachms are still Attic. It would appear, from the comparison of its monograms and letters with those of the Fourth Coinage, that, so far as we know, it was wholly struck in Cyprus. Possibly it was local, and if so, for a time current with the Fourth Coinage issued elsewhere; but it may, though locally struck, have been intended to supply the monetary needs of the whole state. Its peculiarity of a double standard of weight, Attic and Rhodian, would be due to its place as a link between the wholly Attic Second Coinage and the wholly Rhodian Fourth, unless the Rhodian drachms were introduced to exchange with tetradrachms in the same standard of the Fourth Coinage elsewhere in circulation.

Third Coinage. (Pl. i. 2–4.) Tetradrachms, Attic standard; Drachms, Rhodian. Ptolemy gov. for Alex. IV., B.C. 316-311, or Interregnum, 311-305. Wholly struck in Cyprus (?) within interval, 315-306.

In the Third Coinage, copper money occurs with the head of Alexander the Great, horned and uncovered, and the regular Ptolemaïc reverse, now appearing for the first time as a separate type, the eagle on the thunderbolt.

Copper.

This coinage, which is a peculiarly transitional series, seems from its scantiness to have been soon abandoned.

Transitional.

The Fourth Coinage is of Rhodian weight, tetradrachms alone being known, and the Attic standard thus disappears from Ptolemy's coinage. It will be seen, that under the Fifth Coinage the Rhodian weight is in turn supplanted by the Phoenician, after gradually descending to which the standard was fixed for the rest of the rule of the Ptolemies.

Fourth Coinage. (Pl. i. 5–8.) Tetradrachms, Rhodian: Δ on some: Ptolemy governor for Alex. IV., or Interregnum.

ARRANGEMENT.

This natural order is confirmed by the appearance on the aegis of Alexander, in some coins of the Fourth Coinage, of the letter Δ, which on the coinage here classed as the Sixth of Ptolemy I. and the First of Philadelphus, is seen behind Ptolemy's ear. This can only be an engraver's signature, and the two coinages must therefore be near together in date. It might have been thought best to place the coins of Alexander IV. with the Δ at the end of the Fourth Coinage, but it is not certain that the letter is characteristic of a special issue, as in the case of the Sixth Coinage of Ptolemy I. and First of Philadelphus, in which it is seen on all gold coins large enough to admit it, and on all silver coins, and farther it cannot be determined whether it was not sometimes in the die, but too near the edge to appear in a coin; besides which, it is also often hard to distinguish the letter from a scale of the aegis.

Δ engraver's mark.

This coinage was probably issued throughout Ptolemy's dominions. It contains coins which appear to be of Cyprus, and others probably of the Cyrenaïca. The money of Cyprus presents a monogram which it can scarcely be doubted indicates Paphos and another which may indicate Salamis, and, like the supposed Cyprian money of the Third Coinage, it has a special copper issue. But the Fourth Coinage contains far more distinctly Cyprian coins than the Third. Its silver bears some symbols found on later coins of Cyprus, but not, with very rare exceptions, of other parts of the Ptolemaïc dominions, the helmet, the aplustre, and the star. These three symbols may not improbably indicate three great offices, those of strategos, admiral, and high-priest of the island, all held at once by a strategos under the Ptolemies, as we learn from an inscription. (Boeckh, C.I.G. 2622.) It may be conjectured that the strategos was *ex officio* admiral and

Fourth Coinage general.

Cyprus, within interval B.C. 315-306.

Paphos, Salamis?

Symbols of offices of strategos of Cyprus?

high-priest. These symbols cannot be assigned to any towns especially; they are not local, but general.

There are two tetradrachms here attributed to the Cyrenaïca,
Cyrenaïca, within interval B.C. 308-305, Magas governor; tetradrachms. of which one (no. 55) bears two monograms occurring on a gold coin of that province, struck by Ptolemy as king (no. 93); the other (no. 54) three monograms found on two similar gold coins, one monogram being common to both, the other two being found, one on each of the pieces compared.* As Ptolemy lost the Cyrenaïca in B.C. 312, and did not regain it until B.C. 308, he could have struck money there in the name of Alexander IV., either between the years B.C. 316-312 or B.C. 308-305. It is evident, from the occurrence of the monograms of his regal coinage, that the issue, as far as it is known to us, belongs to the later interval; and it is not impossible that it was continued after his accession as king.

A remarkable autonomous coin of Cyrene struck under Ptolemy's rule should be here mentioned. It is the gold stater
Gold stater, with name of Ptolemy. with Alexander's types, formerly only represented in the French National Collection, but of which a second specimen has lately been acquired by the British Museum.

The description is as follows, made out from the two specimens:

Obv. Head of Pallas r.

Rev. ΚΥΡΑΝΑΙΟΙ
ΠΤΟΛΕΜΑΙΩ Nike holding wreath and standard, l.;
to l. ΕΥ (Pl. xxxii. 1).

Unfortunately neither specimen is complete in the ends of the words. The last letter but one of the first word may be either O or Ω in both specimens: in that of the British Museum it looks like Ω altered to O in the die. The last letter, only seen in the Paris specimen, may be I or the first limb of N. Again, there is no certainty that

* The two gold coins last mentioned are in the possession of M. Feuardent.

Ω ends the second word; it could have been followed by an *iota subscriptum*. The true reading may be discovered by comparing the autonomous coins of Cyrene of the period immediately preceding. In them the ethnic name is always ΚΥΡΑΝΑΙΟΝ, and the magistrates' occur in the genitive with the Doric form in Ω. (Müller, Numismatique de l'Ancienne Afrique, p. 113, on the second point.) This evidence would give us ΚΥΡΑΝΑΙΟΝ ΠΤΟΛΕΜΑΙΩ. A similar inscription is found on a remarkable tetradrachm of the usual types of the Third and Fourth Coinages, in the Demetrio Collection, kindly communicated to me by M. Feuardent: it reads ΑΛΕΞΑΝΔΡΕΙΟΝ ΠΤΟΛΕΜΑΙ[ΟΥ?] (Pl. xxxii. 3). While the form is grammatically similar, there is a difference of meaning: the coin is "of Alexander," not "of the Alexandrians," but this does not militate against the reading in the case of the stater of Cyrene. The one is a civic coinage, the other a regal one. Ptolemy in both cases is the magistrate who controls or issues the coinage. Thus the coinage could be one in which the Cyrenaeans who issued it paid honour to Ptolemy, who thus allowed them a privilege of autonomy. This is quite consistent with the appearance on their late autonomous coins of the same magistrates' names as those which occur on Cyrenæan money of Ptolemy as king. (Cf. Müller, Num. de l'Anc. Afr., i., tab. 1. See Id., p. 53, 70, 71, iii. 189, on the whole question.)

This coin must have been issued before Ptolemy took the title of king; either during his first rule of the Cyrenaïca, B.C. 322–312, or his second, B.C. 308–305. The historical circumstances of each period are too much alike for us to be able to choose between them. In 322, as in 308, the rule of Ptolemy succeeded a local tyranny from which the Cyrenaeans must have rejoiced to escape. However anxious for autonomy, many citizens must have welcomed Ptolemy as a very different ruler from Thimbron, Ophellas, and Agathocles.

If we examine the series of gold coins issued during Ptolemy's rule in the Cyrenaïca bearing his name, we may find a clue to the period of issue. They show four distinct transitions of inscription, and two of type:—

1. Stater, Attic, Alex. the Great's types, **KYPANAION ? ΠΤΟΛΕΜΑΙΩ** magistr. **EY.** (p. xx.)

2. Hemi-stater „ Same types, **ΠΤΟΛΕΜΑΙΟΥ**, magistr. **EYΦPI.** (Müller, Suppl. p. 24, no. 359, A.)

3. Tetrobol „ Head of Ptolemy: Rev. of Alexander, **[ΣΩ]ΞΛΙΞΑΒ ΠΤΟΛΕΜΑΙΟΥ.** (Tables, p. 11.)

4. Didrachm, Phoenician, Ptolemy's types, **ΠΤΟΛΕΜΑΙΟΥ ΒΑΣΙΛΕΩΣ.** (Ibid.)

It can scarcely be doubted that the coin inscribed **ΠΤΟΛΕΜΑΙΟΥ** was issued during the Interregnum, after Ptolemy had recovered the Cyrenaïca, therefore B.C. 308-305. The name of Ptolemy could not appear on any earlier coin except as a magistrate, as might be the case with the first issue, where the people also appears in an equally prominent manner. If this classing be correct, the magistrate's name **EYΦPI** in the second issue compared with **EY** in the first, supported by the identity of type, would lead us to assign both to the same period. Should this be admitted, most probably Ptolemy, not the people, struck the first coin. The change from the earlier types to those of the reign of Ptolemy would thus be unbroken.

It will be necessary to recur to the subject of the coinage of the Cyrenaïca at the close of this section, where the whole currency of the dependency, from B.C. 305 to the accession of Berenice II. as Queen of Cyrene, will be examined.

ARRANGEMENT.

Period of Fourth Coinage, probably most part of interval B.C. 316-305.

The Fourth Coinage probably occupied the greater part of the periods during which Ptolemy was governor for young Alexander, and independent during the Interregnum. It is connected by the engraver's mark Δ with the money of Philadelphus, and by the remarkable moneyer's monogram ⊕ with that of Alexander the Great. The Second and Third Coinages were merely tentative, and the Third may have been local, preceding the Fourth in Cyprus only. On the other hand, the Fourth Coinage is shown by its importance to have had a long as well as wide existence; and thus it probably covered nearly the whole period from B.C. 316 to 305, and may for a time have been the silver currency of Ptolemy as king.

Second and Third Coinages tentative.

To the Interregnum may be classed without hesitation local copper money of Cyprus, bearing the name of Ptolemy unaccompanied by any title. One type is certainly of Paphos, another possibly of Salamis. The date of Ptolemy's attempted coinage of his own, craftily united with a special issue of the Cyprian cities, tyranny in the guise of autonomy, may be conjecturally placed late in the Interregnum (B.C. 311-305), but before Cyprus was lost for a few years (B.C. 306). This attribution in time would agree with that of the gold hemi-stater struck in the Cyrenaïca, having the same inscription, which was almost certainly issued between B.C. 308 and 305.

Local coinage with name of Ptolemy.
(Pl. i. 9, 10.)
Interregnum (B.C. 311-305).
Cyprus, Paphos, Salamis ?
Struck within interval, B.C. 311-306, towards close ?

It is evident that when Ptolemy had taken the title of king a reform in the coinage was speedily effected. All regal coins of the Ptolemies in gold and silver, from his downwards, were struck according to the Phoenician standard; and the last step in the depreciation of

Reform of coinage under Ptolemy as king.

weight was then reached. Towards the end of the monarchy there was a further descent, not in weight, but in purity of metal. In the new coinage, the copper money acquired greater importance, but it was not till the reign of Philadelphus that we have reason to suppose that it attained the high position it afterwards continued to hold.

Phoenician standard finally adopted for gold and silver.

Increased importance of copper.

That Ptolemy I. struck coins in his own name as king cannot be doubted. The analogy of his hieroglyphic inscriptions, which successively present the names of Philip Aridaeus, Alexander IV., and Ptolemy, each with the protocol of the Pharaohs, cannot be set aside, nor can the custom of the other kings who simultaneously assumed the diadem. What, however, can we assign to Ptolemy in the vast mass of silver money, issued for over two centuries and a half, which bears, with insignificant exceptions, his portrait, and in the majority the title king, in the minority the title Soter? To make our selection of Ptolemy's own regal coinage, we have two guides, style, and the presence of monograms and letters denoting moneyers common to the coinage of Alexander IV. and a portion of the Ptolemaic regal currency. The gold and silver coins of the earliest style fall into two great groups: (1) those with the inscription ΠΤΟΛΕΜΑΙΟΥ ΒΑΣΙΛΕΩΣ, the larger section of which has the engraver's mark Δ behind the king's ear, on all silver and all large gold coins; (2) with ΠΤΟΛΕΜΑΙΟΥ ΒΑΣΙΛΕΩΣ soon changed to ΠΤΟΛΕΜΑΙΟΥ ΣΩΤΗΡΟΣ, bearing the monograms, &c., of Phoenician and Palestinian coast-towns; both being the earlier coins of a series from the later of which they are clearly distinguishable. Of these, the first group, with the title king, is connected with the money bearing the name of Alexander IV. by the oc-

Determination of regal coins of Ptolemy I.

Earliest Ptolemaic regal coins, gold, silver.

Group with title king; mostly with Δ.

Group with king's style changed to Soter, of Phoenicia;

currence of the same moneyers' monograms, &c., and the reappearance of the engraver's mark Δ. The dates presented by the second group, with for the most part the title Soter, range from the 20th year to the 39th, of one reign, and as far as the 6th year of another reign immediately following. They would therefore be consistent with the reigns of Ptolemy I. and II., or Ptolemy II. and III.*

struck under Ptolemy II. and III. That, however, they were undoubtedly struck under Ptolemy II. and III. appears, from the issue at the same mints, by the same moneyers, in years of both reigns, of gold octadrachms of Arsinoë II., which fact forbids us to suppose the issue of any part of the series by Ptolemy I. It is to be remarked that one of the undated coins immediately anterior to this group (p. xxxiv.) presents K instead of Δ behind the king's ear. (Demetrio Coll., communicated by M. Feuardent: pl. xxxii. 4). It

Title Soter given to Ptolemy I. by Ptolemy II. in his 25th year, B.C. 261-0. may be added that the researches of M. Revillout have shown that the title Soter is first given to Ptolemy I. by Philadelphus in Egyptian official documents dated between his 22nd and 29th years. This is in accordance with the appearance of the title in lieu of that of king on the coins of the 25th year, which may thus be accepted as the actual date at which it was conferred (p. xxxv.). The attribution of these coins to the second and third Ptolemies is historically consistent, whereas the rule of the first in Phoenicia was too short and disturbed for the issue of a consecutive coinage of many years.

The group of coins of which the chief section is characterized **Coins of group with Δ. (Pl. iii.)** by the Δ has now to be noticed. Leaving out for the present the insignificant fraction wanting this sign, it is obvious that we cannot assign so large a class to Ptolemy.I.: yet we cannot deprive him of a fair share of it, or his rule as king

---

* The 39th year seems in excess of the reign of Philadelphus by one year; but this may be explained as due to a different mode of reckoning in Phoenicia and Egypt.

would be almost a blank in numismatics. Having assigned the small gold and copper corresponding to the large gold and silver with the Δ, by the occurrence of the same or similar monograms and letters of moneyers, in combination with those of mints, we are struck by the undoubted fact that this is a new general currency.

Mints of Asia Minor. We next note that it presents a long series of mints not represented in any earlier or later coinage, and which, since they are not of Cyprus, Phoenicia, or the Cyrenaïca, and cannot all be of Egypt, must in part be of Asia Minor, Europe being highly improbable, as the Ptolemies would have been careful to maintain Hellenic privileges. This conjecture seems confirmed by the appearance of the well-known monogram of Miletus, and other monograms equally suiting the maritime dominions of Philadelphus. If these attributions be correct, the

Coinage partly of Philadelphus: his First Coinage; coinage must have been in part struck by Philadelphus, Ptolemy I. not having had an opportunity of continuously coining money in Asia Minor. Thus it must be partly the First Coinage of Philadelphus, and

partly of Ptolemy I.: his Sixth Coinage. would seem also to be partly the Last or Sixth of Ptolemy I. The occurrence of a magistrate's monogram common to the Fourth Coinage (cf. p. 6, no. 54; p. 20, no. 56) is in favour of dating it in part before Philadelphus: so also is the sequence of the coins of the Cyrenaïca (p. 11, 12, 37, *seqq.*). It is also to be noticed that the Cyprian issues of Ptolemy's Fourth Coinage, and of that with the Δ, are connected by the copper money of the island, which will be seen to belong to the Fifth or intermediate coinage, this copper, *inter alia*, presenting monograms of both. There can therefore be no great distance of time between the latest issues with the types of Alexander IV., and the earliest of Ptolemy I. bearing the Δ, or the Fourth and Sixth Coinages.

The types of gold and silver are the head of Ptolemy and the eagle on the thunderbolt: the obverse of the copper presents on the larger coins the head of Zeus Ammon, on the smaller that of Alexander in the elephant's skin.

It is necessary now to discuss the limited class of silver without the Δ, which does not belong to this section, and forms the exceptional part of the whole group. Its coins are marked by the absence of the Δ, and the obverse-type of the corresponding copper is a head of Alexander with the horn of Ammon, and long hair instead of the short hair of the Third and Fourth Coinages; this copper, moreover, being of different denominations to that of the Ptolemaïc regal series with the Δ. As this type of the copper never returns in either of its varieties, all later coins which present the head of Alexander showing it clad in the elephant's skin and aegis, and as, moreover, the denominations do not recur, there can be no doubt that this money, with its corresponding silver and gold, should immediately follow the Fourth Coinage, and precede the coinage with the Δ. The Cyrenaïc coins also indicate a similar intermediate issue (p. 11, nos. 95, 96). This coinage would thus be the Fifth of Ptolemy I. It is especially to be noted that the Cyprian symbols conjectured in the Catalogue to mark three great offices (p. xix.), first appear on the silver of the Fourth Coinage, are continued in the copper of the Fifth, which alone we possess of Cyprus of that issue, and then disappear for a century. It is also noticeable that the silver coins set apart as the Fifth Coinage seem in some cases of an earlier style than those of the coinage with the Δ, and that correspondingly the head of Ptolemy does not seem so aged on the supposed earlier as on the supposed later issue. It might, of course, be urged that it is unreasonable to intercalate the Fifth Coinage between the coins with the types of Alexander IV., which have the Δ, and those regal Ptolemaïc coins characterized in the same way, and that in con-

Group without Δ.

Fifth Coinage of Ptolemy I. (Pl. ii. 1–8.)

sequence the coinage here called the Fifth of Ptolemy I. should follow instead of precede the similar series with the Δ. The answer to this objection is, that the copper money with the head of Alexander, which corresponds to the silver of the Fifth Coinage, would under the changed arrangement present an inexplicable recurrence to a previous coinage after the issue of one in a more complete system into which it would break.

To sum up:—the Fifth Coinage appears to have been the first attempt at a new currency by Ptolemy as king. It may have been local: certainly it was not of long duration. Part of the coinage with the Δ, as Ptolemy's Sixth Coinage, marks the final completion of the reform. Partly issued by Ptolemy I., it was no doubt mostly struck as the first general coinage of Philadelphus.

Coinage of Cyrenaica.
(Pl. ii. 9–11.)

The coinage of the Cyrenaïca, under Ptolemy as king, must here be noticed separately, as it stands almost alone, and it will be necessary to take in the same view that of the time of Ptolemy II. until the accession of Berenice II. as Queen of Cyrene, B.C. 258, referring the reader here from the notice of the money of Philadelphus.

Historical data.

The historical facts of the period from the first acquisition of the Cyrenaica to the accession of Berenice are as follows, it being best to go back for the moment to Ptolemy's governorship.

The Cyrenaïca was acquired by Ptolemy B.C. 322, and apparently held, notwithstanding a rebellion B.C. 313, until B.C. 312, when Ophellas successfully revolted, and ruled it independently until his death, B.C. 308, shortly after which Ptolemy recovered the province. The successful general was his stepson Magas, son of Berenice I., who as governor, and for a time as independent king, ruled for fifty years, until B.C. 258. He was governor so long as Ptolemy I. reigned, but revolted against his half-brother Ptolemy II., and became king, for how long we do not know, peace being ultimately made by the submission of Magas, and the betrothal of Berenice II., his heiress, to Ptolemy Euergetes, son and ultimately successor of Philadelphus. This engagement was evaded by the mother of Berenice, but in vain, and the young queen was at last married to Ptolemy. The marriage appears to have taken place about B.C. 255, Berenice having ruled as queen till that date from her father's death, and her husband becoming, as we may infer, king consort rather than king of Cyrene.

The date of the revolt of Magas, and the length of his reign, are obscure. In the war with Philadelphus, Antiochus I., king of Syria, was in alliance with Magas. Consequently this war must have occurred within the limits of the Syrian king's reign, B.C. 280-262. The last date is two years later than the lowest that modern writers have assigned to the revolt, B.C. 264; the first is identical with the highest.

The numismatic evidence may narrow the question. Ptolemy Philadelphus was involved in a war with Antiochus I., as partizan of Magas. It must have been thus that the Egyptian king acquired Phoenicia. He struck dated coins for Tyre from B.C. 266-5 (no. 44), to his death, B.C. 247. A prior undated coinage was issued at Tyre and Sidon (no. 32, *seqq.*), to which we may assign at least two more years, and place the first issue of coins of Phoenicia by the Ptolemies not later than B.C. 268-7. Making allowance for the preparation for war, and the time needed for the conquest and reorganization of Phoenicia, so that mints could be established, we may venture to add two years more, and obtain as the most probable lower limit for the war with Antiochus I., B.C. 270-69. Thus the period of uncertainty as to this war, and equally as to the revolt of Magas, would not exceed the years B.C. 280 to 269.

Evidence of coins.

The probable order of the coins of the Cyrenaïca struck during the period from the accession of Ptolemy I. as king, B.C. 305,

Probable order of coins.

to that of Berenice II. as queen of the Cyrenaïca, B.C. 258, may now be stated, in order that the problem may be farther elucidated.

It may be well to observe that the earlier coins struck by Ptolemy

Name of Magas wanting on earlier coins.

in the Cyrenaïca after its reduction by Magas, give no indication of the authority of the successful general and governor, whether struck during the Interregnum, or after Ptolemy had taken the royal title.

There are two local gold coinages of Ptolemy as king; (1) Attic

Coins of Ptolemy as king.
Local gold.
First Coinage, Attic standard.
(Pl. ii. 9.)
Second Coinage, Phoenician standard.
(Pl. ii. 10, 11.)

tetrobols having his head, and on the reverse Nike carrying a wreath and palm, a type which is clearly derived from Alexander the Great's identical but unusual type of gold stater; and (2) Phoenician didrachms with the head of Ptolemy, and on the reverse the remarkable type of a beardless figure (Alexander the Great?) in the character of Zeus, in a quadriga of elephants. There is no corresponding silver of Ptolemy. It is to be observed that the autonomous coinage of

Autonomous Coinage of Cyrene; same period, silver, copper.

Cyrene closes for a time with a gold, silver and copper currency, the gold of Attic weight, the denominations being the tetrobol and obol, the silver of Rhodian didrachms, the weight apparently falling to Phoenician, as if influenced by a parallel coinage (the Egyptian) of that standard. These coins are connected by their monograms with Ptolemy's gold coinages just mentioned, and they must represent the autonomous issues of the period before he was king, whether Cyrene was subject to him or not, continued into his reign in the case of the silver and also the corresponding copper. If so, the silver coins of Alexander IV. already noticed (p. xx.) must have been issued under Ptolemy's governorship, together with another silver coinage, the autonomous of Cyrene just mentioned, which survived into his reign. The autonomous copper of Cyrene of this

ARRANGEMENT. xxxi

Local coinage. Copper.
Sixth coinage. Copper.

group is interrupted by a local Ptolemaïc coinage distinguished by the head of Apollo, and by the coinage considered to be the Sixth of Ptolemy I. and First of Philadelphus, having a remarkable variety, a large denomination, with the head of Ptolemy I. for obverse-type. This last coinage would seem to be of Ptolemy I. rather than Ptolemy II., as it presents the beginning of a magistrate's name IΓ (p. 12, nos. 97, 98) common to the second gold coinage of Ptolemy I. (p. 11, no. 93) as king for the Cyrenaïca, as well as to the autonomous silver of Cyrene. (Müller, Num. de l'Anc. Afr. i. tab. 1.) It may be here suggested that a concurrent coinage of Ptolemy and the city of Cyrene may indicate that the king left a privilege of autonomy to the head of the Pentapolis, while not allowing it to the other towns.

The coinages described above are followed by copper with the

Period of Philadelphus. Local coinage of Magas as governor.
(Pl. vi. 5, 6.)

monograms of Magas only, to be carefully distinguished from his later copper with his monograms, all the old magistrates' names now disappearing. Here is a distinct innovation, dating, to judge from the number of types of coins anterior to it, and the unlikelihood of any such change under Ptolemy I., rather early in the reign of his successor than late in his own. It would thus appear that the first pretensions of Magas were advanced not long after the accession of Philadelphus, though the coinage would indicate that he did not at once declare himself independent. This view would favour an early year in the period B.C. 280–269 for the revolt, and accordingly B.C. 280 (?) is given in the tables.

New coinage of Magas as king, and governor second time.
(Pl. vi. 7-10.)

A new coinage in copper, having for the obverse-type the head of Ptolemy, and for the reverse that of Libya, would appear to mark the revolt of Magas and its suppression. It may be classed as follows :—

1. Obv. Head of Ptolemy, Rev. inscr. ΒΑΣΙΛΕΩΣ ΜΑΓΑ.
2. ,, ,, Magas, ,, ,, ,, ,,
3. ,, ,, Ptolemy, ,, ,, ΒΑΣΙΛΕΩΣ ΠΤΟΛΕΜΑΙΟΥ.

The only difficulty is as to the order. If, however, we recollect that the first coins with the monogram of Magas are earlier, this sequence is most natural, representing rebellion following on previous encroachment, and it would be difficult to find room for the abundant issue here called the third before the revolt of Magas, while it is needed after that event. The rarity of the regal money of Magas would indicate that his reign was very short.

Later coins of Magas as governor, second time. (Pl. vi. 11.) A coinage of silver and of copper, with the recurrence of the monogram of Magas (p. 39, nos. 25, *seqq*.), is placed last, as its obviously later style than the other series with his monogram indicates a revival of his pretensions towards the close of his reign, when the betrothal of Berenice to young Ptolemy would have made the king of Egypt less tenacious of his rights.

Coins of Berenice, queen of Cyrene. See p. xlv. This review brings us to the accession of Berenice as queen of Cyrene, B.C. 258. Her coinage will be considered later (p. xlv.).

Coins of Ptolemy II., Philadelphus.

Two great groups of the money of the second Ptolemy have been assigned to him in the previous section. These are:—(1) part, presumably the greater part, of the series marked by the Δ behind the king's ear on the larger gold and the silver coins, struck as the Sixth Coinage of Ptolemy I., and continued as the First General Coinage of his

Divisions of coinage.

successor; and (2) the silver tetradrachms of Phoenicia, with which must be classed corresponding copper issued during the second half of the reign of Philadelphus.

The earlier series, or First General Coinage of Philadelphus, has been already described under Ptolemy I. (p. xxv., supra). It will be farther noticed under the section on Mints.

First General Coinage (see Ptolemy I.).
(Pl. iii.)

The later series, or the First and Second Phoenician Coinages of Philadelphus, is of silver and copper. The copper includes the large piece which has been thought to be the Egyptian pound struck as a coin. The gold is to be sought in other series. Accordingly, we find gold octadrachms of Arsinoë II. struck in Phoenicia during this period. The heavy coins, indeed, in all metals, octadrachms of Arsinoë II., and those with the portraits of Ptolemy I. with Berenice I., and Ptolemy II. with Arsinoë II., the silver decadrachms of Arsinoë II., and the rarer silver octadrachms of Ptolemy I. of the Δ series, as well as the heavy copper of both Egypt and Phoenicia, seem to have had their origin under Philadelphus, and also to have been struck in the second part of his reign, except the octadrachms of Ptolemy I., which can only be of the first half.

Thus there is a marked change in the coinage of Philadelphus in the middle of his reign, characterized by the issue of large gold coins, of silver decadrachms in large numbers, and of heavy copper money. The change was, however, restricted to Phoenicia and Egypt. In Cyprus, except that a few gold octadrachms of Arsinoë II. may have been issued, the old types continued in a Second Coinage of gold, silver, and copper of later style, characterized by the buckler as symbol, and in the gold and silver and the copper in part by the monogram Σ or $\mathcal{I}$, shown by later coins to read $\leqslant\Omega$. These coins clearly next follow the series with the Δ, which

Monetary change in middle of reign.

Cyprus, Second Coinage.
(Pl. iv. 1–6.)

Monogram ΣΩ.

ceases by the middle of the reign of Philadelphus; and there is no reason to assign any of them, except perhaps a few of the copper, the latest, to Euergetes.

The appearance of the buckler on the coins of Cyprus as a constant symbol is of much importance. It also characterizes some of the Egyptian coins, which stand in the same relation as those of Cyprus to the series with the Δ, and also the earliest coins with the four portraits. There can, therefore, be no reasonable doubt that it is a badge introduced by Philadelphus. This symbol does not usually recur later except in the series of the four portraits, where, it must be remarked, it is specially associated with the busts of Philadelphus and Arsinoë II.

<small>Symbol, buckler.</small>

The coinage of Phoenicia must be more specially noticed, as it presents some noteworthy peculiarities, and affords an important chronological indication.

<small>Phoenicia.</small>

This silver coinage seems to have formed the bulk of the ordinary silver currency of Philadelphus in the second half of his reign, to judge from the abundance that has come down to our time, and from the certainty that in several years more than one die was used for the coinage of the same town. It appears that this coinage was struck at a central mint, for the five cities, Sidon, Tyre, Ptolemaïs, Joppa, and Gaza. We observe, that on the whole the type of the head of Ptolemy I. changes very remarkably year by year throughout the five cities, that some coins bear the mint-letters of Joppa and Gaza together, and that a reverse-die of Joppa, year 33, was altered to suit Tyre, year 34 (no. 97).

<small>Peculiarities of minting.</small>

The Phoenician coinage is farther remarkable for the title Soter given to Ptolemy from the year 25 inclusive, showing that it was issued commemoratively in his honour. It is of three classes, under two groups, here called the First and Second Coinages of Phoenicia.

First Coinage.
The First Coinage has the style ΠΤΟΛΕΜΑΙΟΥ ΒΑΣΙΛΕΩΣ, and is at first undated (A), of Sidon, Tyre, and Ace-Ptolemaïs. Then follows a dated series (B) of Tyre,

Undated.
(Pl. v. 7-9.)
years 20 to 24, the dates after 20 appearing in monograms. There is no certain coinage parallel

Dated.
(No. 10.)
with this of the other cities, which probably did not then issue money, or it would have been dated

Second Coinage.
(Pl. v.)
like that of Tyre. The Second Coinage is of Sidon, Tyre, Ptolemaïs, Joppa, Gaza, and Joppa with Gaza.

The change of style from ΠΤΟΛΕΜΑΙΟΥ ΒΑΣΙΛΕΩΣ to ΠΤΟΛΕΜΑΙΟΥ ΣΩΤΗΡΟΣ is accounted for by

Title Soter.
M. Revillout's discovery that the worship of the first Ptolemy with the title Soter was introduced by Philadelphus between the 22nd and 29th years of his reign. (*Revue Égyptologique*, i. 15, *seqq.*). These Phoenician coins show that the actual date was the 25th year, B.C. 261-0. As the head of Ptolemy I. was retained on the coinage, it was not unnatural to associate it with his special honorary title. It is, however, remarkable that no coins known to have been struck out of Phoenicia by Philadelphus or his successors present the style ΠΤΟΛΕΜΑΙΟΥ ΣΩΤΗΡΟΣ. In all other cases, therefore, the head of Ptolemy I. on the obverse is associated with the name of the reigning king on the reverse. It is obvious that the issue of the Phoenician coinage in the 25th year of Philadelphus seems to indicate a more complete organization of the country than does the earlier money. It may be conjectured that the king of Egypt allowed his new subjects, wrested from the Syrian dominion, some degree of autonomy, and by this commemorative coinage indicated this favour, and the final success of his father's efforts to subdue them under cover of deliverance. This conjecture may account for the concurrent use of the style ΠΤΟΛΕΜΑΙΟΥ ΒΑΣΙΛΕΩΣ and ΠΤΟΛΕΜΑΙΟΥ ΣΩΤΗΡΟΣ by Philadelphus; but there is a farther phenomenon which may explain it more fully

the usage of the coins of Cyprus under the same king. In the First Coinage, the silver has the ordinary style ΠΤΟΛΕΜΑΙΟΥ ΒΑΣΙΛΕΩΣ. In the Second Coinage, the monogram ⟍ for ΣΩ appears on the gold and silver coins, and some copper ones. This monogram does not stand for the name of a city or a magistrate, as no city corresponds, and no magistrate could have held office during the three successive reigns in which it is first constant and then frequent. Can it be connected with the Phoenician style, ΠΤΟΛΕΜΑΙΟΥ ΣΩΤΗΡΟΣ ? The coins of Phoenicia may solve this question. At first, under Ptolemy II. and III., they present the inscription ΠΤΟΛΕΜΑΙΟΥ ΣΩΤΗΡΟΣ, once combined with ΣΩ on a coin of Ptolemaïs, where similar coins present ΑΣ and ΞΕ, as though these inscriptions stood for cognate titles of the city, Ἄσυλος, Ξενία, and Σώτειρα. Under Ptolemy IV., the two styles ΠΤΟΛΕΜΑΙΟΥ ΣΩΤΗΡΟΣ and ΠΤΟΛΕΜΑΙΟΥ ΒΑΣΙΛΕΩΣ occur side by side, but the second form (Sidon) is ΠΤΟΛΕΜΑΙΟΥ ΒΑΣΙΛΕΩΣ ΣΩ (p. 64, no. 23); and ΠΤΟΛΕΜΑΙΟΥ ΦΙΛΟΠΑΤΟΡΟΣ ΣΩ (Tyre, no. 24), the form being $\frac{\Omega}{\Sigma}$, also occurs. It seems, therefore, possible that in these coins ΣΩ, except in the singular case of its use apparently for a city title, is a survival of ΣΩΤΗΡΟΣ. Against this might be urged the occurrence of these letters on the coin with the title Philopator, and on another of the same king, also of Tyre, with the style ΠΤΟΛΕΜΑΙΟΥ ΣΩΤΗΡΟΣ (no. 25); but this might be accounted for as the effect of long use. If we might suppose that the letters ΣΩ in Cyprus at least are an abbreviation of ΣΩΤΗΡΟΣ, the Cyprian style would be a link between the Phoenician and the Egyptian, and read ΒΑΣΙΛΕΩΣ ΠΤΟΛΕΜΑΙΟΥ ΣΩΤΗΡΟΣ. It would seem, therefore, as if Ptolemy Philadelphus, in order to conciliate the Phoenicians, issued the coinage commemorative of his father, in harmony with special privileges, that in Egypt, where the regal power was always absolute, and most emphatically so with the natives, he struck in his own name; but that in Cyprus a conces-

ARRANGEMENT. xxxvii

sion was made, and the Phoenician style was adopted in a modified form, so as not to disturb the long-existing coinage.

A few words must be added as to the new copper coinage of Phoenicia and Egypt. It is marked by very large pieces for its highest denomination, of which the weight nearly corresponds, in the heaviest examples, to the native Egyptian pound, or uten, of about 1480 grains. As this was the chief weight of the Egyptian system, it has been supposed that the coinage was adjusted to it, especially as copper was the principal currency among the natives under the Ptolemies, the money of Egypt in this metal having a special importance in their issues, as may be seen in a moment if we compare the Ptolemaïc with the Seleucid or Macedonian currencies. Since M. Revillout's researches doubt has been cast on this hypothesis. For the information of the reader, the weights of the Egyptian copper are given later. (Section, Weights.)

New copper coinage, Phoenicia and Egypt. (Pl. v. 7–9.) *Probably of Egyptian standard.* (Pl. vi. 4.)

The obverse-type of both Phoenician and Egyptian copper is the head of Zeus Ammon. The Egyptian coins present the new reverse-type of the Eagle on the thunderbolt with open wings, looking back. The largest Phoenician coins have two eagles for the reverse, indicating the two Adelphi or Philadelphi, Ptolemy and Arsinoë II., like the double cornucopiæ on the coins of Arsinoë II. The coins of the next size have the eagle with open wings, the smaller, the ordinary Ptolemaïc eagle. (See pl. v., nos. 7—9.) The style is ΠΤΟΛΕΜΑΙΟΥ ΒΑΣΙΛΕΩΣ. With very few exceptions, of which the most important are the Cyrenaïc issues of Ptolemy Euergetes II. and Soter II., all copper coins of the Ptolemies bear only the titles ΒΑΣΙΛΕΥΣ or ΒΑΣΙΛΙΣΣΑ. The absence of the portrait of Ptolemy Soter would account for the absence of his title in the Phoenician copper, and it should be remembered that money in this metal was always of less importance in reference

f

to the authority by whom it was issued than that in the precious metals.

The heavy copper money of Egypt above described appears to belong to the reign of Philadelphus only, a new reverse-type being issued by Euergetes: that of Phoenicia was continued for a while with the silver under the later king.

Coins with busts of Ptolemy II. with Arsinoë II., and Ptolemy I. with Berenice I.

To the reign of Philadelphus we must assign the first issue of two series of coins of a medallic character, which were long continued under later sovereigns. The one is principally of gold octadrachms. It bears the busts of Ptolemy II. with Arsinoë II., and Ptolemy I. with Berenice I. The other is principally of gold octadrachms and silver decadrachms. It bears the bust of Arsinoë II. No such great gold coins are known of Ptolemy I., who issued pentadrachms; the first step in the direction of these heavier issues having been made by the coinage of the very rare silver octadrachms of the series with the Δ, most probably by Ptolemy II. It is consistent with the magnificence of the reign of Philadelphus, and true to his policy that these medallic family coins should have been first issued by him.

Two series of medallic coins first issued by Philadelphus.

The coins with the four portraits, on the obverse those of Ptolemy II. with Arsinoë II., and the inscription ΑΔΕΛΦΩΝ, and on the reverse Ptolemy I. and Berenice I. with the inscription ΘΕΩΝ, must be first noticed. The portrait of Philadelphus may be compared with that in the Hunter Collection (pl. xxxii. 5). The earliest in style are charac-

Coins with four portraits: Ptol. II. Arsinoë II. Ptol. I. Berenice I.

First group, Ptolemy II., III. (Pl. vii. 1–4.)

terized by the buckler on the obverse, as in the general coinages of Philadelphus. They are not inconsistent in style with his other coinages, and with the gold octadrachms of Arsinoë II. of his reign, and that of his successor Ptolemy III., to be discussed under the next head. That these coins were first issued under Philadelphus appears from the titles ΘΕΟΙ and ΑΔΕΛΦΟΙ; Ptolemy I. and his consort already deified, but not Ptolemy II. and Arsinoë II. Of a slightly later style are coins with the same symbol. These may be a later issue during the same period. Thus the mass of these coins would probably be of Ptolemy II. or III., or both. Of a markedly different style are others with, as symbol, a spear-head on the reverse, and on the obverse the monogram ℞. Monogram and symbol occur together on coins of Ptolemy Epiphanes (pl. xxxii. 7, xvii. 3), and the heads of Ptolemy I. on the octadrachms, are of about the same age. This issue may therefore be reasonably attributed to Epiphanes. A still later group, for so its inferior style would seem to indicate, characterized by the buckler only, is probably of Philometor, or perhaps Physcon, the head of Ptolemy I. resembling a type of their time. There is also a small silver coin with the same types, too ill-preserved to be classed according to style. All these coins are probably of Egypt: if this is admitted, their general inferior fabric could be explained.

Second group, Ptolemy V. (Pl. vii. 5, 6.)

Third group, Ptolemy VI. or VIII. (Pl. vii. 7.)

Coins of Arsinoë II., Philadelphos.

The coins which bear the portrait and name of Arsinoë Philadelphos are mainly octadrachms in gold and decadrachms in silver. The gold coins probably range through a period of about a century and a half;

Coins with bust of Arsinoë II.

First group, Ptolemy II. and III.
(Pl. viii. 1-5.)

the silver ones are, without exception, of one time only. The earliest dated specimens are those in gold which correspond in their dates and mint-letters, monograms, &c., to the Phoenician currency of the latest part of the reign of Ptolemy II. and the earliest of Euergetes. They are therefore of Arsinoë II., second wife of Ptolemy II. His first wife, Arsinoë I., daughter of Lysimachus, was divorced in B.C. 277, in his eighth or ninth year. There are no coins in the series which can be reasonably attributed to her, and the undated coins bearing the name of Arsinoë of the same or similar fabric and style to those of the cities of Pheonicia may be assigned to the same period, and therefore classed to Ptolemy II. or III.

There is a solitary coin (pl. viii. 1) presenting a difference of style **Variety of type.** rather than of portrait, and varied in the type by the want of the sceptre. The style limits us to the reigns of Ptolemy II., III., and IV. If placed after the first issues of this period, the coin would show that the sceptre was dropped and resumed: consequently it seems reasonable to place it provisionally at the head of the whole class.

Second group, Ptolemy V.
(Pl. viii. 6.)

Like the gold coins with the four portraits, those of Arsinoë in gold were again struck long after their first great issue. The reissue appears to have similarly begun under Epiphanes, of whose queen we have no gold octadrachms, as we have of her successive predecessors, Arsinoë II., Berenice II., and Arsinoë III. The attribution to Epiphanes is on these grounds:—The use of L for "year," as on the coin in question, is not known before Philopator's coinage of Cyprus, and the style of the octadrachms will scarcely allow a later date than Epiphanes. Farther, as Philopator struck money for his queen Arsinoë III., he is not likely to have issued this of the earlier queen of that name. Thus Epiphanes probably resumed the coinage. The next issues may be assigned to Philometor and

ARRANGEMENT.

Third group, Ptolemy VI. and VIII., or later (Pl. viii. 7-10.) Physcon, and perhaps one or both of his sons, when the portraits of living queens on the gold money are equally wanting. The coin in the French Collection of Paphos, year 33 (pl. xxxii. 6), cannot be doubted to be of Philometor or Physcon, more probably the earlier. Allowing for the Egyptian fabric, always inferior, one coin engraved (pl. viii. 7) may be assigned with probability to Philometor, the rest to **Portrait assimilated to that of later queens.** Physcon, while one or more of the latest may be of Soter II. or even Alexander I. It is quite possible that in the coins later than the reign of Epiphanes, the features of Arsinoë may be assimilated to those of one or more queens reigning when they were issued. Indeed the likeness of one head, in this part of the series (no. 8), to the portrait of Cleopatra, Queen of Syria (Cat. *Seleucid Kings of Syria*, pl. xxiii. 1), suggests that it may represent her sister, Cleopatra III. of Egypt, second wife of Physcon. The subsequent coins (pl. viii. 9-10) might then **Third group ends under Cleopatra III. and Alexander I., or Soter II.** show the same portrait at later ages, and bring us down to the joint-reign of Cleopatra III. and Ptolemy Alexander I., or the subsequent sole reign of Soter II., after which it is most unlikely that Egypt had any gold coinage.

The silver decadrachms of Arsinoë, unlike the gold pieces, are all of one period, that of the earlier gold issue, the reigns of Philadelphus and Euergetes. They cannot be more precisely limited, though it is probable, from their want of variety, that they were struck within a few years. The silver tetradrachm (pl. viii. 3) appears to be of the reign of Euergetes.

On reviewing the evidence for the dates of the two classes of medallic **Summary of evidence of medallic coinage.** coinage just noticed, it would appear that Ptolemy Epiphanes restored the gold money of Philadelphus which had fallen into disuse during or after the reign of Euergetes, and that his successors struck no other gold coinage but this. The cultus of their ancestors under the Ptolemies, and more especially of the earlier and more fortunate princes, partly explains this, which is consistent with the use by most of the later kings of the distinctive titles of the earlier.

Coins of Ptolemy III., Euergetes I.

The coinage of the Third Ptolemy falls into two great classes, due to the political history of his reign. First, he continued the issues of his predecessor, at least in Cyprus and Phoenicia: then, no doubt in consequence of the financial pressure of his great war with Syria, it became necessary to strike rapidly in central positions, and thus Egypt appears to have a new monetary importance, and the Phoenician issues are simplified: at the same time these innovations produce various changes in the types of the coinage.

Classes of coinage of Ptolemy III. due to political causes.

The First Coinage of Euergetes in Cyprus is fixed by the data which interpose a limited Second Coinage between it and the money of the next reign, implying an earlier currency under the present one. It is the sequence in style of the Cyprian money of Philadelphus; and some of its pieces are characterized by a monogram, ⚹, occurring in the next coinage. This Second Coinage is fixed (1) by the occurrence of a portrait, which can only be that of Euergetes, since it much more nearly resembles his known head than that of any other king, but perhaps Philadelphus, for whom the style of the coins is too late; (2) by the presence in its copper, the latest of the style originating with the Δ coinage, and superseded under Ptolemy IV. by a new style, of a monogram 𐅜, apparently common to the later Egyptian money of Euergetes (Second Coinage), and certainly to that of Philopator. It must be borne in mind that under Euergetes there is a recurrence to the wide use of a

Cyprus, First Coinage, silver, copper. (Pl. ix. 1–3.)

Second Coinage, silver, copper. (Pl. ix. 4–7.)

ARRANGEMENT. xliii

moneyer's name which marks the series with the Δ: consequently even a common monogram is not likely to mean two names in the same period.

Phoenicia,
First Coinage,
silver, copper.
(Pl. x. 1, 2.)

Gold, Arsinoë II.

The First Coinage of Phoenicia continues that of Philadelphus, and apparently ceases with the sixth year of Euergetes. The metals are silver and copper, the type in copper being that with the two eagles; and the corresponding gold pieces are octadrachms of Arsinoë II.

Second Coinage,
silver, copper;
Ptolemaïs, &c.
(Pl. x. 3–8.)

The Second Coinage is mainly of Ptolemaïs, where a class of coins seems to have been hastily issued, with the obverse-types of old dies of the Second Coinage of Philadelphus, combined with reverse-types bearing various monograms. With these coins may be classed others of similar style in silver and copper which bear no mint-letters, but only the monograms or initials of magistrates. This may be regarded as a local unimportant issue.

Third Coinage,
silver, copper.
(Pl. xi. 1–8.)

The Third Coinage of Phoenicia is characterized in the silver pieces by a late head of Ptolemy I., and a style of work consistent with the time of Euergetes and superior to that of Philopator, whose Phoenician coinage is certain, combined with a copper issue, which, in the case of Tyre, closely corresponds with the bulk of the Egyptian money of Euergetes, the two eagles on the largest coin here giving way to the single eagle; but the correspondence is in the matter of style rather with his Second than his First Coinage in Egypt. The silver pieces of this Third Coinage of Phoenicia are characterized in the case of Tyre and Ptolemaïs by the monogram ₥ to the right. The copper is marked by a variety of type in the case of that which is probably of Sidon, and by a prominent town-symbol at Ptolemaïs, Joppa, and Berytus, in addition to the symbol of Tyre, the club already in use. At the close of the Phoenician series is placed a remarkable tetradrachm (pl. xi., no. 9), with the symbol of an agalma, apparently of the Asiatic Artemis, which in the portrait of Ptolemy I. resembles in style a barbarous coin of Ptolemaïs of the First Coinage, and the earlier coins of the series of the Era (pl. xxv., nos. 1, 2). It is probably of Phoenicia or Syria.

The First Coinage of Egypt consists, as far as we know, of a series of bronze pieces, remarkable for the fineness of their metal, which present generally one obverse-type and one reverse-type of all denominations, the head of Zeus Ammon and the eagle with a cornucopiæ before it. The smaller denominations have also Alexander's head in the elephant's skin. The whole series is marked by the occurrence of the monogram ⚹, which is also found on the silver money of Berenice II. struck in the Cyrenaïca. So peculiar a monogram can scarcely have occurred more than once within the course of two reigns, for this is the utmost limit fabric would allow for the coins bearing it, and we must remember the wide use of a single monogram at this time. It is therefore reasonable to class the copper series to Euergetes, the husband of Berenice, for of course we could not connect a Cyrenæan moneyer of Berenice with Philadelphus. Moreover there is a cognate and more limited series with similar reverse-types, which is undoubtedly of the same age as the copper coins just discussed, and which bears on the obverse the laureate bust of Euergetes.

Egypt, First Coinage, copper. (Pl. xii. 1, 2.)

The Second Coinage of Egypt is marked by the new gold money which bears the bust of Euergetes, with a radiate diadem, and over his shoulder a sceptre-trident; and, on the reverse, a radiate cornucopiæ. The copper coinage is simply an inferior continuation of the common type of that which preceded it, except that in the smaller denomination the constant types are the head of Alexander in the elephant's skin, and the eagle with spread wings. Throughout the gold and larger copper we find the moneyer's

Second Coinage, gold, copper. (Pl. xii. 3-7.)

letters Δϊ; in the smaller copper, (with Alexander's head), Δ, E, Є and E, probably for Ɛ, which we find in the Second Coinage of Cyprus. It is to be remarked that the copper Tyrian coins of the Third Coinage of Phoenicia, which are strikingly like the heavier copper coins of Egypt of the Second Coinage, bear in higher denominations the letters Δϊ. Thus we have two certain instances of prevalent moneyers' letters in ✳ and Δϊ. It is indeed in this and the succeeding two reigns that this recurrence of prevalent moneyers' letters or monograms, as in the various mints of the coinage with Δ, is particularly to be noted.

It must also be observed that the cornucopiæ begins to be a characteristic symbol of large groups of coins under Euergetes. Its position is usually in front of the eagle: under later sovereigns the type is varied by the reintroduction of the double cornucopiæ of Philadelphus, and its place is also changed from time to time.

Cornucopiæ as symbol.

The only coins here assigned to the Cyrenaïca of the reign of Ptolemy Euergetes are copper pieces analogous to the smaller pieces of his Second Egyptian Coinage in size and style, making allowance for local fabric, and having for types the head of Zeus Ammon and the eagle with open wings. One of these coins was acquired from a Tunis collection rich in Cyrenaïc pieces. It is not to be expected that more coins of this king should be assigned to the Cyrenaïca, as will be obvious from the next section.

Cyrenaïca, Copper. (Pl. xiii. 1.)

Coins of Berenice II., Euergetis.

Berenice II. is the first Egyptian queen who bears her title, βασίλισσα, on the coins. The second Arsinoë takes her husband's surname, Philadelphos: similarly Arsinoë III. is not queen but Philopator. Cleopatra I. in her own coinage struck by her as regent after the death of Ptolemy Epiphanes is called queen, and

Coinage of Berenice II. Title of βασίλισσα; its import in the Ptolemaic Coinage.

the same is the case with the only other Egyptian queens whose names occur on coins, Cleopatra II. or III. as wife of Ptolemy Physcon, Cleopatra III. as his widow, and Cleopatra VII., the last and most famous of that name, when sole queen, and when co-regent with Ptolemy Cæsar. It is to be remarked that each of these queens had a hereditary right. Berenice II. inherited the Cyrenaïca; Cleopatra I. brought with her the claim to Cœle-Syria and Phoenicia, her dowry; Cleopatra II. was treated as co-heiress by her brothers; Cleopatra III. was heiress of Philometor; and the last Cleopatra was co-heiress of Auletes, striking money with the regal title, as sole sovereign, or coregent with a junior. It was necessary to premise this, lest it should be supposed that all the coinage of Berenice II. as queen should be limited to her reign in Cyrenaïca, from the death of her father Magas, B.C. 258, to the accession of Ptolemy Euergetes, B.C. 247, when, or a little later, the diadems of Egypt and the Cyrenaïca were united by the marriage of Ptolemy and Berenice.

It will be best to begin the study of the coinage of Berenice II.

Cyrenaïca. with that of the Cyrenaïca, as this class could alone comprise specimens of her currency as queen before the reunion of the province to Egypt.

The Cyrenaïc coinage is limited to Cyrene and Euesperides, or Berenice, new-named after the queen. The coins of Cyrene are gold and silver, and remarkable as affording divisions peculiar to them of the Phoenician weight-system. The gold coins are the tridrachm and its fifth and tenth, whereas the regular Ptolemaïc coins are, first the pentadrachm, didrachm, and hemidrachm, then the octadrachm and tetradrachm. The silver coin is a hexadrachm, a denomination unknown to the true Ptolemaic currency. It is therefore evident that this is a special coinage. It may be conjectured that the system was adopted with the object of harmonizing the Ptolemaïc standard with the Attic standard previously current in the Cyrenaïca. It will be observed that the fifth

Cyrene.
Gold, Silver.
(Pl. xiii. 4-6.)

of the Ptolemaïc tridrachm is an Attic hemidrachm, and the tenth of the tridrachm the quarter of the Attic drachm. In the gold coinage issued before the rule of the Cyrenaïca by the Ptolemies, the hemidrachm occurs, and possibly its half. The hexadrachm in silver is an Attic pentadrachm, equally with it an entirely new denomination.

Do these peculiar coins belong to the sole reign of Berenice II.,
<small>Date of issue.</small> or to her joint reign with Ptolemy Euergetes? The coinage in precious metal of the Ptolemies after the settlement of the standard has but one great change, the substitution of the gold octadrachm and tetradrachm for the pentadrachm and hemidrachm. It seems therefore very unlikely that after the union of the crowns Berenice should have innovated, particularly as her money struck out of the Cyrenaïca is uniform in system with that of her husband. On the other hand, it must be remarked that the monogram ✱ found on a silver hexadrachm (p. 60, no. 8) characterizes what I believe to be the first issue of Ptolemy Euergetes in bronze, and this would indicate that Berenice's coins of Cyrenaïca are part of those of the empire, and thus not of her sole reign. The question must for the present remain undetermined.

The coins of Euesperides-Berenice are probably of the queen's
<small>Euesperides-Berenice. (Pl. xiii. 7, 8.) Date of issue.</small> first or sole reign. The portrait is youthful, and the fabric poor. They present the monogram of Magas.

The rest of Berenice's coinage presents nothing exceptional but the Cyprian money bearing her name as well as that of Ptolemy.
<small>Other parts of empire. (Pl. xiii. 2,3,9,10.)</small> The gold octadrachm struck at Ephesus, and the Egyptian silver decadrachm, are simply a new issue on the principle of the great gold and silver coins of Arsinoë II. The Cyprus coins are copper, assigned on the evidence of the provenance of a similar coin and the fabric of all.

Note on the coins of Cyrene with the inscription **KOINON**.

The series of the Cyrenaïca presents a gap in regal money between

Berenice II. and about the time of Ptolemy V., and is interrupted by an autonomous issue in silver and copper characterized by the inscription KOINON. The weight is Phoenician, and there are no names of magistrates. The description of both silver and copper is as follows:—

Note on Cyrene coins with KOINON.

Head of Zeus Ammon r., diademed. Rev. KOINON Silphium.

In style these coins are good. The head of Zeus Ammon resembles that of the first Egyptian coinage of Ptolemy Euergetes I., the fabric that of the Cyrenaïc coins classed to Ptolemy V.

History explains the appearance of this new coinage, relating how Ecdemus and Demophanes, having been sent for by the Cyrenæans, governed them and preserved their liberty (ἔτι δὲ Κυρηναίων αὐτοὺς μεταπεμψαμένων, ἐπιφανῶς προὔστησαν καὶ διεφύλαξαν αὐτοῖς τὴν ἐλευθερίαν, Polyb. x. 25. Κυρηναίοις δεηθεῖσαν, τεταραγμένων τῶν κατὰ τὴν πόλιν καὶ νοσούντων, πλεύσαντες εὐνομίαν ἔθεντο καὶ διεκόσμησαν ἄριστα τὴν πόλιν, Plut. Philop. i. 1). Unfortunately the date is not given, but Thrige cannot be far wrong in placing the events between B.C. 250 and 220 (Res Cyrenensium, p. 240, 241). The lowest possible limit is B.C. 216, when Livy, speaking of the detention at Cyrene of the ship carrying Decius Magius of Capua, states not only that the city was under royal rule but that an appeal to Ptolemy was possible. (Navem Cyrenas detulit tempestas, quæ tum in ditione regum erant. ibi quum Magius ad statuam Ptolemaei regis confugisset, deportatus a custodibus Alexandriam ad Ptolemaeum, etc., xxiii. 10.) The accession of Ptolemy III. took place B.C. 247, that of Ptolemy IV. B.C. 222.

The evidence of the regal coins seems to show that during the reign of Euergetes scarcely any coins were struck in the Cyrenaïca in his name. The coinage may have been Berenice's, if her money was issued in the Cyrenaïca after her husband's accession. But it seems most probable that Berenice conceded a certain degree of autonomy to Cyrene, which included the right of coining; when a Ptolemy, probably Philopator, withdrew the one privilege he may not have interfered with the other. (On the whole question, see Thrige p. 239, seqq.; on the coinage here discussed, Müller, Numismatique de l'Ancienne Afrique, i. 37, seqq., iii. 187.)

Coins of Ptolemy IV., Philopator.

Coinage of Ptolemy Philopator: political influences.

The coinage of Ptolemy Philopator presents that confusion which we should expect in a reign marked by a great war, causing the temporary loss of the eastern provinces, and characterized by bad government.

Cyprus. Silver countermarked. (Pl. xiv. 1.)

The money of Cyprus appears to fall into three groups: first the reissue of the Cyprian tetradrachms of Ptolemy Philadelphus, with countermarks for Salamis and for Citium. These coins are presumably later than the Cyprian coinages of Euergetes, which, it will be remembered, complete the old series (to an earlier part of which these countermarked coins belong), and add to it another with that king's portrait. They are certainly anterior to the reign of Ptolemy Epiphanes, under whom a new coinage of Cyprus was issued immediately on or very soon after his accession, which coinage was continued by his successors. It is also unlikely that old coins would have been thus recirculated in the prosperous reign of Euergetes. These countermarked pieces are therefore probably of Philopator, and if so they may be reasonably placed before the issue of the dated series, and therefore in his first and second years.

Silver and copper dated. (Pl. xiv. 2-5.)

The second, or dated series, consists mainly of copper, the Museum containing one silver coin that may be here classed with probability. The copper pieces are dated in the third and fourth years. They bear on the obverse the monogram $\mathbb{R}$ or the letter K; on the reverse, in the field (l.) $\stackrel{\Omega}{\leqslant}$, and (r.) the date preceded by the symbol L. The obverse type of the largest denomination is the head of Zeus Ammon, of the next that of the bearded Herakles, and of the smallest that of Pallas.

INTRODUCTION.

The reign is probably fixed by the occurrence of $\frac{\Omega}{\Xi}$ for the earlier Σ or Ξ of Cyprus, as on the coin of Tyre (pl. xiv., 10) which bears the king's title (ΠΤΟΛΕΜΑΙΟΥ ΦΙΛΟΠΑΤΟΡΟΣ). This combination has been conjectured in the earlier part of this essay to be the abbreviation of ΣΩΤΗΡΟΣ (p. xxxv). The symbol L for the year is here first seen: we find it in the Cyprian coinage of Epiphanes, and thenceforward on nearly all silver coins, ultimately of Egypt as well as of Cyprus.* The silver coin of Salamis dated in the fourth year, and with the owl as symbol in the field (l.) (pl. xiv., 2), is here placed on account of its being, both on obverse and reverse, of a finer style than the coins of Cyprus of Epiphanes. It might, but for its style, have been attributed to the regency of Cleopatra I., on a silver coin of which the same symbol occurs. (Berl. Zeitsch. iii., Taf. ix. 15.)

The third group, which was probably contemporary with the other two, is the beginning of a series evidently issued through several reigns in Cyprus, the fabric and provenance being equally in favour of this attribution. The obverse-type is the king's bust as Dionysus, clad in the nebris, his diadem entwined with the ivy-wreath, and the thyrsus over his shoulder. The unmistakable portrait on the earliest coins of the series (pl. xiv., 6, 7), those here classed to Philopator, and that king's known attachment to the worship of Dionysus, fix these coins to him as their originator. Thus, as in the cases of Alexander the Great, Ptolemy Soter, Arsinoë II., and later, Cleopatra I., the portrait of Ptolemy Philopator was retained in later currency. The Dionysiac type of Philopator recalls the story in the third book of Maccabees, of this king's persecution of the Jews, characterized by his ordering them to be branded with the ivy-leaf; though this story may be a combination in a dramatic form of the persecution by Antiochus Epiphanes, and that attempted by Ptolemy Physcon, with which indeed it has been connected. It may also

Dionysiac silver. (Pl. xiv. 6, 7.)

---

* Most probably it is the Egyptian demotic symbol for 'year.'

ARRANGEMENT.

be remarked that the Dionysiac Guild of the οἱ περὶ τὸν Διόνυσον τεχνῖται was of some consequence in the island (Boeckh, C. I. G. 2619, 2620). If Boeckh's restoration of the first of the two inscriptions referred to be correct, the office of Secretary of the Guild was at one time held by a Strategos, who was also admiral and high-priest of Cyprus (2619). According to the second inscription, this guild was at another time connected with the cultus of the Euergetæ, whether Euergetes I. and Berenice II. or Euergetes II. and one or both of the Cleopatras, cannot be proved (2620). If we could infer that the Secretaryship of the Guild was held ex officio by the governor of Cyprus, then the recurrence of a Dionysiac coinage marked by the symbols (with others) of the supposed offices of the Strategos would be very significant. In the present state of knowledge all that can be done is to point to a possible connexion of the Guild and the coinage.

The Phoenician money of Ptolemy Philopator falls into two classes,

Phoenicia. which I have termed the First and Second Coinages.
First Coinage, Silver. To the First Coinage I have assigned a tetradrachm
(Pl. xiv. 8.) represented in the National Collection by two specimens from the same die, which differs from the latest or Third Coinage of Euergetes in having the inscription ΒΑΣΙΛΕΩΣ instead of ΣΩΤΗΡΟΣ. The fabric is remarkably similar, but the portrait of Ptolemy I. is varied. The letters in the field to left appear to be ΘΕ ΣΙ ΣΤΡΑ, which I would conjecturally read ΘΕΟΔΟΤΟΥ ΣΙΔΩΝΟΣ or ΣΙΔΩΝΙΩΝ ΣΤΡΑΤΗΓΟΥ, Theodotus having been governor of Phoenicia and Cœle-Syria from B.C. 222 to 219. To the right in the field there are traces of letters which appear to be ΣΩ, equivalent to $\overset{\Omega}{\Sigma}$ on coins of Cyprus and a coin of Tyre to be presently noticed. This coinage would have been naturally interrupted by the temporary success of Antiochus III., B.C. 219—217.

Second Coinage, Silver. The Second Coinage would follow the recovery of the Asiatic provinces after the Battle of Raphia, B.C.
(Pl. xiv. 9, 10.) 217. The ordinary silver coins assigned to this coinage

are merely a continuation of the usual Phoenician series of the earlier kings with the inscription ΣΩTHPOΣ, the inferior work of which would induce us to put them as late as possible, and thus to Philopator's second rule in Phoenicia, there being no place for them in the Phoenician money of Epiphanes. The coinage of Tyre is represented by a coin of this group, equally barbarous with the rest, having the monogram and symbol of the city in the field (l.), and the letters $\overset{\Omega}{\Sigma}$ (r.), as well as by a coin with the king's portrait and the inscription ΠΤΟΛΕΜΑΙΟΥ ΦΙΛΟΠΑΤΟΡΟΣ, the letters $\overset{\Omega}{\Sigma}$ occurring in the field as before (pl. xiv., 10). A coin classed to Sidon is a link between this coinage and the First Coinage. The obverse bears the king's portrait: the reverse has the title ΒΑΣΙΛΕΩΣ; in the field (l.) are the letters ΣΩ, while ΣΙ, here presumably the mint-name, appears between the eagle's legs, a very unusual place (no. 9). The reverse of this coin is closely similar to that of the Phoenician and Egyptian silver coinage of Ptolemy Epiphanes. The irregularity of the Second Coinage may be explained by the disturbance caused by the temporary loss of Phoenicia to Antiochus III. It may be added that the head of Ptolemy Soter on this group is similar to that on coins of the Era Series (cf. pl. xxv., 3–5), probably struck in Phoenicia or the neighbouring territory, which it is reasonable to class to about the same period.

Philopator's copper money of Phoenicia is classed as later than that of Euergetes, and earlier than that of Epiphanes:

Copper.

it cannot be said to which of his two coinages in silver it corresponds. The pieces are small and scanty. That of Ptolemaïs is interesting as offering the symbol of the tripod as well as the monogram of the town.

In the gold assigned to Egypt the octadrachms bear the king's

Egypt, Gold.
(Pl. xv. 1, 2.)

bust and the eagle, with the title Philopator, like the silver coin of Tyre noticed above. The copper coinage is attributed to this reign as naturally following the latest of

ARRANGEMENT.   liii

Ptolemy Euergetes, and bearing between the eagle's legs sometimes
Copper.   a letter and sometimes the monogram Ɛ̄, which is
(Pl. xv. 3-5.)   probably identical with Ɛ̄ in the issue of Euergetes
just mentioned. It is characterized by the reverse-type of the
eagle looking back and bearing a cornucopiæ on his left wing.
A similar coinage, probably from its inferiority issued after this,
shows the eagle looking forward with open wings. The two are
connected by their mint-letters. In both issues the head of
Alexander in the elephant's skin takes the place of that of Zeus
Ammon on smaller coins.

Coins of Arsinoë III., Philopator.

Gold octadrachms were struck for Arsinoë III. in continuation of
Coinage of Arsi-   those of Arsinoë II. and Berenice II. They are
noë III.   remarkable for the absence of the veil. The cornu-
(Pl. xv. 6, 7.)   copiæ, as in the case of Berenice II., is single, but
accompanied by a single star above it. This star being a common
symbol in the money of Cyprus might indicate a Cyprian mintage,
but on the whole it seems most probable that the coins were struck in
Egypt. There are also small copper coins found in Cyprus bearing
what appears to be the portrait of this queen, and on the reverse the
name of Ptolemy with a double cornucopiæ.

Coins of Ptolemy V., Epiphanes.

The coinage of Ptolemy Epiphanes is marked by the great
Coinage of Pto-   disaster of his reign, the loss of the eastern pro-
lemy Epiphanes: vinces, and, in consequence, his issues after the
political influ-
ences.   earlier years are mainly limited to the mints
of Cyprus and Egypt.

h

Cyprus.

The Cyprian Coinage of Epiphanes is the true commencement of a series of dated silver tetradrachms, with the symbol L, which were issued by the three chief towns of Cyprus, Paphos, Salamis, and Citium, with little interruption, one period excepted, at least at one mint, generally at all three, until the disturbed condition of the island under the rule of Ptolemy Lathyrus after his expulsion from Egypt by his mother. The important interruption is in the troubled early period of the reign of Philometor. The classification depends on the dates the coins bear and their style. The portrait of Ptolemy Soter, although greatly varied, must be taken into consideration, as similar types of this portrait are repeated at the same mint during several years, though there is a change every few years, without departure from the general type.

Beginning of series of dated tetradrachms.

The starting-point for the arrangement of the whole series is the reign of Physcon after the death of Philometor. Certain silver coins bearing the dates from 41 to 54 can only be of him, no other Ptolemy having reigned so long. This series presents the mint-letters ΓΑ, ΣΑ, and ΚΙ, for Paphos, Salamis, and Citium. Two distinct styles of work, and consequently two mints with the letters ΓΑ, will be found to be due to an Egyptian and no doubt Alexandrian issue with the well-known letters of the Cyprian mint.

Bases of arrangement of series: coins of Physcon.

Mints of Cyprus.

ΓΑ, for Egyptian mint, Alexandria.

Having once determined a Cyprian coinage of Physcon, it becomes possible to class the money of earlier and later kings.

Later coinages of series.

The later issues of the series will be seen to follow according to the sequence of style, there being some difficulty in the case of the Cyprian coinage of the first four years of the two sons of Physcon, Lathyrus, and Alexander I.

ARRANGEMENT. lv

The coins struck before Physcon's undoubted money fall into two groups. One of these is clearly of later style than the other, and contains certain pieces which from their high dates can only be of Philometor or Physcon. By a careful comparison, based on the undoubted coinages of Philometor and of Physcon, those coins which bear dates suited to either king may be classed with probability.

Earlier coinages.

There remains the earlier group of Cyprian coins. This resembles the group assigned to Philometor, but is unquestionably antecedent to it. The dates range from year 2 to year 20. Such a series would suit Epiphanes, the predecessor of Philometor, his reign having lasted 24 years, and would not suit the next earlier king Philopator, who reigned 17 only. They cannot possibly be anterior to Philopator. It must be added that a single coin (pl. xiv., 2) previously assigned to the 4th year of Philopator would, if this be the true attribution, be the earliest instance of dated money of Cyprus marked by the symbol L. The comparatively continuous series begins with Epiphanes.

Coins of Epiphanes. Silver.
(Pl. xvi. 1, 2, 4-8.)

This determination of the ordinary silver staters of Epiphanes struck in Cyprus is supported by a coin with his bust (known to represent him by its being elsewhere accompanied by his distinctive title ΠΤΟΛΕΜΑΙΟΥ ΕΠΙΦΑΝΟΥΣ pl. xxxii., 7), and the letters in the left of the field ΓΟ corresponding to ΓΟ on a coin of Paphos, undated, but probably of his first or second year, judging from the style. The letters are unusual, and may be conjectured to indicate Polycrates, governor of the island until B.C. 196. The Cyprian copper money of this reign may be determined by a comparison of the series here assigned to Paphos and Citium with the copper coinage of the island under Philopator, which is of similar but better work. The supposed copper of Salamis appears to be of the same time as the two groups classed to Paphos and Citium.

Copper.
(Pl. xvi. 3, 9, 10.)

During the short period for which Epiphanes held Phoenicia (B.C. 204–198) his chief mint appears to have been the federal city of Tripolis. The occurrence of the stars of the Dioscuri on the reverse of the gold octadrachms here assigned to Tripolis is likely to create a doubt whether the same symbols on the gold coins struck by Berenice II. in the Cyrenaïca should not weaken the present attribution. It is, however, to be remembered that no symbols would be more likely at Tripolis than these, and that a silver stater presents the united monogram and symbol ⚓, TP and palm, which can scarcely be of any other mint. In the silver coinage with the head of Ptolemy Soter, the style ΠΤΟΛΕΜΑΙΟΥ ΣΩΤΗΡΟΣ still appears giving way in this class to ΠΤΟΛΕΜΑΙΟΥ ΒΑΣΙΛΕΩΣ. This would be the natural effect of the portrait-coinage of Epiphanes, which could not well bear a reverse with the legend of Ptolemy Soter. The copper coinage of Tyre is classed here on account of its late style and the occurrence of the monogram ₳, which appears on the coinage of Epiphanes (nos. 53, 54, cf. pl. xxxii. 7).

Phœnicia. Gold Silver and Copper. (Pl. xvii. 1-4.)

The Egyptian gold and silver coinage is classed to that country on grounds that seem conclusive. The series of Cyprus is determined, and that of Phoenicia must have been necessarily very limited. Indeed, if the letters in the left of the field of some coins of the remaining group are dates, their Phoenician attribution would be impossible, as some of them would fall after the loss of the province. It is not likely that any city of the Cyrenaïca was chosen as a principal mint, and thus probability limits us to Egypt, the only country left for their issue. This conjecture is supported by the style of the coins, which is rather Egyptian than of any other part of Ptolemy's dominions. The letters in the left of the field are A, B, H, Θ, and either denote years or mark a series of issues. There is, however, no certain instance of a mere mint-number on the reverse of any Ptolemaic coin, and

Egypt. Gold and silver. (Pl. xvii. 5.)

ARRANGEMENT.　　　　　　　lvii

the occurrence of dates would well correspond with the contemporary issue of dated coins in Cyprus.

Copper.
(Pl. xvii. 6,
xviii. 1-3.)

The copper money here assigned to Egypt under Epiphanes is of two classes. The First Coinage is simply an inferior repetition of the Second, or last, Coinage of Euergetes; the Second Coinage similarly repeats in its larger coins the Second Coinage of Philadelphus, the smaller size presenting a type which varies the type of Philopator. The distinctive types are of course those of the reverses. (i.) Eagle l.; in front, cornucopiæ. (ii. a.) Eagle l., wings open, looking back. (ii. β.) Eagle l., on left wing double cornucopiæ. These classes are connected by the common use of the letters ΣE, separate or in monogram. The double cornucopiæ probably indicates the marriage of Epiphanes in B.C. 193. A small coin, with the reverse-type of the eagle with open wings looking back, is interesting as having for the obverse-type the head of Nilus (pl. xviii., 3). It is evident that these coins are later than the time of Philopator, as one retains in a varied form a type of his copper, and is connected with the rest, while all show a decline in style. Are they, however, earlier than the reign of Philometor? in other words, are they of Epiphanes? A careful comparison of the new issues of the regency of Cleopatra I., widow of Epiphanes, and of the coinage of her sons Philometor and Physcon, gives a general support to the classification, as also does the coinage of Cyrenaïca here attributed to the present reign.

Cyrenaica.
Copper.
(Pl. xviii. 4-6.)

The later Cyrenaïc coins with the types of the heads of Ptolemy I. and Libya, are all, but the latest, here classed to Epiphanes. Like the coins attributed to Egypt, they are characterized by the single and double cornucopiæ on two classes. They also bear the letters ΣE in monogram and ME. They must be later than the coinage of Berenice II. and the autonomous copper coinage with **KOINON**, which may be assigned to the period including the reigns of Euergetes and Philopator (p. xlvii). They are anterior to the rule of Physcon, whose title Euergetes (II.) occurs on all his Cyrenaïc money. Allowing a few of the class under consideration, in its latest style, and a coin of the regency of Cleopatra I. of a different character, to the period between the accession of Philometor, B.C. 181, and the separation of Cyrenaïca under Physcon's rule, B.C. 164-3, it is obvious that the coins attributed to Epiphanes could only be of him or Philopator. That they are of Epiphanes is almost certain, from the presence of both ME and ƧE (monogram), the first also occurring on a silver coin of this king, assigned to Egypt, the second on the Egyptian copper which is most probably his.

It may be well to observe that the gold octadrachms attributed to Phoenicia and to Egypt, and some of the silver staters of both countries, present the bust of Epiphanes, with (in gold) a radiate diadem, this type combined with a radiate cornucopiæ on the reverse, a diadem adorned with an ear of corn, and (in silver) a plain diadem, as in the solitary coin of Cyprus with his portrait. It may be remarked that the plain diadem only occurs on this Cyprus coin supposed to have been struck while Polycrates was governor, and if so, between B.C. 204 and 196, and on an Egyptian stater which is here supposed to be of the 8th year (B.C. 198-7), on which the ear of corn appears to have been effaced on the die. The divinity to whom Epiphanes is assimilated by the radiate diadem and the ear of corn is probably Sarapis, who, as a form of Osiris, would be solar, and connected with the idea of productiveness. Certainly Sarapis appears as the consort of Cleopatra I., the widow of Epiphanes, represented on her coins in the character of Isis.

Types.

ARRANGEMENT. lix

Coins of Ptolemy VI., Philometor.

Ptolemy Philometor. Periods of reign.

It is necessary in this reign and those of Euergetes II. and his sons to begin with a table of the periods of which they consist :—

1. Regency of Cleopatra I., B.C. 181—circ. 174.
2. Regency of Eulæus and Lenæus, B.C. circ. 174—170.
3. Usurpation of Antiochus IV. } B.C. 170—168.
   Ptolemæus VIII., Euergetes II. (Physcon) King }
4. Joint reign with Ptolemæus VIII., B.C. 168—164-3.
5. Sole reign, B.C. 164-3—146.
6. Joint reign with Ptolemæus VII., Eupator, B.C. 146.

The reign of Ptolemæus VIII., Euergetes II., has the following periods during his brother's reign :—

Contemporary periods of reign of Ptolemy Euergetes II.

1. Sole King, B.C. 170—168.
2. Joint reign with Ptolemæus VI., B.C. 168—164-3.
3. King of Cyrene, B.C. 164-3—146.

Coinage of Regency of Cleopatra I.
Cyprus. Copper.
(Pl. xviii. 7.)

The coinage of the Regency of Cleopatra I. is, in part, easily determined by the fact that the earliest in style of the four portraits of Queens occasionally accompanied by the name Cleopatra is copied on the Egyptian copper money of Antiochus IV. Epiphanes, brother of Cleopatra I., struck during his usurpation. His Egyptian coinage is clearly imitated from earlier issues of Egypt, no actually new type being introduced but the head of Antiochus himself. The second denomination has for obverse-type the head of a Queen in the character of Isis (Cat. Seleucidæ, pl. xii., no. 12), a head which we find on copper money of Cyprus and Egypt. One of the earliest in style of the Cyprian coins in question has on the obverse the inscription ΒΑΣΙΛΙΣΣΗΣ ΚΛΕΟΓΑΤΡΑΣ, and on the reverse ΓΤΟΛΕΜΑΙΟΥ ΒΑΣΙΛΕΩΣ (pl. xviii., 7). This Cleopatra can only be the first of that name, striking with the title Queen probably as heiress of Cœle-Syria and Phoenicia, in association with her son Philometor, for whom she was regent.

The interesting staters with the busts jugate of Sarapis and Cleopatra as Isis appear to have been the special silver issue of this regency. The two busts are repeated, but separately, on the Egyptian coinage of Antiochus Epiphanes; and the reverse-type, the eagle looking back, with a double cornucopiæ resting on and passing under his right wing, only differs from the usual reverse of the Cyprian copper with the head of Cleopatra just noticed in the cornucopiæ being double. The association of Cleopatra with Sarapis implies the protection of the most popular Egyptian divinity of the time, just as Apollo, who shared with Ammon a similar position with the Greeks of the Cyrenaïca, appears with Cleopatra on her Cyrenaïc coinage, to be next noticed. The usual representation of Epiphanes with the diadem adorned with the ear of corn has been already shown to be a link with the Osiris cycle to which Sarapis belongs; but this must not be too strongly insisted upon. From their fabric, these silver staters with the two busts are probably of Egypt. To the same country are here assigned copper coins which are identical with those of Cyprus without the name of Cleopatra, except that they are of Egyptian fabric.

Egypt. Silver, with busts of Sarapis and Cleopatra as Isis. (Pl. xviii. 8.)

Copper. (Pl. xviii. 9.)

A single copper coin represents the Cyrenaïc currency under Cleopatra I. The obverse has the busts of Apollo and Cleopatra as Artemis, jugate; the reverse, the head of Ptolemy I., with the inscription ΒΑΣΙΛΕΩΣ ΠΤΟΛΕΜΑΙΟΥ (p. 79, no. 13). Here Apollo and Artemis take the place of Sarapis and Isis.

Cyrenaïca, Copper.

The issue of coins with the head of Cleopatra seems to have been interrupted by the Regency of Eulæus and Lenæus. The later pieces with this head, but a different reverse-type, are here classed to the sole reign of Physcon after the death of Philometor.

Recurrence of type of Cleopatra's head.

ARRANGEMENT. lxi

Classification of Cyprian currencies of Philometor and Physcon.

It is necessary to state briefly the reasons for attributing certain coins of Cyprus to the reign of Philometor, as it will be seen that according to the arrangement proposed the earliest date of these coins falls in the year which was the last of the Regency of Cleopatra, and the first of that of Eulæus and Lenæus,—by whom the coin was probably struck,—the point now reached.

Bases.

There can be no doubt that there are some coins in the Cyprian series of Philometor, and others of Physcon. The dated series from year 41 to 54 can be of no other Ptolemy than Physcon, he alone of his family having reigned above 38 or possibly 40 years; and considering that they are of a class which can only be of Philometor or Physcon, as Philometor reigned 36 years, the dates assigned to Physcon may be extended as far as 37 inclusive, giving years 37–54 inclusive for his undoubted coinage. Similarly all coins dated before year 25 of like fabric can only be of Philometor, Physcon having become ruler of Cyprus in his own 25th year. But as Philometor reigned 36 years, all coins of this group dated year 25 to 36 may be of either Philometor or Physcon. The discrimination is extremely difficult. By comparing the coins of Philometor before year 25 with later specimens of the series, and similarly by carrying up a comparison of Physcon's coins later than 37, it is possible to establish two groups, 28–34 probably of Philometor but possibly of Physcon, and 25–36 probably of Physcon but possibly of Philometor. Although the period from the 36th year of Philometor to the 36th of Physcon is only eleven years, a difference in style is to be expected. Such a difference we certainly find in Physcon's undoubted coinage within as short a period. At the same time there are insuperable difficulties in the way of a final division of the coins of the doubtful groups. A careful study of those of the class year 25–36, attributed to Physcon probably or Philometor possibly, shows that the same obverse-die was used in later years for the same and another town.

i

(Thus the obverse-die of Salamis year 31 is used with two different reverse-dies of Salamis 32 and with another of Citium 32 : again, an obverse-die of Citium year 31 is repeated with several different reverse-dies, and another of 32 with a different reverse-die, p. 90–92.) It follows that coins which are apparently of two classes, the obverse resembling Philometor's undoubted currency, the reverse Physcon's, may be reissues of Philometor's obverse-types by Physcon. It is even possible that Physcon reissued Philometor's reverse-types for the corresponding years of his own reign, though the actual proof cannot be expected.

Another difficulty must be here noticed, that due to the fact that from the time that Egypt and Cyprus were separate monarchies, B.C. 114, the mint-letters of Paphos ΓΑ, were also used for a mint of Egypt, presumably Alexandria, a point to be considered under the coinage of Physcon. This is proved by the occurrence of these letters on coins with the double dates of Cleopatra III. and Ptolemy Alexander I. of four years within the period B.C. 107-6—99, when those princes did not hold Paphos except perhaps for a year or two, and thus actually of dates when Cyprus was lost to them. The Egyptian style can apparently be carried back to the 25th year of Physcon, although between that date and 36 there is a difficulty. There can be little doubt that Physcon had an Egyptian coinage of later years than 36 : it will be seen that Philometor appears to have issued such coinage with Eupator in his 36th year. If any of the coins conjecturally assigned to an Egyptian mint were a Cyprian issue, they would be of a rougher fabric than that of Paphos or the other mints of the island, and this of course favours the attribution to the mint of Alexandria here preferred.

Mint-letters ΓΑ also used for an Egyptian mint, presumably Alexandria. Proof of this position.

The style of Philometor's certain coins is better than that of the certain coins of Physcon. The head is usually larger and in

ARRANGEMENT.

lxiii

Styles of Philometor and Physcon. higher relief, and has a nearer resemblance in many cases to that of the later coins of Epiphanes of Salamis. The eagle is generally better designed, and has a fuller form and larger stride.

To return to the currency of the reign of Philometor under the **Regency of Eulæus and Lenæus**: the regular issue of the silver coins of Cyprus with the traditional portrait of Ptolemy I. seems to have marked the beginning of the period, as we have coins (p. 80, nos. 14, 15) dated in the 7th year (B.C. 175–4). This year corresponds to the close of Cleopatra's Regency, and as she appears to have used special types of her own, the reissue would mark their abandonment, as we shall see was the case with the copper of Egypt. It may be observed that the thunderbolt is winged as on one of the two specimens of the next issue dated year 19 (Pl. xix. 5, p. 83, nos. 31, 32 and 33).

Regency of Eulæus and Lenæus.
Cyprus, Silver.
(Pl. xix. 1.)

A new copper coinage was issued in Egypt under this regency. It bears the head of Zeus Ammon and the eagle, under whose left wing in the larger denomination is a sceptre, while in the left of the field is a lotus, the prevailing symbol on Philometor's copper money, according to the classification of this catalogue; between the eagle's legs are the letters **EYΛ** for Eulæus. Were there any doubt as to the attribution of these coins, it would be removed by their being countermarked by Antiochus IV. in Egypt with the Seleucid anchor, a circumstance which has additional value in showing them to have been a currency of Egypt. The occurrence of the name of Eulæus to the exclusion of that of his colleague is of historical value.

Egypt. Copper.
(Pl. xix. 2.)

The usurpation of Antiochus IV. was marked not only by the countermarking of the current copper just noticed, but also as already observed by the issue of a new copper currency for Egypt with his own name, two of the obverse-types of which, the heads

Coinage of usurpation of Antiochus IV.
Egypt. Copper.

of Sarapis and Isis, were borrowed from his sister's, the regent Cleopatra's, money.

Coinage of joint reign of Philometor and Physcon.
Cyprus, Copper.
Egypt, Copper.
(Pl. xix. 3.)

The joint reign of Philometor and Physcon B.C. 168-164-3 may perhaps be commemorated by the issue in Cyprus and Egypt of hastily-struck copper coins which have the air of money of necessity. There appear to have been two issues in Egypt, the first repeating the largest denomination of Eulæus, without the lotus, the second a barbarous reissue of the same types (pl. xix., no. 3). Possibly part or all of this group should be classed to Physcon's first sole reign, B.C. 170—168.

Cyrenaica.
Coinage from first Regency to separation of Cyrenaica.
Copper.
(Pl. xix. 4.)

To the period between the death of Cleopatra I. and the close of the joint reign of the two kings, when Physcon became king of Cyrene and issued a special coinage, we may conjecturally assign the latest copper coins with the heads of Ptolemy I. and Libya, which have some analogy in size and fabric with the Egyptian coins of about the same period.

Sole reign of Philometor, B.C. 64-3—46.
Cyprus, Silver.
(Pl. xix. 5-8; xx. 1, 2.)
Copper.
(Pl. xx. 3-5.)

The Cyprian silver coinage assigned to Philometor during his sole reign has been already discussed. Certain copper coins of Cyprus with the types of the head of Zeus Ammon and the eagle on thunderbolt, with closed wings, and dates ranging from 26 to 36, are classed to this period. Most have the lotus in the field left, beneath the date, but one bears a star above the date (cf. pl. xx., nos. 4, 5). The lotus is markedly consistent with the attribution, the star is consistent, and the dates correspond to those of the issue of Cyprian silver in the series assigned to Philometor. One large coin in copper of the maximum Egyptian size (pl. xx., no. 3) is here classed to Cyprus, on account of its provenance and style, and its similarity in the reverse, not excepting in the form of the lotus, to the dated pieces. It should be remarked that the lotus in the Egyptian money classed to the same king had usually a different form (cf. pl. xx., nos. 3, 4, 5 with 8 and xix. 2, 3). This occurrence of copper of the largest size out of Egypt is very unusual. It also occurs in Phoenicia under Ptolemy II. and III., and the Cyrenaïca under Physcon with Cleopatra II. and III.

Two coins of the Dionysiac series are assigned to Philometor's reign in Cyprus between B.C. 164-3 and 146, as one bears two symbols, both of which occur separately on the regular silver coins assigned to this period, and both are marked by their characteristic striding eagle (pl. xx., 6).

Dionysiac series. Silver. (Pl. xx. 6.)

The short reign of Philometor in Phoenicia from the date of his capture of Ptolemaïs B.C. 148-7 to his death B.C. 146 is commemorated by two coins, the silver tetradrachm represented in the Bibliothèque Nationale at Paris, and the Hague, and a copper coin in the British Museum. Both bear the diademed portrait of the king, as a king of Syria, not of Egypt, for they lack the aegis; and this is in accord with the statement of the historians that Philometor was offered at Antioch the diadem of Syria, to which it may be added his maternal descent from the Seleucids gave him a claim, though one inferior to that of Demetrius II. Nicator, in whose favour he appears to have resigned.*

Phoenicia. Silver and copper. (Pl. xxxii. 8; xx. 7.)

Portrait of Philometor as a Seleucid.

There is therefore nothing surprising in the occurrence of coins of Ptolemy Philometor in the character of a Seleucid king. These

---

* Πτολεμαῖος, ὁ τῆς Συρίας βασιλεὺς, κατὰ τὸν πόλεμον πληγεὶς ἐτελεύτησε τὸν βίον, Polyb. xl. 12. ἐλθὼν δὲ πρὸς τοὺς Ἀντιοχεῖς Πτολεμαῖος βασιλεὺς ὑπ' αὐτῶν καὶ τῶν στρατευμάτων ἀναδείκνυται, καὶ ἀναγκασθεὶς δύο περιτίθεται διαδήματα, ἓν μὲν τὸ τῆς Ἀσίας, ἕτερον δὲ τῆς Αἰγύπτου, Jos. Ant. xiii. 4, § 7. καὶ εἰσῆλθε Πτολεμαῖος εἰς Ἀντιόχειαν, καὶ περιέθετο δύο διαδήματα περὶ τὴν κεφαλὴν αὐτοῦ, τὸ τῆς Ἀσίας καὶ [τὸ τῆς] Αἰγύπτου, 1 Macc. xi. 13. So far there is no difference: Josephus adds that Ptolemy at once resigned at Antioch in favour of Demetrius II. Nicator.

coins might have been struck by him as a claimant to the throne of Syria on his invasion, or under the circumstances of his receiving the Syrian diadem at Antioch, or indeed for Phoenicia alone, to which he had an undoubted right.

The coins may be thus described:—

Head of Ptolemaeus VI. r. diademed.
Rev. ΠΤΟΛΕΜΑΙΟΥ [ΒΑΣΙΛ]ΕΩΣ ΦΙΛΟΜΗΤΟΡΟΣ ΘΕΟΥ.
Eagle l. on winged thunderbolt; under r. wing corn-stalk; to r. m̊; between eagle and thunderbolt IΔ ˥ A. Æ.
Struck at Ptolemaïs. (Pl. xxxii., no. 8.)

The Syrian style of the inscription is particularly to be noticed.—The type of the eagle and corn-stalk was first correctly described by Dr. Imhoof-Blumer (Zeitschrift für Numismatik iii. 352. Taf. ix. 16).

Head of Ptolemy VI. r. diademed; countermark ₭.
Rev. ΠΤΟΛΕΜΑΙΟΥ ΒΑΣ . . . . . Eagle l. on thunderbolt, wings open; in front, dolphin r., downwards. Æ.
(Pl. xx., no. 7.)

This coin, struck at some coast-town of Phoenicia, Palestine, or Syria, bears a countermark which seems peculiar to Cyprus.

The Egyptian coinage of Philometor as sole king from B.C. 164–3 to 146 probably comprised gold octadrachms of Arsinoë II. (supra, p. xl.). The copper money here classed to him is characterized by his supposed distinctive symbol the lotus, and is remarkable as containing the latest known example struck in Egypt of the heaviest piece in this metal (pl. xx., no. 8). In style this copper stands between the coinages assigned to Epiphanes and to Physcon.

Egypt.
Gold ?
Copper.
(Pl. xx. 8.)

It is necessary here to notice a remarkable coin, apparently with double dates, which appears to be of Philometor and his son Eupator.

There has been a difference of opinion as to Ptolemy Eupator, some considering him to have been an elder brother and immediate predecessor of Philometor, others as Philometor's young son and successor, put to death, after a reign of a few months or days, by his uncle Physcon. An inscription copied at Apello in Cyprus determines the question. It is as follows:—

Ptolemy VI. Philometor, and Ptolemy VII. Eupator. (Pl. xxxii. 9.)

Βασιλέα Πτολεμαῖον, θεὸν Εὐπάτορα,
Τὸν ἐγ Βασιλέως Πτολεμαίου καὶ Βασιλίσσης
Κλεοπάτρας, θεῶν Φιλομητόρων, ...
. . . .

(Le Bas et Waddington, iii. 1, p. 646, no. 2809.) The date of Eupator is therefore B.C. 146, and I have numbered him Ptolemy VII., as intermediate in the legitimate succession between Philometor and Physcon.* Professor Lepsius had, however, ascertained that Eupator was associated during his father's life with him in the dynastic worship (Ueber einige Ergebnisse der aeg. Denkmäler für die Kenntniss der Ptolemäergeschichte, Berlin Acad., 1852, p. 464), and this M. Revillout explains in an unpublished paper in the Revue Égyptologique, kindly communicated by him, to be a mode of designation for the heir to the throne. The coin referred to, first published by Mr. Reichardt in the Numismatic Chronicle (N. S., iv. 189), appears to show an actual association of Eupator with Philometor on the throne. It may be thus described:—

Coin which appears to commemorate their association. (Pl. xxxii. 9.)

Obv. Head of Ptolemy I.
Rev. ΠΤΟΛΕΜΑΙΟΥ ΒΑΣΙΛΕΩΣ Eagle; in field l. and r.
L ΑΣ ΚΑΙ
Α   ΓΑ   (Pl. xxxii. 9.)

---

* M. Waddington numbers Eupator Ptolemy VIII., and I regret to have inadvertently adopted a different numbering, although on reasonable grounds.

This coin is evidently related to a group classed in the tables to Alexandria with the mint-mark ΓA, ranging from year 25 to 36, probably of Physcon, possibly of Philometor. The type of the head is most like that of the coins with the extreme dates. As the 25th year of Physcon was the 36th of Philometor we have here an agreement of type, however we attribute the group.* If we are justified in reading LΛΕ ΚΑΙ Α, as a double date as in the coins of Cleopatra III. and Alexander I., where the years are arranged in the same manner without the conjunction, we have to choose between Philometor and Physcon. If the coin is of Philometor it would indicate that at the close of his reign he endeavoured to strengthen the position of his heir by direct association, only a slight step beyond the association in the family cultus. On the other hand, there is nothing in the reign of Physcon which would explain a double date in his 36th year. The presence of καί might be urged against this reading, but a magistrate's name would be more strange in this part of the series; and if, as is likely, this was an innovation, the presence and subsequent dropping of the conjunction would be quite natural.

Thus this exceptional coin cannot reasonably be doubted to be of Philometor and Eupator; thus furnishing us with a coregency, which is a new fact in history; and it is not unlikely that it begins the Egyptian series with ΓA.

Coins of Ptolemy VIII., Euergetes II. (Physcon).

The reign of Ptolemy Physcon comprises the following periods:—

Ptolemy Physcon. Periods of reign. 1. King of Egypt B.C. 170–168 (during usurpation of Antiochus IV.).

---

* Thus the coin cannot affect the classification. It may be noted, however, that the piece dated year 36 has a worn die on the obverse, and may be an instance of the reissue of old obverse-dies by Physcon, which the coins of the same period of Salamis and Citium illustrate, though it is not certain that under this king such dies were so used except of his own coinage.

ARRANGEMENT. lxix

2. Joint reign with Ptolemæus VI., Philometor, B.C. 168-164-3.
3. King of Cyrene B.C. 164-3-146.
   α. Before revolt B.C. 164-3-circ. 156.
   β. After revolt B.C. circ. 156-146.
4. King of Egypt B.C. 146-117.
   α. Sole king B.C. 146-127.
   β. Joint reign with Cleopatra II. and III. B.C. 127-117.
      1. With Ptolemæus IX., Philopator II., Cyprus only, year 50, B.C. 121-0.
      2. With Philopator II., whole kingdom, years 52-54, B.C. 119-8-117.

It will be noted that in this list only those periods which are supported by numismatic evidence are inserted.

The coinages which may possibly be of the first and second periods have been already noticed (p. lxiv).

There are no silver coins which can be assigned with certainty to Physcon's rule in the Cyrenaïca, B.C. 164-3-146, or during the later part of his reign after Philometor's death B.C. 146-117. It is most probable that he had a silver coinage during the earlier of these periods, when he held no territory but the Cyrenaïca; and it will be seen that an uncertain group, to be noticed immediately after his assignable coinage, may be in part or wholly the wanted series, but the evidence is as yet slight (p. lxxiii).

The whole copper coinage of the Cyrenaïca should be here noticed,

Cyrenaïca. Copper. (Pl. xxii. 7—9; xxiv. 1.)

as we cannot separate the coins struck after Physcon's succession to the whole kingdom B.C. 146 from the earlier currency, except those struck during the last period of his reign, that is while Cleopatra II. and III. were associated with him B.C. 127-117. This copper coinage is determined by its provenance to the Cyrenaïca and by the occurrence of the title ΕΥΕΡΓΕΤΟΥ to the rule of Physcon. It is of three classes. All have for obverse-type the head of Zeus Ammon—rev. 1. Eagle looking

k

back; before him Φ (pl. xxii., no. 7). This is of the earliest fabric. 2. Eagle with expanded wings, letters Φ, ΘΕ, and Κ (pl. xxii., nos. 8, 9); the order being determined by the occurrence of Φ in the previous class and the intermediate character in this class of the coins with ΘΕ. The class is large and of careful execution. 3. Two cornucopiæ united with fillet. The last class is shown by its type to belong to the joint rule of Physcon and the Cleopatras, B.C. 127-117. It is remarkable as containing the last examples of the largest copper coin of the Ptolemies (pl. xxiv., no. 1). The exact attribution to particular periods of the other classes is as yet uncertain.

The silver coinage of Cyprus and Egypt during Physcon's reign,

Period 4, Cyprus; Egypt. Silver.

after Philometor's death B.C. 146—117, has been noticed in discussing the coinage of Philometor. Here it is necessary to add the reasons for considering the Egyptian mint that adopted the mint-letters ΓΑ of

ΓΑ for Alexandria.

Paphos to be Alexandria. It might seem at first sight improbable that the well-known mint-letters of Paphos should have been adopted by another city. We have, however, an instance of a like usage in the imitations of the money of Athens, and an exact parallel in the appearance of the mint-letters of Constantinople, CON or COM, at one time, on the whole gold coinage of the Roman Empire. But the occurrence of the letters ΓΑ on coins of Cleopatra III. and Alexander I., with dates at which Cyprus was not subject to their rule, establishes a distinct principle. It only remains for us to ascertain what mint or mints the Egyptian ΓΑ represents. It must be remembered that the silver coinage of the Ptolemies was emphatically that intended for their Greek subjects, the copper money obtaining a growing importance with the native Egyptians. Consequently, Alexandria would be the natural mint-city of the staters, apart from its importance as capital. If we could distinctly trace two fabrics we might assign a second mint to the only other great Greek city,

ARRANGEMENT. lxxi

Ptolemaïs; but there is not sufficient evidence to justify this hypothesis. At one time, under Ptolemy Alexander I. and Cleopatra III., one might be tempted to suggest it.

At first there does not appear to have been a double coinage at Paphos and Alexandria, and it would seem probable that for some time after Physcon succeeded Philometor, apparently until the joint reign with Cleopatra II. and III., very little money was coined at Paphos, Alexandria having superseded it with the same mint-letters, ΓΑ. It is indeed possible that Philometor in his last year, 36, or Physcon on succeeding him, transferred the mint of Paphos to Alexandria, and did not at once resume the Paphian currency.

Period 4a.
Sole reign.
Cyprus, Egypt.
Silver, copper.
(Pl. xxi.; xxii.1-6.)

The silver money of the two periods of Physcon's reign after Philometor's death may be separated by the dates, the copper by the types. The only copper money that can reasonably be attributed to Cyprus (Paphos) and Egypt during the first period, B.C. 146—127, Physcon's sole reign, presents the head of his mother Cleopatra I. and the eagle with open wings. The Cyprian group has the monogram ⟨A⟩ of Paphos (pl. xxi., no. 3); the Egyptian group wants the monogram, and is further characterized by its style (pl. xxii., nos. 5, 6). The obverse-type is clearly derived from the money of Cleopatra's regency. That money is succeeded by the coinages of Eulæus, of Antiochus IV. in Egypt, and by those coins which repeat the types of Eulæus, and lastly by the coins of Cyprus which it is reasonable to attribute to Philometor's later years. It is obvious that a coinage resuming the type of Cleopatra which only recurs once before, in a denomination of Antiochus IV.'s money in the group just noticed, cannot well be earlier than the succession of Physcon. Two different series of later style seem to correspond to the joint rule of Physcon with Cleopatra II. and III. B.C. 127—117, and to the subsequent coregency of

Cleopatra III. with Lathyrus or Alexander, or probably both. The important copper coinage resuming the portrait of Cleopatra I. would thus suit the sole reign of Physcon B.C. 146—127, and there is no other copper money we could attribute to that time.

The copper coinage of the second part of this period, the joint reign of Physcon and the Cleopatras, is probably a new series, with the head of a Cleopatra, probably Cleopatra III., wearing stephane and elephant's skin on the obverse, the eagle with open wings on the reverse. The coins are of Paphos and Egypt. The Paphian coins have the mint monogram ꟼꟼ, and occasionally on the obverse ΒΑΣΙΛΙΣΣΗΣ ΚΛΕΟΓΑΤΡΑΣ (pl. xxiii., no. 3). The Egyptian coins have no mint-monogram and no obverse-inscription, and are of clearly Egyptian fabric (no. 10). As the joint reign of Cleopatra III. with Lathyrus, and possibly that with Alexander, has coins with the same obverse-inscription, of Egyptian fabric, and another type (Head of Zeus Ammon), and that coinage is long continued, there can be no doubt that the arrangement here proposed of the series with the head wearing the elephant's skin, itself most probably of earlier fabric than the series last noticed, is correct; but these coins may possibly be of Cleopatra II. and Ptolemy Philometor.

Coregency. Cyprus; Egypt. Silver, copper. (Pl. xxiii.)

Coins of Citium with the head of Zeus Ammon and the eagle with open wings, having Κ between his legs, are from their bad fabric probably of late date in Physcon's reign, but cannot be certainly attributed in point of time (pl. xxiii., no. 8).

A very interesting coin throws light upon the obscure history of Ptolemy Philopator II., a young prince associated in the worship of the sovereigns in Physcon's 52nd year. We may regard him as then definitely recognized as heir of the old king; and as he was set aside by Cleopatra III. he was probably her brother, who stood in the way of her sons. This information is due to the researches of M. Revillout, who has most generously communicated them before publication in the Revue Archéologique. A coin of Physcon's 50th year, struck at Paphos, described in the tables, p. 96, no. 99, presents on the reverse L N Γ A (pl. xxiii., no. 4). The conjunction of N (50) and A (1), ⁂ ⁂ precisely as ΛΓ and A, on a previously noticed coin, A but without the καί, indicates, it would seem, a coregency; and M. Revillout is of opinion that a previous association in Cyprus in the 50th year of Physcon preceded that of the 52nd year in Egypt. Of course, as before, the actual occurrence of a regnal year on a coin would prove more than an association as heir, but a coregency for Cyprus only.

Uncertain Coins of, and anterior to, the period of Ptolemy VI. and Ptolemy VIII.

There are two groups of silver coins, the one of about the period of Philometor and Physcon, the other extending from an earlier time and terminating about that time, which should be noticed here.

A. The group of uncertain coins of about the period of Philometor and Physcon should be first examined, as it is possible that it represents the coinage of Physcon during his sole reign in the Cyrenaïca, B.C. 164-3–146.

Uncertain Coins about time of Ptolemy VIII. (Pl. xxiv. 4–7.)

These coins are the only group in the class of Ptolemaïc silver money which have no indication of mint or moneyer, nor any certain indication of date. They have a general resemblance, but it may be that they do not all belong to one part of the empire. Unfortunately no satisfactory evidence of their provenance as a group has come to light. There seems, however, to be negative evidence that they are not Egyptian, as I do not know of their occurring in collections formed in Egypt. Their style appears to forbid Cyprus, and less certainly Phoenicia: their age as indicated by style would exclude the idea that they were struck in Greece. Consequently the Cyrenaïca is not impossible as their source, and Physcon's reign between B.C. 164-3-146 is not only the most likely period, but one favoured by the similarity observable in one of these coins and his supposed Egyptian coinage from B.C. 146. (Compare pl. xxiv. 6 with pl. xxii. 1, 2). They may be reasonably classed as two coinages.

B. The second group is one of much greater importance. It is Coins of an Era. dated throughout, but the only other letters which (Pl. xxv.) occur (ΕΙ or Ε) on three specimens do not seem to be connected with a mint. The succession of dates and styles leaves no doubt that the group is of one sequence.

The provenance, as in the case of the previous class, is obscure. Similarly, however, the coins do not to my knowledge occur, with rare exceptions, in collections formed in Egypt, and the style excludes Cyprus while the length of the series excludes Greece or Asia Minor. Here, however, a difference is to be noted. Instead of the ordinary inscription ΠΤΟΛΕΜΑΙΟΥ ΒΑΣΙΛΕΩΣ, the reverses bear up to year 90 inclusive the Phoenician variety of style ΠΤΟΛΕΜΑΙΟΥ ΣΩΤΗΡΟΣ. It is also remarkable that all coins with the title ΣΩΤΗΡΟΣ are tetradrachms, all with ΒΑΣΙΛΕΩΣ didrachms. There is no indication of mint or magistrate except on three didrachms, ΕΙ occurring on the thunderbolt on one of the coins of year 109 and on that of 110, and Ε, probably for the same word, on another of year 115. Occurring on two coins of successive years, ΕΙ cannot be a date. No mint seems to agree with ΕΙ or Ε, and consequently it probably stands for a magistrate's name. The chief varieties in the type are in the place of the date, which is first between the eagle's legs, then in the field left, then in the exergue, then in the field left again, then in the earliest didrachms on the thunderbolt, and lastly across the field. The thunderbolt is occasionally winged from year 88, and from year 112 is always winged. The types show a curious degradation with a recovery on the reverse in year 88: the didrachms are uniformly of better style. (See pl. xxv.)

The Era must be regal or civic. A civic Era is almost excluded by the absence of indications of the mint. If regal, it would first appear that we should choose between the Era of Philip B.C. 324 and that of Dionysius, or of Ptolemy Philadelphus, B.C. 285. The Era of the Seleucidæ seems wholly out of the question. The choice of the Era depends upon the style of the coins as well as the territory in which they were struck. If we conclude them to be of Phoenicia or a neighbouring province, no known Era but that of Philip would suit. The highest date on the coins is year 117: thus we should have 116 years before B.C. 199 when Ptolemy V. lost Phoenicia, or B.C. 315 for the latest date of the beginning of the Era. If, however, we reckon from B.C. 324 or 315 the style of the coins which would fall about the time of Philadelphus (years 48, 50, 71, 72, 74, 75 ?, 77) with the dated coins of this king struck in Phoenicia, the arrangement is destroyed by the evidence of style. If we arrange them by style, the Era of Dionysius would suit, and most modifications of type in the place of the date would indicate a change of reign. The alteration of style ΣΩΤΗΡΟΣ to ΒΑΣΙΛΕΩΣ would suit either Era. The style of the coins seems as surely to point to the East as the inscription ΠΤΟΛΕΜΑΙΟΥ ΣΩΤΗΡΟΣ, and if we accept the Era of Dionysius, there is a remarkable agreement between the coins here attributed to the reign of Euergetes and his Phoenician issues, particularly those of barbarous style. But if the coins were struck in the East and dated by the Era of Dionysius, some maritime city must have been held by Epiphanes after he had lost the rest of his Oriental provinces. This is so doubtful that a third but very hazardous hypothesis may be suggested. The cultus of Ptolemy I. as Soter appears to have been introduced in the year 25, B.C. 261–0, when the new title begins in the Phoenician silver currency, the title 'king' being dropped for a long time. If the coins were thus religious, and dated from this event, which we may place B.C. 261–0, we could understand their being struck until the conquest of Egypt by Antiochus Epiphanes, when by this arrangement there is a gap; and the title ΣΩΤΗΡ disappears. Again, their reissue with the title ΒΑΣΙΛΕΥΣ from the early part of the sole reign of Philometor until his death, and perhaps into the next year if we date from B.C. 261-0, is equally possible, for it is quite reasonable to suppose he recovered some border-towns of Phoenicia before his conquest of the country at the close of his reign, and Physcon may not have instantly lost all his brother gained. This arrangement is most consistent with the style of the coins as compared with the known Phoenician issues, and failing these, with those of Cyprus.

Coins of Ptolemy X., Soter II. (Lathyrus), Ptolemy XI., Alexander I., and Ptolemy (Apion) King of Cyrene.

The coins of the sons of Physcon must be treated together, as their reigns were mainly contemporary, and in the cases of Lathyrus and Alexander I. interchanging with the interchange of the kingdoms of Egypt and Cyprus. The following are the chronological data:—

Coins of sons of Physcon. Periods.

Ptolemaeus X. Soter II. Lathyrus.
1. Joint reign with Cleopatra III.
    B.C. 117-111.
    α. Rules whole kingdom B.C. 117-114.
    β. Rules Egypt and Cyrenaïca? B.C. 114-111.
2. Sole king of Egypt and Cyrenaïca? B.C. 111-107-6.
3. King of Cyprus B.C. 107-6?-88.
4. King of Egypt and Cyprus B.C. 88-81.

Ptolemaeus XI. Alexander I.
1. King of Cyprus B.C. 114-107-6?
2. King of Egypt B.C. 107-6-88.
    α. Joint reign with Cleopatra III. B.C. 107-6-99.
    β. Sole reign B.C. 99-88.

Ptolemaeus Apion.
King of Cyrene B.C. 107-6?-96?

ARRANGEMENT. lxxvii

Coinages of Lathyrus and Alexander.

It is the most easy method to take first the Cyprian, and then the Egyptian coinages of Lathyrus and Alexander, and last the money of the Cyrenaïca here classed to Lathyrus and Apion. The Egyptian and the Cyprian coinages are markedly distinct: the chronological sequence in each country would be equally clear were it not that both Lathyrus and

Cyprus, Silver.
Lathyrus, Per. I.
(Pl. xxvi. 1, 2.)
Alexander, Per. I.
(Pl. xxvii. 5–11.)

Alexander may have coined at Cyprus during their regnal years 1 to 4, the 1st year of Alexander being the 4th of Lathyrus. Consequently all Cyprian coins dated 1 to 4 may be of either king. The strictest principle of arrangement would be to class to Lathyrus probably, Alexander possibly, those coins of these dates which closely resemble the latest coins of Physcon, and to Alexander probably, Lathyrus possibly, those which closely resemble Alexander's undoubted later Cyprian coinage. It will be seen by examining the plates that there is a sufficient difference of style to justify a more positive arrangement.

There is a difficulty in the Cyprian series. The supposed coinage of Alexander closes at Paphos and Citium with coins of year 9, the Museum having two specimens of Paphos (one engraved, pl. xxvii. 7) and one of Citium of this date. It is, however, quite certain that Alexander was sent for by Cleopatra III. in the previous year and appointed her coregent in Egypt, where coins were struck with the joint dates 11 (of Cleopatra) and 8 (of Alexander). Nothing is better determined in the coinage of the Ptolemies than the attribution of the double-dated coins which begin with those bearing the years just mentioned. There does not, however, seem to be any proof that Alexander abandoned Cyprus, and Lathyrus took possession of the island, when the change of sovereigns took place in Egypt. On the contrary, Justin states that Cleopatra sent a force to Cyprus against Lathyrus, who in consequence left the island. (Nec filium regno expulisse contenta bello Cypri exulantem persequitur. Unde pulso interfecit ducem exercitus sui, quod vivum

l

lxxviii   INTRODUCTION.

eum e manibus dimisisset, quanquam Ptolemaeus verecundia materni belli non viribus minor ab insula recessisset. xxxix. 4.) It is quite certain that Lathyrus was in full possession of Cyprus B.C. 105, in his 12th or 13th year, the 9th or 10th of Alexander (Jos. A. J. xiii. 12. 2). It is confirmatory of the proposed modification of the usual view of the history of the time, that one of the two coins of year 8 (Paphos) in the Museum and the three of year 9 present an appearance of hasty striking (pl. xxvii., no. 12). One coin of the Dionysiac series is classed with the group of Alexander; it may be of Lathyrus (pl. xxvii. 12).

The Cyprian copper coinage assigned to the first reign of Lathyrus in the island is similar to the Egyptian copper coinage of about the same period (pl. xxvi. 7, 8), which sometimes bears the name Cleopatra, and can only begin with Cleopatra III., but is characterized by the mint-letter K for Citium between the legs of the nearer eagle (no. 3). There are two copper coins of comparatively good style which are conjecturally assigned to Lathyrus in Cyprus: both are engraved (pl. xxviii. nos. 6, 7).

Copper. (Pl. xxvi. 3; xxviii. 6, 7.)

The second coinage of Lathyrus in Cyprus, struck while he was king of the island, is very scanty. Its attribution cannot reasonably be doubted on account of the dates, years 18, 19, 20, and 21, which could be otherwise only of the reign of Philometor, with whose coins the style does not agree.

Lathyrus, Period III. (Pl. xxvii. 3, 4; xxxii. 10.)

The Egyptian coinage of Lathyrus and Alexander presents no difficulty, as the order is determined by the agreement of the gradually debased style under the sequence of years with the middle portion which is fixed by the double dates of Cleopatra III. and Alexander. The double-dated coins are of $\frac{11}{8}$, $\frac{12}{9}$, $\frac{13}{10}$, and $\frac{16}{13}$, or B.C. 107–6, 106–5, 105–4, and 102–1.

Egypt, Silver. Lathyrus, (Pl. xxvi. 4–6; xxviii. 8.) *Alexander,* (Nos. 1–5.) *Double dates of Alex. and Cleopatra III.* (Nos. 1, 2.)

ARRANGEMENT. lxxix

In the series with the double dates we find two characteristically different heads of Ptolemy I., one of which preserves the head on the latest Egyptian coins of Physcon (cf. pl. xxviii., no. 2, with xxiii. 9), and the other shows a variety found only after his time. During the joint reign of Lathyrus and Cleopatra III. (B.C. 117—111) the first type alone occurs in the Egyptian coinage (xxvi. 4, 5, 6). During the sole reign of Lathyrus (B.C. 111—107-6) the second type, with straighter features (xxvii. 2), is found side by side with the old one (no. 1). In the joint reign of Alexander and Cleopatra III., as already indicated, the two types continue, but during the sole reign of Alexander, so far as we can judge from the coins, which become much debased in style, only the older Egyptian type is maintained (xxviii. 3, 4, 5). The one coin of Lathyrus after the time of Alexander is simply a copy of Alexander's latest currency (no. 8).

Copper of Lathyrus and Alex. (Pl. xxvi. 7, 8.) The copper coins of Egypt during the whole period under consideration begin with those bearing the head of Zeus Ammon and the inscription ΒΑΣΙΛΙΣΣΗΣ ΚΛΕΟΠΑΤΡΑΣ, and for the reverse two eagles and ΠΤΟΛΕΜΑΙΟΥ ΒΑΣΙΛΕΩΣ, with, between the legs of the nearer eagle, ΠΑ, and in front, a double cornucopiae. The origin of this type is, as already shown, to be placed in the joint reign of Cleopatra III. and Lathyrus, the style repeating this Queen's or her mother's as coregent, and Cleopatra I. her grandmother's as regent. The monogram on coins of undoubted Egyptian fabric is valuable as connecting Paphos with an Egyptian mint. The comparison of fabric with the Cyprian coins of Lathyrus and Cleopatra III. is most instructive (xxvi. 3). In Egypt the Queen's name and the mint-monogram seem to have speedily disappeared (no. 8), but the coinage was probably prolonged at least until the death of Lathyrus. It was appropriate during the two joint reigns, and not inappropriate to the sole reigns of Lathyrus and Alexander, Ptolemy

Philadelphus having set the example of indicating his consort by a second eagle as by a second cornucopiæ.

The Cyrenaïc coinage presents three reverses, noticed in order of size, the obverse being always the head of Zeus Ammon; reverse (1) two eagles, (2) double cornucopiæ; in field, ΣΩ ΘΕ, (3) head-dress of Isis; beneath, ΣΩ. The appearance of a title, ΣΩ[THPOΣ] with or without ΘΕ[ΟΥ] is characteristic of the Cyrenaïc issues, as in Physcon's case. (Müller, Numismatique de l'Ancienne Afrique, Suppl. p. 29, on Physcon's Cyrenaïc money). The second type preserves that of Physcon during the last coregency with the Cleopatras. The coins are attributed by their provenance. The chronology presents some difficulty. It has been hitherto held that Apion immediately succeeded Physcon at Cyrene. The number of the coins apparently of Lathyrus, besides some undoubtedly his, would make the most reasonable date of the accession of Apion that of the exile of Lathyrus, B.C. 107-6.

Cyrenaica, Lathyrus. Copper. (Pl. xxvi. 9–12.)

To Ptolemy Apion I have conjecturally assigned the small copper coins apparently of Cyrenaïc fabric with the inscription B A for BAΣIΛEΩΣ. Perhaps some or all of the coins assigned to Lathyrus which bear no title are Apion's.

Ptolemy Apion. (Pl. xxviii. 9.)

Coins of Ptolemy XIII., Neus Dionysus (Auletes).

There is no difficulty in arranging the coins of Ptolemy Auletes. The baseness of the metal, which is almost potin, is far below that of any other Ptolemaïc series, and connects this money with the Roman potin of Alexandria, to which it should stand nearest. The known dates, with a break for the rule of Cleopatra VI. with Berenice IV. and Berenice alone, exactly suit the reign of Auletes, and the type is the same as that of the silver coin of Cleopatra

Coinage of Ptolemy Auletes. (Pl. xxix. 1–3.)

VII., struck in her sixth year, therefore not long after the death of Auletes (pl. xxx., no. 5). It is worthy of remark that on his restoration Auletes appears to have issued a better coinage. From the beginning of his reign to his expulsion there is evidently a growing debasement accompanied by degradation in work, but during his second reign the quality of the metal is evidently better and the work more careful. (Cf. Feuardent, Coll. Demetrio i. p. 111, 112.) The weight throughout is irregular, and M. Feuardent (l. c.) seems to be in error in stating that it becomes more uniform in the second reign: the majority of the coins are, however, then higher in weight than before; yet the low weights of 182.8 and 147.6 occur in the ten tetradrachms of the Museum collection belonging to the second reign.

Coins of Ptolemy, king of Cyprus.

There is a series of silver coins which must, to judge from their style, be subsequent in date to Ptolemy Lathyrus, and as they extend without break from the 1st to the 23rd year, they can only be of Ptolemy Auletes or of his younger brother Ptolemy king of Cyprus (B.C. 81—58). No other Ptolemy after Lathyrus had so long a reign. The fabric of the coins is rather Cyprian than Egyptian, though the converse seems to be true of the style. The obverse-type at first resembles the later Cyprian money of Lathyrus and the earlier Egyptian of Auletes. The reverse-type follows the extreme simplicity of the Egyptian coinages before Auletes, there being no symbol, nor any palm beside the eagle. The provenance is sometimes Egyptian, but some of the Museum specimens come from sources which would rather point to Cyprus as the origin of the coinage. Strangely, however, I know personally of no instance of these coins being brought from Cyprus. M. Feuardent, however, states that they

Coinage of Ptolemy, king of Cyprus.
(Pl. xxix. 4-8; xxx. 1-3.)

are largely found there. The attribution would be balanced between the first reign of Auletes and his brother's reign as king of Cyprus but for circumstances which seem to point in favour of the Cyprian attribution. The types, except those of the obverses in the earliest years, are different in style and work from those of Auletes, and the reverse-types are markedly distinct. Besides the difference in style and work, the silver is much better in the doubtful series. It is thus safest to accept, as most probable, M. Feuardent's attribution of these coins to Ptolemy, king of Cyprus. (Coll. Dem. p. 116—118.) Certain copper coins of undoubted Cyprian fabric have been here classed to the same king (pl. xxx., nos. 1—3). They are obviously very late in date, and those which bear the palm-branch under the eagle's wing and the monogram of Cyprus ₭, are thus connected with the time of Auletes and the early part of the reign of Cleopatra VII. by the type, and with the Cyprian coinage of Cleopatra by the monogram (xxx. 6). The attribution of these pieces is therefore probable, and the others cannot be much out of place.

Coins of the Successors of Auletes.

Coinage of successors of Auletes.

It is not probable that the reigns of the successors of Auletes were commemorated by any but a scanty issue of Egyptian money sufficient to show their exercise of the regal right of coinage. The earlier part of the period was disturbed; in the later, the Roman or virtually Roman coinage, issued throughout the foreign provinces over which Cleopatra held a joint rule with Antony, must have provided an ample gold and silver currency even for Egypt.

Cyprus copper.

It will be best to take the Cyprian coinage of the whole period before the Egyptian. Cyprus was restored by Cæsar to the Ptolemaïc family, and the two younger of the children of Auletes, Ptolemy XV. and Arsinoë IV., made joint

ARRANGEMENT.   lxxxiii

sovereigns B.C. 47. This arrangement was broken in the same year, when after the death of her elder brother Cleopatra VII. was associated with the younger, Ptolemy XV., on the Egyptian throne. The young king was murdered in B.C. 44, and Ptolemy XVI., Cæsar, taken as colleague by his mother Cleopatra, their joint reign lasting until the overthrow of the Ptolemaïc dynasty B.C. 30. Whether Cyprus was handed over to any representatives of Ptolemy XV. and Arsinoë is not clear: they never appear to have gone to the island. It seems to have fallen into the hands of the Romans soon after the arrangement which gave it to the young sovereigns, and to have been retained by them until about B.C. 44, when Cleopatra seized it and held it until B.C. 41. Antony gave the island to Cleopatra and Ptolemy Cæsar B.C. 36, and it thenceforward remained part of the Ptolemaïc kingdom. (Cf. Engel, Kypros. i. p. 455 seqq.) Thus it is possible that Ptolemy XV. and Arsinoë may have issued coins in Cyprus, and even that the same king and Cleopatra may have done so. To the

Cleopatra.
(Pl. xxx. 6.)

interval B.C. 36—30 no doubt belongs the copper coinage with the obverse-type of Cleopatra as Aphrodite holding on her arm Ptolemy Cæsar as Eros, and the reverse-type of a double cornucopiæ, with the inscription

Ptolemy XV.
and Arsinoë IV.1
(Pl. xxx. 4.)

ΚΛΕΟΠΑΤΡΑΣ ΒΑΣΙΛΙΣΣΗΣ and the monogram of Cyprus ₧. There are, however, other coins with the head of Zeus Ammon, and the two eagles, with the headdress of Isis in front, either with (no. 4) or without a stand, or else no symbol: these coins must refer to a joint reign, and seem later than the coins with the single eagle assigned to Ptolemy King of Cyprus in this Catalogue. Probability would be in favour of assigning them to Cleopatra and Ptolemy Cæsar, were it not that the bulk of the Egyptian coinage, copper, of the period of their joint reign bears her head and name alone, the double reign being merely indicated by the double cornucopiæ, and that similarly in the copper coinage of Cyprus before noticed the young colleague simply appears in the inferior character of Eros. Thus these coins should rather be assigned to the joint reign of Ptolemy XV. and Arsinoë, but with hesitation, as we want proof that the island was actually under the rule of these coregents.

The Egyptian coinage of the successors of Auletes presents no difficulties. In her 6th year, B.C. 47–46, Cleopatra struck silver money of which the Museum has a specimen, a drachm with her portrait and the reverse-type of Auletes. As there is no allusion to any Ptolemy, a most exceptional phenomenon in ordinary silver money of the dynasty, it is probable that this coin was issued before Ptolemy XV. became her colleague, which took place B.C. 47, after the death of Ptolemy XIV. in December B.C. 48 (Lepsius, Königsbuch, Syn. Taf. 9): therefore it may be dated B.C. 47. The copper coinage is no doubt of the joint reign with Ptolemy Cæsar (B.C. 44—30), the double cornucopiæ indicating the coregency. The larger coins bear the mint-mark Π for ΓΑ, the smaller Μ (or Μ), which may possibly indicate Memphis. A single copper coin of very late style is assigned to Ptolemy Cæsar.

Cleopatra.
Egypt.
Silver, copper.
(Pl. xxx. 5, 7, 8.)

Ptolemy Cæsar,
Copper.
(Pl. xxx. 9.)

II. Mints.

The letters, monograms, and symbols indicating mints are more constant and regular in the coinage of the Ptolemies than in any other series of Greek regal money.

Indications of Mints.
The place of the mint-name is usually in the field of the reverse, and if the coin is dated, the mint-name and date are on opposite sides of the field. The rare positions of the mint-name are the space between the eagle's legs, and the rare positions of the date the exergue, and the thunderbolt.

Cyprus.
(1) Coins of Cyprus. In the sequence of coins dating from the time of Ptolemy V. Epiphanes to that of Ptolemy X. Lathyrus and XI. Alexander I., the three chief cities of Cyprus are indicated as follows:—

	Paphos.		Salamis.	Citium.	
	Æ	Æ	Æ	Æ	Æ
Ptolemy V.	AΠ, Γ	⌧	≤A	KI	K
,, VI.	ΓA	,,?	,,	,,	
,, VIII.	,,	,,	,,	,,	K
,, X.	,,	,,	,,	,,	,,
,, XI.	,,	,,	,,	,,	

In coins of Egyptian fabric, ΓA (Æ) and ⌧ (Æ) stand for an Egyptian mint, no doubt Alexandria (pp. lxii., lxx., lxxi., above). Under Cleopatra VII. Π (Æ) occurs. It is obvious from this list that whenever we find these letters in the usual mint-places on coins of Cyprian fabric, or such fabric as we may fairly think to be Cyprian, struck by other Ptolemies ruling the island, we may assign the coins to these cities. Two monograms probably of Paphos ⋈, ⋈, of the Third Coinage of Ptolemy I. (p. 2), and a probable one of Salamis ⋈ of his Fourth (p. 4), suggest a classification to these cities. The first attribution is confirmed by comparison with coins

lxxxvi INTRODUCTION.

of Paphos (⧫) of the next class, a second monogram being common to both (cf. p. 2, no. 10, and p. 3, no 19).

The symbols occurring on the coins of Cyprus, already noticed as probably indicating offices of the strategos, are not connected with any special mints. The same appears to be the case with other symbols in the Cyprian series from Ptolemy Epiphanes downwards.

(2) *Coins of Phoenicia and the neighbouring coast.* The basis of classification is to be found in the coins of Ptolemy II. Philadelphus: its reasonableness will appear from the following table, after short explanation of a few points.

Phoenicia.

	Sidon.		Tyre.		Ptolemais.		Joppa.		Gaza.	Berytus.	Tripoli
	Æ	Æ	Æ	Æ	Æ	Æ	Æ	Æ	Æ	Æ	Æ
Ptol. II.	⧫		⚚	⚵	⑪	⊓		᠀⏐ ⏐⫙	⌇		
„ III.	„	Type diff on prow.	„	⚵	ΓT	„	⚶ tripod.	ΙΟΓ	„	⫙ „	⫙
„ IV.	„	„	„			⚶ „					
„ V.		„	„							⨳	⚵
„ VI.						⚶					

The coins of Ptolemaïs are classed by their similarity in fabric to the rest of the group. To Ptolemaïs in the Thebaïs coins are given of Ptolemy I. and II. with mint-letters ΓT and monogram ⊓. They are of different fabric and of a connected series: as Ptolemy I. did not hold Phoenicia, they cannot be of that country.

Most of the attributions to Phoenicia are obvious. The harpa is assigned to Joppa on account of the myth of Perseus. The trident associated with B is appropriate to Berytus. It will be observed that the symbol almost always occurs alone without a monogram on the copper money.

There is a remarkable deviation from the general system of the

Ptolemaïc coins in those Phoenician pieces in copper which bear a new type, a female figure, a city, facing, on an advancing prow. These coins are reasonably assigned to Sidon.

It is evident that under Ptolemy II. and III. the coins of Phoenicia, though having the mint-marks of the various cities, were usually struck at a central mint, as stated in the previous section (p. xxxiv). Coins with mint-marks which cannot be connected with any of the coast-cities are probably of a common currency struck at the central mint, and are therefore assigned to it.

(3) Coins of Egypt. In the coins of Egypt there are the following mints:—

	ALEXANDRIA.		PTOLEMAIS.	DAPHNÆ?
	Æ	Æ	Æ	Æ
Ptol. I.	A?		ΓT	
,, I. II.	,,		,, ⋔	Δ
,, VIII.	ΓA	Ⱥ		
,, X.	,,	,,		
,, XI.	,,			
,, XIII.	,,			
Cleop. VII.	,,			

The attribution of coins to the town of Ptolemaïs in the Thebaïs, which as the Greek centre of Upper Egypt would probably have had a mint, has been already explained. The mint-mark Δ is conjecturally assigned to Daphnæ, because the coins of Alexander with the same monogram have an Egyptian symbol. A mint on the eastern border, where the Ptolemies must have maintained one or more large Greek garrisons, is very likely.

The paucity of mints we can assign to Egypt may be explained by the limited Hellenization of the country, and the concentration of the administration in Greek centres. Indeed the general absence of mint-names on the money of Egyptian fabric probably indicates that it was for the most part struck in Alexandria.

(4) Coins of the Cyrenaïca. Most of the Ptolemaïc coins of the Cyrenaïca are without evidence of mintage. Some, however, have indications by which they can be attributed to special cities. Under Ptolemy I. the crab appears to indicate Apollonia, and the silphium Cyrene. In the coinage of Magas the crab is again found. Under Berenice the star probably indicates Cyrene, and her coinage of Euesperides-Berenice has the reverse-type enclosed in an apple-wreath, and as symbols the trident and silphium. Other coins show the apple-branch certainly or probably as the symbol of the latter town.

(5) Coins of Asia Minor? and doubtful mints. Under the coinages of Ptolemy I. in which he bears the title king, his Fifth and Sixth (the Sixth continuing under Philadelphus as his First, and being the great issue marked with the Δ), we find, besides the certain and probable indications of Cyprus and Egypt as well as of the Cyrenaïca, a number of mint-letters and monograms not characteristic of any other Ptolemaïc money.

In this doubtful class the Fifth Coinage is represented by a limited number of coins which, judging from the provenance of certain copper specimens, would appear to be of Caria or the neighbouring countries. Most are characterized by the club, indicating a local worship of Heracles. It is possible that this symbol may be of Cos.

The coinage with the Δ is as a whole difficult of classification. It seems to be connected with the last by the recurrence of the club symbol. But there is a great variety of distinctive monograms or letters, some of which may be classed to cities of Asia Minor, if the coins bearing them be of Ptolemy II. The series in general has a double set of mint-marks, one indicating the issue, the other perhaps the mint. The marks of the issue are ⩘, P, Φ for silver, and ⩘, A for copper. These general marks run through the whole coinage, wherever struck, being combined with the special mark supposed to indicate the mint. Thus the general marks A/ and P are combined with the special mark ᛏ on silver coins. At present the classification of these coins must remain obscure. It is a significant circumstance that the general mark does not extend to the coinage of the Cyrenaïca of this class (p. 12, nos. 97, 98). It might therefore seem possible that its range was still more limited than its varieties would indicate, and that instead of being classed to Asia Minor possibly and Egypt, it should be wholly assigned to Egypt. However, the monogram M, which is identical with that of Miletus, and the absence of any mint-letters easily referable to Egypt, except Alexandria, Daphnæ? and Ptolemaïs, do not favour this view.

A certain number of coins are classed to territories, not mints, on account of their bearing letters or monograms of moneyers which are found on coins attributed to mints of those territories, though they are without the distinctive mint-letters, or for other obvious reasons.

III. Weights.

It is necessary to state briefly what standards the Ptolemies are known to have used, and to give the data afforded by the Museum Collection for the elucidation of the only obscure part of the question, that relating to the copper coinage.

Ptolemy I. first coined gold and silver on the Attic standard, then introduced, perhaps in a local currency, the Rhodian for drachms, while still issuing Attic tetradrachms, next adopted the Rhodian standard, and ultimately chose the Phoenician, henceforward used by all his successors.

The table here given shows the denominations, and their probable standard weights.

Weights of Gold and Silver Coins.

	ATTIC.		RHODIAN.		PHOENICIAN.	
	Actual.	Normal.	Actual.	Normal.	Actual.	Normal.
Decadrachm.					546	560
Octadrachm.					429	448
Hexadrachm.*					326	336
Pentadachm.*					275	280
Tetradrachm.	265$^{grs.}$	270$^{grs.}$	243	240	228	224
Tridrachm.*					164	168
Didrachm.		(135)		(120)	109	112
Drachm.*		(67·5)	53	60	54	56
Tetrobol.*	43	45		(40)		(37)
Hemidrachm.		(33·7)		(30)	27	28

The denominations marked with an asterisk occur only under one or two reigns, those within parenthetic marks are not found.

The copper coinage of the Ptolemies seems to follow the same system of divisions throughout their rule. If the standard was reduced at one or more times the individual weights appear to have remained the same, a lower denomination representing a higher one of an earlier period. The following table gives the average or individual weights of the well-preserved specimens in the National Collection, the notes supplying all necessary information as to the countries of issue, and specifying exceptional weights.

The supposed normal weight is given as Attic. If we adopt Egyptian it would have to be raised, the Egyptian pound (*uten*) having weighed 1400 grs., and its main division (the *ket*), being the tenth, 140 grs. The subdivisions would rather suggest the Attic system, and it is unlikely that an Egyptian one would have been forced on the inhabitants of Cyprus and the Cyrenaïca. The difference is, however, too small to be of consequence in the comparison, considering the irregularity with which the copper money was struck. M. Revillout's discussion of the evidence of the demotic papyri, in the Revue Égyptologique for 1881, just published, is of the highest value for the solution of the problem.

xcii   INTRODUCTION.

Supposed denomination.	Normal Weight.	Ptolemy I	Ptolemy I. and II.	Ptolemy II	Ptolemy III	Ptolemy IV	Ptolemy V.	Ptolemy VI.	Ptolemy VIII.	Ptolemy X.	Later.
20	1340			1445^j 1128^k	1082^t		1023^{ao}	1340^{ar} 1413^{ba}	1308^{bk}		
10	670			693^l	752^u	711^{ae}	684^{ap}	656^{bb}			
8	540				530^v	486^{ah}	504^{aq}				
5	335	325^a		368^m 332^n	323^w	330^{ai}	316^{ar}	354^{bc} 316^{bd}	468^{bl} 552^{bm}	550^{bw}	299^{ce}
4	270	262^b		254^o	214^x 242^y	248^{aj}	240as	268^{be}	354^{bn}	370^{bx}	262^{cf}
2½	168·75		248^h		168^z	171^{ak}	170^{at}	161^{bf} 190^{bg}	256^{bo} 230^{bp}	195^{by}	151^{cg}
2	135	131^c	125^i	104^p	109^{aa}	128^{al}	113^{au}	128^{bh}	151^{bq}		116^{ch}
1½	101·25				87^{ab}	96^{am} 79^{an}	80^{av}		111^{br}	113^{bz} 131^{ca}	
1	67·5	65^d 53^e		66^q	65^{ac} 50^{ad}		53^{aw}	67^{bi}	91^{bs}	73^{cb}	
	45	47^f			40^{ae}		43^{ax}		52^{bt}		
⅓	33·75				29^{af}		32^{ay}	33^{bj}		38^{cc}	
¼	22·5			21^r					30^{bu}		
⅙	16·87	14^g		15^s					18^{bv}	23^{cd}	20^{ci}

^{a} Ptolemy I. no. 98 Cyrenaica. ^{b} 97, Cyr. ^{c} 56, 57 Cyprus. ^{d} 17, 18 aver. wt. 57·6, Cypr.?; 59-61, wt. 66; 62-71, 73, wt. 70·2, Cypr.; 80-83, Asia Minor? wt. 56·6. ^{e} 95, 96, Cyr. ^{f} 72, Cypr. ^{g} 37-39, Cypr.? 52, 53, uncertain; 58, Cypr. ^{h} Ptol. I. and II. 12, 13, 21, 22, 29, 32, 36, 37, 41-3, 45, 58, 61. ^{i} 7, 39, 46, 66, 67.—J Ptolemy II. 157-163, Egypt. ^{k} 102, 103, 124, Phoenicia. ^{l} 104, 105, Phoen. ^{m} 43; Phoen. ^{n} 106, 107, Phoen. ^{o} 3, 14-19, 20-22, 23-26, 27-31, Cypr. ^{p} Cyr. local 4-9, wt. 110; 11, wt. 113; 12, wt. 84; 17, 18, wt. 131·5; 26-30, wt. 108·4. ^{q} Cyr. local 1, 2, wt. 61; 3, wt. 78. ^{r} Cyr. local 13, 14, 15, 19, 20. ^{s} Cyr. local 16, 21, 22.—^{t} Ptolemy III. 24, 29, 30, 49, 50, 64 and dupl., Phoen.; 87, 88, 107, 108, Eg. ^{u} 84, Phoen. ^{v} 65, 66, Phoen.; 89, 90, 109, 110, Eg. ^{w} 51-53, 67, Phoen.; 92, Eg. ^{x} 5-10, 15, 16, Cypr. ^{y} 57, 58, Phoen. ^{z} 59, 68, 69, 75, 76, Phoen.; 93, wt. 180; 100, wt. 157; 111-114, Eg. ^{aa} 11, wt. 118, Cypr.; 54, wt. 105; 60, wt. 100, Phoen. ^{ab} 99, wt. 132; 115-120, wt. 106·6, Eg.-; 121, wt. 106, Cyr. ^{ac} 60, wt. 100, 70, 71, wt. 92·5, 77, wt. 85, Phoen.; 95, wt. 80; 101, wt. 75, Eg.; 123, wt. 85, Cyr. ^{ad} 96, Eg. ^{ae} 122, 124-127, Cyr. ^{af} 61, 62, wt. 45; 72, 73, wt. 39; 78, 79, wt. 40, Phoen. ^{ag} 80-82, wt. 27·3, Phoen.; 94, wt. 35, Eg.—^{ah} Ptolemy IV. 35-38, Eg. ^{ai} 43, Eg. ^{aj} 39, Eg. ^{ak} 4-9, Cypr. ^{al} 40-42, Eg. ^{am} 10-13, Cypr. ^{an} 29, Phoen. ^{ao} Ptolemy V. ^{ap} 73-76, Eg. ^{aq} 56-59, wt. 510, Phoen.; 72, wt. 494, Eg. ^{ar} 77-81, Eg. ^{as} 28, 29, Cypr.; 89-94, Cyr. ^{at} 9, 10, 44-47, Cypr. ^{au} 30, wt. 134, Cypr.; 83, 84, wt. 104; 95, wt. 126, Cyr. ^{av} 82, Eg. ^{aw} 11, wt. 80, Cypr.; 96-99, wt. 54·5; 100, wt. 54, Cyr. ^{ax} 48, wt. 46, Cypr.; wt. 40, Cyr. ^{ay} 12-15, wt. 27·7, Cyr.; 31-36, wt. 35·1 Cypr. ^{az} 59, Cypr. ^{ba} 71, Eg.—^{bb} Ptolemy VI. 72-74, Eg. ^{bc} 23, 24, Cypr.; 16, 17, Eg. ^{bd} 13, Cyr. ^{be} 20, 21, Eg. ^{bf} 58, 60-67, wt. 160·4, Cypr.; 18, 19, wt. 162·5; 22, wt. 175, Eg. ^{bg} 28, 29, Cyr. ^{bh} 9-12, Eg. ^{bi} 1-4, Cypr. ^{bj} 5, 6, Cypr.—^{bk} Ptolemy VIII. 132, Cyr. ^{bl} 67, 68, 74-76, Eg. ^{bm} 78, Cyr. ^{bn} 117-120, wt. 350. Cypr.; 86, 87, wt. 364, Cyr. ^{bo} 6-11, wt. 248·3, Cypr.; 69-73, wt. 278; 130-131, wt. 242·5, Eg. ^{bp} 80, Cyr. ^{bq} 127, 128, wt. 147·5, Eg.; 1, wt. 168; 81, wt. 143, Cyr. ^{br} 94-97, wt. 108·7, Cypr.; 79, wt. 122, Cyr. ^{bs} 82, 83, Cyr. ^{bt} 98, Cypr. ^{bu} 84, Cyr. ^{bv} 85, Cyr.—^{bw} Ptolemy X. 36, 37, Cyr. ^{bx} 20-23, wt. 363·5; 27-30, wt. 362·5; 24-26, wt. 391, Eg. ^{by} 88, Cyr. ^{bz} 5, 6, Cypr.; 39-41, Cyr. ^{ca} 31-34, Cyr. ^{cb} 42-48, wt. 70, Cyr.; 57, 58, 87·5, Cyr. ^{cc} 49-52, Cyr. ^{cd} 63-66 Cyr.—^{ce} Cleopatra VII. 4, 5, Eg. ^{cf} 2, 3, Cypr.; 6-11, Eg.—^{cg} Ptolemy King of Cyprus? 47-58, Cypr.—Ptolemy XV. and Arsinoë II.? 1, 2, Cypr.—^{ci} Ptolemy King of Cyrene? 1-4, Cyr.

STEMMA PTOLEMAEORUM.

Ptolemaeus (Lagus) m. 2. Antigone d. Cassander. 1. Arsinoë.

- Philippus m. Berenice I. m. Ptolemaeus I. — Ptolemaeus I. m. 3. Eurydice d. Antipater. m. 4. Berenice I. d. Ptolemaeus (Lagus). — Menelaus.
  - Magas m. 1. Apame, d. Antiochus I. m. 2. Arsinoë. Ptolemaeus Ceraunus. Ptolemaeus II. m. 1. Arsinoë I., d. Lysimachus. m. 2. Arsinoë II. — Philotera.
    - Berenice II. m. Ptolemaeus III. Ptolemaeus III. m. Berenice II. d. Magas. Lysimachus. Berenice, m. Antiochus II.
      - Ptolemaeus IV. m. Arsinoë III. Berenice. Magas.
        - Ptolemaeus V. m. Cleopatra I. d. Antiochus III. Epiphanes.
          - Ptolemaeus VI. Philometor. Cleopatra II. m. Ptolemaeus VIII. Euergetes II. — Unknown.
            Cleopatra m. Alexander Bala, &c. Cleopatra III. m. Ptolemaeus VIII. Memphites. Ptolemaeus IX. (Neos.) Philopator II. Ptolemaeus Apion.
              - Ptolemaeus VII. m. Cleopatra IV. m. 2. Selene — Unknown. Ptolemaeus XI. m. 1. Unknown. m. 2. Berenice III. m. 3. Cleopatra V. Tryphaena m. Antiochus VIII.
                Eupator. Alexander I. (below).
              - Ptolemaeus X. m. 1. Ptolemaeus XI. m. 2. Ptolemaeus XII. Two Sons. Ptolemaeus XII. m. Berenice III. Daur.
                Soter II. Alexander I. Alexander II. Alexander II.
                - Berenice III. m. 1. Ptolemaeus XII. Cleopatra VII. m. 1. Ptolemaeus XIV. m. 2. Ptolemaeus XV. — Caesar — Antonius. Arsinoë IV.
                  Alexander I.
                  - Berenice IV. Cleopatra VII. m. 1. Ptolemaeus XIV. m. 2. Ptolemaeus XV. Ptolemaeus XVI. Ptolemaeus. Alexander. Cleopatra m. Juba,
                    m. 1. Seleucus, 2. Archelaus. Ptolemaeus XIII. m. Cleopatra VI. Caesar. King of Mauretania.
                    Nea Dionysus.
                    - Ptolemaeus King of Mauretania. Drusilla m. Antonius Felix.

TABLE II.—CHRONOLOGY.

	B.C.
Ptolemaeus I. (Soter) Governor of Egypt for Philip III.	323
,, ,, ,, Alexander IV.	316
,, Independent during Interregnum	311
,, King	305
Ptolemaeus II., Philadelphus	284
Death of Ptolemaeus I.	283 (?)
,, marries Arsinoë I.	281
,, divorces Arsinoë I., marries Arsinoë II.	277
Title Soter given to Ptolemaeus I.	261
Death of Arsinoë II. circ.	249
Ptolemaeus III., Euergetes I.	247
Ptolemaeus IV., Philopator I.	222
Death of Arsinoë III.	209
Ptolemaeus V., Epiphanes	204
,, marries Cleopatra I.	193
Ptolemaeus VI., Philometor I.	181
Death of Cleopatra I. circ.	174
,, taken prisoner by Antiochus	170
Ptolemaeus VIII., Euergetes II. (Physcon). circ.	170
,, Ptolemaeus VI. and VIII. reign together	168
,, Ptolemaeus VI. marries Cleopatra II.	165
Ptolemaeus VIII., King of Cyrene	164-3
Revolt and subjugation of Cyrenaica. circ.	156
Ptolemaeus VII., Eupator	146
Ptolemaeus VIII., Euergetes II., succeeds	146
,, marries Cleopatra II.	146
,, divorces Cleopatra II., marries Cleopatra III.	143-2
,, takes back Cleop. II., reigns with both (till 132)	141
,, expelled	130
Cleopatra II., Philometor	130
Ptolemaeus VIII. returns, reigns with both Cleopatras (till 117).	127
Ptolemaeus X. marries Cleopatra IV.	127
Ptolemaeus IX. (Neos), Philopator II., coregent in Cyprus.	121-0
Coregent, whole kingdom (till 117)	119-8

CHRONOLOGY.

	B.C.
Cleopatra III., Philadelphos	117
Ptolemaeus X., Soter II., taken by Cleopatra III. as colleague	117
Ptol. X. divorces Cleop. IV. and marries Selene	116
divorces Selene . . . circ.	114
Ptolemaeus XI., Alexander I., king of Cyprus	114
Ptolemaeus Apion, king of Cyrene . . circ.	114?
Cleop. III. and Ptol. X. take titles Philometores Soteres	114-3
Ptolemaeus X. expelled	107
Ptolemaeus XI., Alexander I., taken by Cleopatra III. as colleague	107
Ptolemaeus XI. still strikes money in Cyprus	106-5
Death of Cleopatra III.	89
Ptolemaeus XI., Alexander I., reigns alone	99
expelled	88
Ptolemaeus X., Soter II., returns to Egypt, reigns alone	88
Berenice III., Philopator	81
Ptolemaeus XII., Alexander II., marries Berenice III.	81
Ptolemy, King of Cyprus	81
Ptolemaeus XIII., Neos Dionysos	81
„ marries Cleopatra VI.	79
„ expelled	58
Cleopatra VI., Tryphaena with Berenice IV.	58
Berenice IV.	57
Ptolemaeus XIII. returns	55
Cleopatra VII., Philopator with Ptolemaeus XIV.	52
Ptolemaeus XIV. alone	49
Cleopatra VII. alone	48
Cleopatra VII. with Ptolemaeus XV.	47
Ptolemaeus XV. and Arsinoë IV. granted Cyprus	47
Cleopatra VII. and Ptolemaeus XVI., Caesar*	45
Death of Cleopatra VII. and Ptolemaeus XVI.	30

NOTE.—This and the previous table are mainly taken from Lepsius (Königsbuch der alten Aegypter, and Ueber einige Ergebnisse der ägyptischen Denkmäler für die Kentniss der Ptolemäergeschichte, Kön. Akad. Berl. Abhand. 1852, p. 503, seqq.). Additional information is supplied from M. Revillout's articles in the Revue Égyptologique and from the coins. A few incidents are omitted having no bearing on coins, such as the joint rule of Cleopatra and M. Antonius, which was practically imperial.

---

* Association in 44, counted back to 45.

xcvi   INTRODUCTION.

TABLE III.
MINTS AND DATES.

King	Year of reign	Year B.C.	Asia Minor	Cyprus				Phoenicia and Palestine									Egypt				Cyrenaica				Mint with the Phoenician		
			Incertae	Paphos	Salamis	Citium	Incertae	Sidon	Tyre	Ace, Ptolemais	Joppa	Gaza	Gaza and Joppa	Berytus	Tripolis	Incertae	Alexandria	Ptolemais	Daphnae?	Incertae	Cyrene	Euesperis Berenice	Apollonia	Incertae	Year, Era of Philip, B.C. 324	Year, Era of Dionysius, B.C. 286	Year, Era of Ptolemaeus I,? B.C. 261
Alexander IV.	20	266·5																									
Interregnum	21	265·4																									
Ptolemy I.	22	264·3		ǀ	?	?	ǀ																				
	23	263·2		ǀ	ǀ	ǀ	ǀ									?											
Ptolemy I., II.	24	262·1	?				ǀ	ǀ								?	ǀ	ǀ			ǀ		ǀ		48		
	25	261·0	?						ǀǀǀǀǀǀ							?			ǀ						50		
Ptolemy II.	26	260·9						ǀ																			
	27	259·8																									
	28	258·7																									
	29	257·6					?	ǀ	ǀǀ	ǀ	ǀ																
	30	256·5						ǀ		ǀ							?										
	31	255·4						ǀǀǀǀǀǀ	ǀǀǀǀǀ	ǀǀǀǀǀ	ǀǀǀ	ǀ	ǀ					ǀ							71		
	32	254·3																							72		
	33	253·2																									
	34	252·1																							74		
	35	251·0																									
	36	250·9																									
	37	249·8						ǀǀǀ																	77		
	38	248·7										ǀ															

Magas Kg. — Berenice II. Queen.

MINTS AND DATES. xcvii

				48 50		
	48 50.			71 72	74 77	80 81
80 81 82 83 84	88 89 90	102	105 106 107	109 110 111 112 113 114 115 116 117		

Ephesus B

Ptolemy III. 247·6 246·5 245·4 244·3 243·2 242·1 241·0 239·8 238·7 237·6 236·5 235·4 234·3 233·2 232·1 230·9 229·8 228·7 227·6 226·5 225·4 224·3 223·2 222·1
1 2 3 4 5 6 7 8 9 10 11 12 13 14 15 16 17 18 19 20 21 22 23 24 25 1

Ptolemy IV. 221·0 220·9 219·8 218·7 217·6 216·5 215·4 214·3 213·2 212·1 211·0 210·9 209·8 208·7 207·6 206·5 205·4
2 3 4 5 6 7 8 9 10 11 12 13 14 15 16 17 18

xcviii INTRODUCTION.

TABLE III.—MINTS AND DATES—*Continued.*

King.	Year of reign.	Year B.C.	Asia Minor	Cyprus				Phœnicia and Palestine									Egypt			Cyrenaica				Mint with the Phœnician			
			Incertae.	Paphos.	Salamis.	Citium.	Incertae.	Sidon.	Tyre.	Ace, Ptolemais.	Joppe.	Gaza.	Gaza and Joppa.	Berytus.	Tripolis.	Incertae.	Alexandria.	Ptolemais.	Incertae.	Cyrene.	Euesperis, Berenice.	Apollonia.	Incertae.	Year, Era of Philip.	Year, Era of Dionysius.	Year, Era of Ptolemaeus I.?
Ptolemy V.	1	204		?																					82	
	2	204-3																					—		83	
	3	203-2																	—						84	
	4	202-1																								
	5	201-0																								
	6	200-9			—		—												—						88	
	7	199-8			—	—													—						89	
	8	198-7				—													—						90	
	9	197-6			—																					
	10	196-5			—	—																				
	11	195-4			—	—																				
	12	194-3			—																					71
	13	193-2																								72
	14	192-1			—																					
	15	191-0																								74
	16	190-9				▲																				
	17	189-8			—																					
	18	188-7																								77
	19	187-6			—																					
	20	186-5			—														—		—		—		102	80
	21	185-4																								
	22	184-3			—																					
	23	183-2			—																					
	24	182-1																								
Ptolemy VI.	1	181-0		⎫	—																				106	81
	2	180-9		⎪																					106	82
	3	179-8		⎬?														—					—			83
Cleop. I., regent to cir. 174.	4	178-7		⎪	—																					84
	5	177-6		⎪	—																				109	
	6	176-5		⎭																					110	

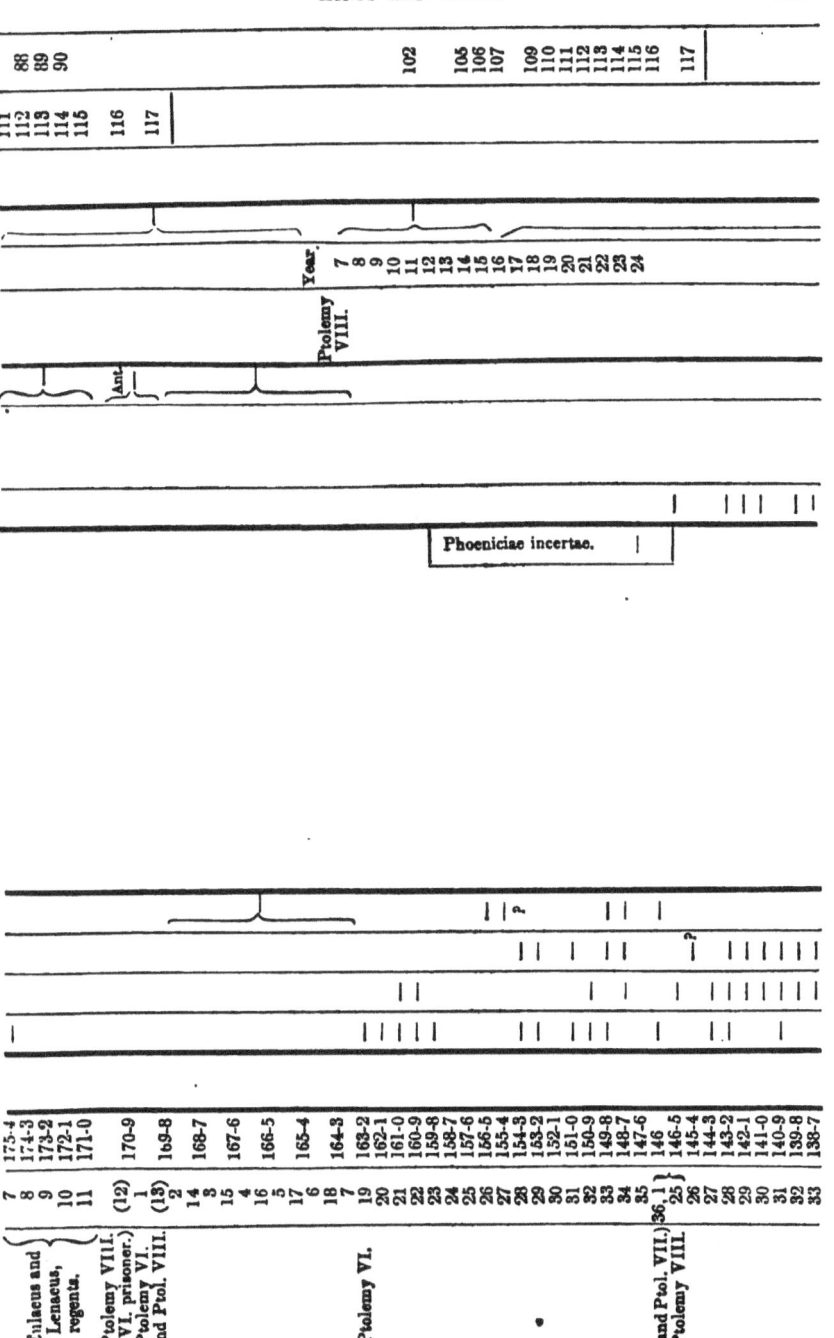

TABLE III.—MINTS AND DATES—Continued.

King.	Year of reign.	Year B.C.	Cyprus.				Egypt.		Cyrenaica.	
			Paphos.	Salamis.	Citium.	Incertae.	Alexandria.	Incertae.	Incertae.	
Ptolemy VIII	34	137-6		|	|		|			
	35	136-5		|	|		|			
	36	135-4		|	|		|			
	37	134-3		|	|		|			
	38	133-2		|	|		|			
	39	132-1		|						
	40	131-0	|							
	41	130-9		|	|					
	42	129-8			|					
	43	128-7		|	|					
	44	127-6			|					
	45	126-5			|					
	46	125-4								
	47	124-3								
	48	123-2								
	49	122-1	|	|	|					
(and Ptol. IX.)	50	121-0	|							
	51	120-9	|	|	|					
	52	119-8		|			|			
	53	118-7	|	|			|			
	54 ⎱	117		|	|		|			
	1 ⎰	117-6					|			
Ptolemy X.	2	116-5	|	|	|		|			
	3	115-4			|		|			
	1	114-3	|		|		|			
Ptolemy XI.	2	113-2			|		|			
	3	112-1	|				|			
	4	111-0					|			
	5	110-9		|	|		|			
	6	109-8	|		|		|			

Ptolemy X. Year 4 5 6 7 8 9

Ptolemy, king of Cyrene.

MINTS AND DATES.   ci

	Cleopatra III. Ptolemy XI.	Ptolemy XI.	Ptolemy X.	Ptolemy XIII.
10, 11, 8, 12, 9, 13, 10, 14, 11, 15, 12, 16, 13, 14, 15, 16, 17, 18, 19, 20, 21, 22, 23, 24, 25, 26, 29				1, 2, 3, 4, 5, 6, 7, 8, 9, 10, 11

	Ptolemy X.		Ptolemy, king of Cyprus.
108-7, 107-6, 106-5, 103-4, 104-3, 103-2, 102-1, 101-0, 100-9, 99-8, 98-7, 97-6, 96-5, 95-4, 94-3, 93-2, 92-1, 91-0, 90-9, 89-8, 88-7, 87-6, 86-5, 85-4, 84-3, 83-2, 82-1, 81-0, 80-9, 79-8, 78-7, 77-6, 76-5, 75-4, 74-3, 73-2, 72-1, 71-0
7, 8, 9, 13, 14, 15, 16, 17, 18, 19, 20, 21, 22, 23, 24, 25, 26, 27, 28, 29, 30, 31, 32, 33, 34, 35, 36, 1, 2, 3, 4, 5, 6, 7, 8, 9, 10, 11

o

TABLE III.—MINTS AND DATES—*Continued.*

King.	Year of reign.	Year B.C.	Cyprus. Paphos.		Year.	Egypt. Alexandria.	Egypt. Incertae.
Ptolemy, king of Cyprus (*Continued.*)	12	70-9	—	Ptolemy XIII. (*Continued.*)	12	—	
	13	69-8	—		13	—	
	14	68-7	—		14	—	
	15	67-6	—		15	—	
	16	66-5	—		16	—	
	17	65-4	—		17	—	
	18	64-3	—		18	—	
	19	63-2	—		19	—	
	20	62-1	—		20	—	
	21	61-0	—		21		
	22	60-9	—		22		
	23	59-8	—		23		
	24	58-7	—		24		
		57-6			25		
		56-5			26		
		55-4			27		
		54-3			28		
		53-2			29		
		52-1			30		
		51-0	Incert.	Cleopatra VII., Ptolemy XIV.	1	—	
		50-9	?		2	—	
		49-8			3	—	
		48-7		Ptolemy XIV. alone. Cleopatra VII. alone.	4	—	
		47-6		Cleopatra VII., Ptolemy XV.	5		
Ptol. XV. Arsinoë IV. }		46-5			6		
		45-4			1		
					7		
				Cleopatra VII., Ptolemy XVI. Caesar.	2		
					8		
					3		
					1	—	

MINTS AND DATES. ciii

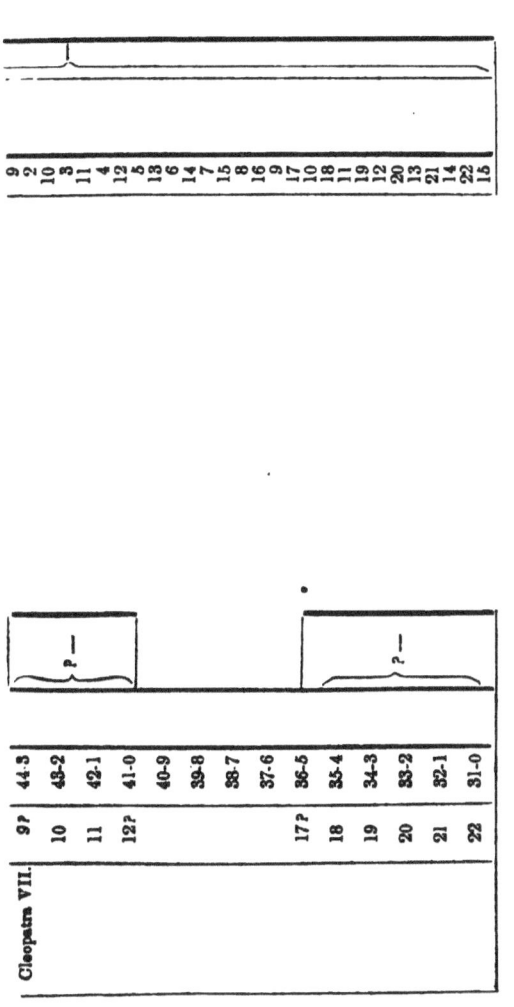

Pages xcvii., xcviii., xcix. A Arsinoë II.; B Berenice II.; Ant., Antiochus IV.
Where coinages (first, second, third) are of uncertain duration, the brackets have been limited according to probability.

ERRATA.

p. xxxvii, line 8, *for* 1480 *read* 1400.

„ lxxx, „ 17, *for* exile of Lathyrus B C. 107–6 *read* loss of Cyprus by Lathyrus B.C. 114.

„ 32, line 13 (from foot), *for* diadem and globe *read* diadem.

„ 36, „ 2, after *Gold* insert SECOND COINAGE.

„ „ under Mint-Date, *for* Alexandria *read* Alexandria ?

„ 45, *for* Ptolemaeus IX. *read* Ptolemaeüs VIII.

„ 47, line 3 (from foot), *for* E *read* E.

„ 57, „ 17, 18, *for* E (E ?) *read* E (E ?).

„ 59, last two lines, *for* Pl. XIV. *read* Pl. XIII.

„ 78, line 5, *for* 174–171 *read* 174–170.

„ 86, „ 4 (from foot), *for* Ptolemaeus VII. *read* Ptolemaeus VI.

„ 96, „ 3, *for* Cleopatra III. *read* Cleopatra II. or III.

„ 105, „ 7, insert β before Egypt.

„ 107, „ 2, *for* 117–111 ? *read* 117–114 ?

„ 109, under Mint-Date, insert Citium above 98–7.

THE PTOLEMAIC KINGS OF EGYPT.

No.	Wt. or Size.	Obverse.	Reverse.	Mint.—Date.
		PTOLEMAEUS I., SOTER I. B.C. 323–284. PERIODS OF REIGN. I. Governor for Philip Aridaeus . B.C. 323–316 II. Governor for Alexander IV. . . 316–311 III. Independent (Interregnum) . . 311–305 IV. King . . . . . . 305–284 (V. Ex-King . . . . . 284–283 ?) FIRST COINAGE. Ptolemy, Governor for Philip Aridaeus, B.C. 323–316. (See Coins of Philip Aridaeus, Catalogue of Kings of Macedon.) *Types of Alexander the Great.* SECOND COINAGE. *Silver; reverse-type of Alexander the Great; Attic Standard.* Ptolemy, Governor for Alexander IV., B.C. 316–311. (See Third and Fourth Coinages.)		
1	Wt. 265·1	Head of Alexander the Great r., with horn of Zeus Ammon, clad in elephant's skin and aegis.	ΑΛΕΞΑΝΔΡΟΥ Zeus Aetophoros seated l. on throne without back, his l. hand resting on sceptre; in front, thunderbolt upwards. beneath throne, OP . [Pl. I. 1.]	Uncert.

No.	Wt. or Size.	Obverse.	Reverse.	Mint. — Date.
		Head of Alexander the Great r., with horn of Zeus Ammon, clad in elephant's skin and aegis.	ΑΛΕΞΑΝΔΡΟΥ Zeus Aetophoros seated l. on throne without back, his l. hand resting on sceptre; in front, thunderbolt upwards.	
2	Wt. 264·3		beneath throne, ⋈.	Uncert.
3	263·7		,, ,,	,,
4	261·1		,, ΑΥ.	,,
5	264·2	(diadem across forehead.)	,, ΡΥ.	,,

THIRD COINAGE.

Silver: Tetradrachms, Attic Standard; Drachms, Rhodian Standard.

Ptolemy, Governor for Alexander IV., B.C. 316–311, or Interregnum 311–305.

Cyprus?

Within interval, B.C. 315–306.

No.	Wt. or Size.	Obverse.	Reverse.	Mint. — Date.
		Head of Alexander the Great r., with horn of Ammon, diademed and clad in elephant's skin and aegis.	ΑΛΕΞΑΝΔΡΟΥ Pallas Promachos r.; in front, eagle r. on thunderbolt.	
6	264·5		to l., ⟑; to r., ΕΥ. [Pl. I. 2.]	Paphos?
7	264·		,, ΔΙ.	Uncert.
8	262·3	Countermark, bee, 🐝.	,, ,,	,,
9	264·3		,, ,, (Ξ for Ξ).	,,
10	263·8	,, scarabaeus?	,, ♣.	,,
11	264·4		,, ΕΥ.	,,
12	264·7	,, ✳.	(Ξ for Ξ).	,,
13	53·8		,, Α; ,, ΕΥ.	Paphos?
14	48·7 worn.		,, ,, ,, ,,	,,

PTOLEMAEUS I., SOTER I. 3

No.	Wt. or Size.	Obverse.	Reverse.	Mint. Date.
15	Wt. 52·2	Head of Alexander the Great r., with horn of Ammon, diademed and clad in elephant's skin and aegis.	ΑΛΕΞΑΝΔΡΟΥ Pallas Promachos r.; in front, eagle r. on thunderbolt. to r., ΔΙ.	Uncert.
16	55·2		,, ΕΥ. [Pl. I. 3.]	,,
			Copper.	
17	Size. ·65	Head of Alexander the Great r., with horn of Ammon, diademed.	ΑΛΕ Eagle l. on thunderbolt, wings open. to l., ΕΥ; to r., Ä . [Pl. I. 4.]	Paphos?
18	·6		,, ,, ,, Δ. (Barbarous.)	,,

FOURTH COINAGE.

Silver; Tetradrachms, Rhodian Standard.

Engraver's mark Δ on some.

Ptolemy, Governor for Alexander IV., B.C. 316–311, or Interregnum B.C. 311–305.

Cyprus.

Within interval, B.C. 315–306.

		Head of Alexander the Great r., with horn of Ammon, diademed and clad in elephant's skin and aegis.	ΑΛΕΞΑΝΔΡΟΥ Pallas Promachos r.; in front, eagle r. on thunderbolt.	

(a) *With mint-monograms.*

19	Wt. 242·6	on aegis, Δ; countermarks, eagle l., ⋈; scarabaeus?	to l., ⋈; to r., ⚵ ⚶ . [Bank Coll.]	Paphos.
20	241·6	on aegis, Δ .	,, ,, ,, ,, ,, ,,	,,
21	240·	,, ,, ·	,, ,, ,, ,, ,, [Pl. I. 5.]	,,

No.	Wt. or Size.	Obverse.	Reverse.	Mint. Date.
22	Wt. 241·1	Head of Alexander the Great r., with horn of Ammon, diademed and clad in elephant's skin and aegis.	ΑΛΕΞΑΝΔΡΟΥ Pallas Promachos r.; in front, eagle r. on thunderbolt. to L, (A); to r., ⚘ ; in ex., ΔΙ. [Pl. I. 6.]	Salamis?
23	229·7 worn.		,, ,, ,, ,, (ex., off field.)	,,
24	240·2*		,, ,, ,, ΔΙ (ex., not visible.)	,,

(β) *With symbols of offices of strategos of Cyprus ?*

No.	Wt. or Size.	Obverse.	Reverse.	Mint. Date.
25	242·		to L, Δ; to r., mon.† ℞. (Ξ for Ξ.) [Bank Coll.]	Uncert.
26	211·7 worn.		,, ΔΙ ,,	,,
27	243·1	on aegis, Δ; countermk., ✳	,, ⚘ ,,	,,
28	240·		,, ,, ,, Phoenician graffito? [Bank Coll.]	,,
29	241·	,, ,,	,, ╟P ,,	,,
30	238·3	,, ,, ,, ❦	,, ,, ,, [Bank Coll.]	,,
31	171·5 plated.		,, ,, ,,	,,
32	222·4		,, K ,,	,,
33	241·7		,, ✕ ,, [Bank Coll.]	,,
34	209·5 plated.		,, ,, ,,	,,
35	237·8	,, ,, ,, ✺ ,,	,, ✳ ; ,, ╟P ,,	,,
36	241·7	on aegis, Δ .	,, ⚘ ; ,, ▮ . [Bank Coll.]	,,

* Since cleaning, Wt. 223·5.   † Mon. defaced in die.

No.	Wt. or Size.	Obverse.	Reverse.	Mint. — Date.
			Copper.	
		Head of Alexander the Great r., with horn of Ammon, diademed.	ΑΛΕ Eagle l., wings open.	
			(a) With mint-letters or mint-symbol.	
37	Size. ·4		to r., Γ.	Paphos?
			ΑΚ Similar.	
38	·45		to l., 𝒫.	Citium?
39	·4		,, ,,	,,
			(β) With symbol of office of strategos of Cyprus?	
			ΑΛΕ Similar.	
40	·4		to l., ✳. [Pl. i. 7.]	Uncert.
			Unattributed.	
			Silver.	
		Head of Alexander the Great r., with horn of Ammon, diademed and clad in elephant's skin and aegis.	ΑΛΕΞΑΝΔΡΟΥ Pallas Promachos r.; in front, eagle r. on thunderbolt.	
41	Wt. 242·6		to r., ⚘ Aρ· [Bank Coll.]	Uncert.
42	235·6		,, ,, ,,	,,
43	241·		,, Α ⱥ· [Bank Coll.]	,,
44	235·		,, Χ Αν· [Bank Coll.]	,,
45	242·3		to l., ⋔ ⿱.	,,

No.	Wt. or Size.	Obverse.	Reverse.		Mint. Date.
46	Wt. 241·9	Head of Alexander the Great r., with horn of Ammon, diademed and clad in elephant's skin and aegis.	ΑΛΕΞΑΝΔΡΟΥ Pallas Promachos r.; in front, eagle r. on thunderbolt. to l., ᛉ; to r., ᛕ.	[Pl. I. 8.]	Uncert.
47	242·	Countermarks, ✳, ᛉ.	,, ,, ,, ᛕ.		,,
48	232·3		,, ,, ,, ,,		,,
49	241·5	on aegis, Δ.	,, ᛉ.	[Bank Coll.]	,,
50	236·2		,, ,,		,,
51	242·7	,, ,,	,, ᛙ.	[Bank Coll.]	,,

Copper.

		Head of Alexander the Great r., with horn of Ammon, diademed.	ΑΛΕ Eagle l. on thunderbolt, wings open.		
52	Size. ·4		to l., ᛤ.		Uncert.
53	·45		ΑΛΕ Similar. to l., ᛰ.		,,

CYRENAICA.

Within interval B.C. 308–305.

Magas, Governor.

Silver.

| 54 | Wt. 240·4 | Head of Alexander the Great r., with horn of Ammon, diademed and clad in elephant's skin and aegis. | ΑΛΕΞΑΝΔΡΟΥ Pallas Promachos r.; in front, eagle r. on thunderbolt. to l., ᛝ; to r., ✕ ᛟ | | Uncert. |
| 55 | 241·2 | on aegis, Δ. | ,, ,, ,, ᛙ ᛰ. | | ,, |

No.	Wt. or Size.	Obverse.	Reverse.	Mint. Date.
		LOCAL COINAGE WITH NAME OF PTOLEMY. Interregnum B.C. 311–305. Cyprus. Within interval B.C. 311–306, towards close? Copper.		
56	Size. ·85	Head of Aphrodite r., wearing ornamented stephanos and earring.	ΠΤΟΛΕΜΑΙΟΥ Eagle l. on thunderbolt; to l., wreath; in ex., wreath. [Pl. I. 9.]	Paphos.
57	·9			,,
58	·45		(inscr. and exergue obscure.)	,,
59	·65	Head of Aphrodite? r., wearing taenia ornamented with leaves placed in it, earring and necklace.	ΠΤΟΛΕ Eagle l. on thunderbolt, wings open. in front, wreath. [Pl. I. 10.]	Salamis?
60	·6	(Taenia plain.)	in ex., wreath?	,,
61	·65	Head of Aphrodite r., wearing ornamented stephane, earring, and necklace.	Same type.	,,

No.	Wt. or Size.	Obverse.	Reverse.	Mint. Date.
		\multicolumn{2}{c}{FIFTH COINAGE.}	
		\multicolumn{2}{c}{*Gold and Silver, Phoenician Standard; Copper, obv. type,*}	
		\multicolumn{2}{c}{*Head of Alexander, hair long.*}	
		\multicolumn{2}{c}{Ptolemy, King, B.C. 305–284.}	
		\multicolumn{2}{c}{(See Sixth Coinage).}	
		\multicolumn{2}{c}{Cyprus.}	
		\multicolumn{2}{c}{Early in interval, B.C. 295–284.}	
		\multicolumn{2}{c}{*Copper; with symbols of offices of strategos ?*}	
62	Size. ·75	Head of Alexander the Great r., with horn of Ammon, diademed; hair long.	ΠΤΟΛΕΜΑΙΟΥ ΒΑΣΙΛΕΩΣ Eagle l. on thunderbolt, wings open. to l., [symbol] [Pl. II. 1.]	Uncert.
63	·7		,, ,,	,,
64	·7		,, ,,	,,
65	·7	Countermark, thunderbolt.	,, ΔΙ.	,,
66	·75		,, [symbol].	,,
67	·65		,, ΚΛ [symbol].	,,
68	·75		,, ,,	,,
69	·7		,, Ⅹ [symbol].	,,
		\multicolumn{2}{c}{Uncertain mints, about same period.}	
70	·7		,, ⚘.	,,
71	·7		,, ⱵP.	,,
72	·55		,, ,,	,,
73	·75		,, ΤΙ.	,,

PTOLEMAEUS I., SOTER I.

No.	Wt. or Size.	Obverse.	Reverse.	Mint. — Date.
			Asia Minor?	
			Gold; with symbol.	
74	Wt. 274·2	Head of Ptolemaeus I. r., diademed and wearing aegis.	ΠΤΟΛΕΜΑΙΟΥ ΒΑΣΙΛΕΩΣ Eagle l. on thunderbolt. to l. H. [Bank Coll. Pl. II. 2.]	Cos ?
			Silver.	
75	215·	Similar.	Similar. to l. H. [Pl. II. 3.]	,,
76	210·2		,, ,, ,,	,,
77	213·6		,, ,, ,,	,,
78	215·		O ,, ,,	,,
79	207·1	Countermarks, H or I and two obscure.	,, ,, ,,	,,
			Copper.	
80	Size. ·6	Head of Alexander the Great r., with horn of Ammon, diademed; hair long.	ΠΤΟΛΕΜΑΙΟΥ ΒΑΣΙΛΕΩΣ Eagle l. on thunderbolt, wings open. to l., H.	,,
81	·6		,, ,, ,,	,,
82	·6		Γ ,, ,,	,,
83	·6		,, ,, ,,	,,

No.	Wt. or Size.	Obverse.	Reverse.	Mint.—Date.
			With monogram.	
			Silver.	
84	Wt. 218·2	Head of Ptolemaeus I. r., diademed and wearing aegis.	ΠΤΟΛΕΜΑΙΟΥ ΒΑΣΙΛΕΩΣ Eagle l. on thunderbolt. to l., ΚΕ. [Pl. II. 4.]	Uncert.
			Copper.	
85	Size. ·45	Head of Alexander the Great r., with horn of Ammon, diademed; hair long.	ΠΤΟΛΕΜΑΙΟΥ ΒΑΣΙΛΕΩΣ Eagle l. on thunderbolt, wings open. to l, ΚΕ.	,,
86	·45		,, ,, [Pl. II. 5.]	,,
87	·45		,, ,,	,,
			No monogram or letter.	
88	·35		(Inscr. obscure.)	,,
			Egypt.	
			Gold.	
89	Wt. 274·6	Head of Ptolemaeus I. r. Countermark, Δ.	ΠΤΟΛΕΜΑΙΟΥ ΒΑΣΙΛΕΩΣ Eagle l. on thunderbolt. to L, Φ A. [Pl. II. 6.]	Alexandria!
			Silver.	
90	218·5	Similar.	Similar. to L, Φ A. [Pl. II. 7.]	,,
91	203·		ΠΤ ◎. ,, ⚹; to r., [Pl. II. 8.]	Ptolemais

No.	Wt. or Size.	Obverse.	Reverse.	Mint. — Date.
			CYRENAICA.	
			Magas, Governor.	
			Local Coinages.	
			Gold.	
			FIRST COINAGE.	
			Attic Standard.	
92	Wt. 43·4	Head of Ptolemaeus I. r., diademed and wearing aegis.	ΠΤΟΛΕΜΑΙΟΥ ΒΑΣΙΛΕ (the latter retrograde). Nike l., bearing wreath and palm. to l., ◆; to r., 𝚰. [Pl. II. 9.]	Apollonia
			SECOND COINAGE.	
			Phoenician Standard.	
		Head of Ptolemaeus I. r., diademed and wearing aegis.	ΠΤΟΛΕΜΑΙΟΥ ΒΑΣΙΛΕΩΣ Quadriga of elephants l., in which Alexander as young Zeus Ammon? holding thunderbolt and reins.	
93	109·9	behind head, ✥?	in ex., Ν̸ ΓΡ. [Pl. II. 10.]	,, ?
94	109·3		,, Χ Ν̸. [Pl. II. 11.]	Uncert.
			Copper.	
		Head of Apollo r., laur.	ΠΤΟΛΕΜΑΙΟΥ ΒΑΣΙΛΕΩΣ Eagle l. on thunderbolt, wings open.	
95	Size. ·65		⌐⊙⌐? to r., Ⓡ. 🪲	Cyrene.
96	·7		to l., ∣⊙∣. 🪲	,,

No.	Wt. or Size.	Obverse.	Reverse.	Mint.— Date.
			SIXTH COINAGE. *Copper.*	
		Head of Zeus r., laur.	ΠΤΟΛΕΜΑΙΟΥ ΒΑΣΙΛΕΩΣ Eagle l. on thunderbolt, wings open.	
97	Size. 1·1		to l., IΓ.	Uncert.
98	1·2	Head of Ptolemaeus I. r., diademed and wearing aegis.	Similar. to l., IΓ.	,,

PTOLEMAEUS I., AND PTOLEMAEUS II.

Ptolemaeus I. Sixth Coinage. B.C. 305–284. (See also Fifth Coinage.)

Ptolemaeus II. First General Coinage. B.C. 284– ?

Gold and Silver, with engraver's mark Δ; Copper, with heads of Zeus and Alexander.

Cyprus.

Within intervals B.C. 295–284, 284– ?

Silver.

No.	Wt. or Size.	Obverse.	Reverse.	Mint. Date.
1	Wt. 216·	Head of Ptolemaeus I. r., diademed and wearing aegis; behind ear, Δ.	ΠΤΟΛΕΜΑΙΟΥ ΒΑΣΙΛΕΩΣ Eagle l. on thunderbolt. to l., EY KΛ.	Uncert.
2	209·3		„ EY KΛ. A	„
3	214·3		„ EY KΕ.	„
4	207·7		„ „ [Countermark, amphora?]	„
5	193·6 worn.		„ EY KΕ. A	„
6	219·		„ EY X·	„

No.	Wt. or Size.	Obverse.	Reverse.	Mint. — Date.
			Copper.	
7	Size. ·8	Head of Alexander the Great r., with horn of Ammon, clad in elephant's skin and aegis.	ΠΤΟΛΕΜΑΙΟΥ ΒΑΣΙΛΕΩΣ Eagle l. on thunderbolt, wings open. to l., EY ⚡︎·	Uncert.
			Silver.	
8	Wt. 211·4	Head of Ptolemaeus I.	ΠΤΟΛΕΜΑΙΟΥ ΒΑΣΙΛΕΩΣ Eagle l. on thunderbolt. to l., ⚡︎·	,,
9	219·6		P ,, ⚡︎·	,,
10	211·9		ΣΤ ,, ⚡︎·	,,
11	227·1		Φ ,, ⚡︎·	,,
			Copper.	
12	Size. 1·	Head of Zeus r., laur.	ΠΤΟΛΕΜΑΙΟΥ ΒΑΣΙΛΕΩΣ Eagle l. on thunderbolt, wings open. to l., A ✕·	,,
13	1·05		Ā ,, ✕·	,,
14	·8	Head of Alexander the Great.	Similar. to l., ✕.	,,

No.	Wt. or Size.	Obverse.	Reverse.	Mint. Date.
			With mint-monograms or letters.	
			Silver.	
		Head of Ptolemaeus I.	ΠΤΟΛΕΜΑΙΟΥ ΒΑΣΙΛΕΩΣ Eagle l. on thunderbolt.	
15	Wt. 220·		to l., P M. ⋈	Paphos.
16	218·		,, P ⋈·	,,
17	216·5		,, ΣΤ ⋈·	,,
18	210·5		,, ΣΤ ⋈·	,,
19	221·3		,, Φ ⋈·	,,
20	229·3		,, Φ ⋈·	,,
			Copper.	
		Head of Zeus.	ΠΤΟΛΕΜΑΙΟΥ ΒΑΣΙΛΕΩΣ Eagle l. on thunderbolt, wings open.	
21	Size. 1·1		to l., A M. ⋈	,,
22	1·1		,, Ã ⋈·	,,

16 THE PTOLEMAIC KINGS OF EGYPT.

No.	Wt. or Size.	Obverse.	Reverse.	Mint, Date.
			Silver.	
		Head of Ptolemaeus I.	ΠΤΟΛΕΜΑΙΟΥ ΒΑΣΙΛΕΩΣ Eagle l. on thunderbolt.	
23	Wt. 228·2		to l., Ɛ. [Pl. III. 1.]	Salamis.

24	214·4		,, ΣΤ
			   ΚΙ .
			   ⚔
				Citium.

25	219·2		,, ΣΤ . ΚΙ	,,
			Copper.	
		Head of Alexander the Great.	ΠΤΟΛΕΜΑΙΟΥ ΒΑΣΙΛΕΩΣ Eagle l. on thunderbolt, wings open.	

26	Size.
	·75
			to l., ΣΤ
			      ΚΙ .
			      ⚔
				,,

Asia Minor ? Egypt ?

Gold; with symbol.

		Head of Ptolemaeus I.	ΠΤΟΛΕΜΑΙΟΥ ΒΑΣΙΛΕΩΣ Eagle l. on thunderbolt.	
27	Wt. 273·		to l., 🯄 ⚔ . [Pl. III. 2.]	Cos ?

With monograms or letters.

Silver.

		Similar.	Similar.	
28	215·9		to l., P Ⱥ . .	Uncert.

No.	Wt. or Size.	Obverse.	Reverse.	Mint. — Date.
			Copper.	
		Head of Zeus.	ΠΤΟΛΕΜΑΙΟΥ ΒΑΣΙΛΕΩΣ Eagle l. on thunderbolt, wings open.	
29	Size. 1·15		to l., 𝔸 𝔸· [Pl. III. 3.]	Uncert.
			Silver.	
		Head of Ptolemaeus I.	ΠΤΟΛΕΜΑΙΟΥ ΒΑΣΙΛΕΩΣ Eagle l. on thunderbolt.	
30	Wt. 232·2		to l., Δ.	,,
31	204·3 worn.		,, 𝒩· Δ	,,
			Copper.	
		Head of Zeus.	ΠΤΟΛΕΜΑΙΟΥ ΒΑΣΙΛΕΩΣ Eagle l. on thunderbolt, wings open.	
32	Size. 1·15		to l., 𝔸. Δ	,,
			Silver.	
		Head of Ptolemaeus I.	ΠΤΟΛΕΜΑΙΟΥ ΒΑΣΙΛΕΩΣ Eagle l. on thunderbolt.	
33	Wt. 208·2 worn.		to l., ⋔. (Ω in inscr. inverted.)	,,
34	219·7		,, ,,	,,
35	212·2		,, ⋔· P	,,
			Copper.	
		Head of Zeus.	ΠΤΟΛΕΜΑΙΟΥ ΒΑΣΙΛΕΩΣ Eagle l. on thunderbolt, wings open.	
36	Size. 1·1		to l., ⋔.	,,
37	1·05		,, ,,	,,

No.	Wt. or Size.	Obverse.	Reverse.	Mint — Date.
38	Wt. 204·7 worn.	Head of Ptolemaeus I.	*Silver.* ΠΤΟΛΕΜΑΙΟΥ ΒΑΣΙΛΕΩΣ Eagle l. on thunderbolt. to l., ⚒ ΔΙ.	Uncert.
39	Size ·9	Head of Alexander the Great.	*Copper.* ΠΤΟΛΕΜΑΙΟΥ ΒΑΣΙΛΕΩΣ Eagle l. on thunderbolt, wings open. to l., ΔΙ.	,,
40	Wt. 219·7	Head of Ptolemaeus I.	*Silver.* ΠΤΟΛΕΜΑΙΟΥ ΒΑΣΙΛΕΩΣ Eagle l. on thunderbolt. to l., P ΕΙ.	,,
41	Size 1·05	Head of Zeus.	*Copper;* ΠΤΟΛΕΜΑΙΟΥ ΒΑΣΙΛΕΩΣ Eagle l. on thunderbolt, wings open. to l., A ΕΙ.	,,
42	1·1		,, A ΕΙ.	,,
43	1·05		,, A Ε.	,,
44	Wt. 198·3 worn.	Head of Ptolemaeus I.	*Silver.* ΠΤΟΛΕΜΑΙΟΥ ΒΑΣΙΛΕΩΣ Eagle l. on thunderbolt. to l., P Ι.	,,

No.	Wt. or Size.	Obverse.	Reverse.	Mint. Date.
			Copper.	
		Head of Zeus.	ΠΤΟΛΕΜΑΙΟΥ ΒΑΣΙΛΕΩΣ Eagle l. on thunderbolt, wings open.	
45	Size. 1·1		to l., A͞ HP.	Uncert.
		Head of Alexander the Great.	Similar.	
46	·85		to l., HP.	,,
			Silver.	
		Head of Ptolemaeus I.	ΠΤΟΛΕΜΑΙΟΥ ΒΑΣΙΛΕΩΣ Eagle l. on thunderbolt.	
47	Wt. 203·		to l., P K.	,,
			Gold.	
		Similar.	ΠΤΟΛΕΜΑΙΟΥ ΒΑΣΙΛΕΩΣ Eagle l. on thunderbolt, wings open.	
48	27·4		to l., M.	Mylasa?
			Silver.	
		Similar.	ΠΤΟΛΕΜΑΙΟΥ ΒΑΣΙΛΕΩΣ Eagle l. on thunderbolt.	
49	227·	Countermark, Δ ?	to l., M.	,,
50	229·8		,, [M ?]	,,
51	217·4		,, P M.	,,
52	224·7		,, Φ M.	,,

No.	Wt. or Size.	Obverse.	Reverse.	Mint. — Date.
			Gold.	
		Head of Ptolemaeus I.	ΠΤΟΛΕΜΑΙΟΥ ΒΑΣΙΛΕΩΣ Eagle l. on thunderbolt, wings open.	
53	Wt. 26·9		to l., Ṁ. [Pl. III. 5.]	Miletus?
54	27·3		,, ,,	,,
			Silver.	
		Similar.	ΠΤΟΛΕΜΑΙΟΥ ΒΑΣΙΛΕΩΣ Eagle l. on thunderbolt.	
55	215·2	Countermark obscure.	to l., Ṁ.	,,
56	228·7		Ạ ,, Ṁ·	,,
57	213·8		P ,, Ṁ·	,,
			Copper.	
		Head of Zeus.	ΠΤΟΛΕΜΑΙΟΥ ΒΑΣΙΛΕΩΣ Eagle l. on thunderbolt, wings open.	
58	Size. 1·1		to l., Ạ̄. Ν?	Uncert.
			Silver.	
		Head of Ptolemaeus I.	ΠΤΟΛΕΜΑΙΟΥ ΒΑΣΙΛΕΩΣ Eagle l. on thunderbolt.	
59	Wt. 219·5		P to l., ΑΡ.	,,
			Copper.	
		Head of Zeus.	ΠΤΟΛΕΜΑΙΟΥ ΒΑΣΙΛΕΩΣ Eagle l. on thunderbolt, wings open.	
60	Size. 1·		A to l., ΑΡ.	,,
61	1·05		A ,, ΠΡ. [Pl. III. 4.]	,,

No.	Wt. or Size.	Obverse.	Reverse.	Mint. — Date.
			Silver.	
		Head of Ptolemaeus I.	ΠΤΟΛΕΜΑΙΟΥ ΒΑΣΙΛΕΩΣ Eagle l. on thunderbolt.	
62	Wt. 224·		to l., 𐤌.	Uncert.
63	215·		,, 𐤌.	,,
			Copper.	
		Head of Zeus.	ΠΤΟΛΕΜΑΙΟΥ ΒΑΣΙΛΕΩΣ Eagle l. on thunderbolt, wings open.	
64	Size. 1·15		to l., 𐤌.	,,
65	1·1		,, ,,	,,
		Head of Alexander the Great.	Similar.	
66	·9		to l., 𐤌. [Pl. III. 6.]	,,
67	·8		,, ,, [Pl. III. 7.]	,,
			Gold.	
		Head of Ptolemaeus I.	ΠΤΟΛΕΜΑΙΟΥ ΒΑΣΙΛΕΩΣ Eagle l. on thunderbolt, wings open.	
68	Wt. 27·7		to l., 𐤌.	,,
69	27·3		,, ,,	,,
			Silver.	
		Similar.	ΠΤΟΛΕΜΑΙΟΥ ΒΑΣΙΛΕΩΣ Eagle l. on thunderbolt.	
70	229·		to l., 𐤌.	,,
71	227·		,, 𐤌.	,,

THE PTOLEMAIC KINGS OF EGYPT.

No.	Wt. or Size.	Obverse.	Reverse.	Mint.—Date.
		Head of Ptolemaeus I.	ΠΤΟΛΕΜΑΙΟΥ ΒΑΣΙΛΕΩΣ Eagle l. on thunderbolt.	
72	Wt. 218·8		to l., P ⩔ ᴔ .	Uncert.
73	219·		,, ,, (*graffito,* A.)	,,
74	206·7 worn.		,, P Σ.	,,
			Copper.	
		Head of Zeus.	ΠΤΟΛΕΜΑΙΟΥ ΒΑΣΙΛΕΩΣ Eagle l. on thunderbolt, wings open.	
75	Size. 1·05		to l., Ⱥ Σ.	,,
76	1·05		,, Ⱥ ΤΙ.	,,
			Gold.	
		Head of Ptolemaeus I.	ΠΤΟΛΕΜΑΙΟΥ ΒΑΣΙΛΕΩΣ Eagle l. on thunderbolt, wings open.	
77	Wt. 27·6		to l., ✦.	,,
			Silver.	
		Similar.	ΠΤΟΛΕΜΑΙΟΥ ΒΑΣΙΛΕΩΣ Eagle l. on thunderbolt.	
78	218·4		to l., P ✦.	,,
			Copper.	
		Head of Zeus.	ΠΤΟΛΕΜΑΙΟΥ ΒΑΣΙΛΕΩΣ Eagle l. on thunderbolt, wings open.	
79	Size. 1·1		to l., A ✦.	,,

No.	Wt. or Size.	Obverse.	Reverse.	Mint.—Date.
			Egypt.	
			Gold.	
		Head of Ptolemaeus I.	ΠΤΟΛΕΜΑΙΟΥ ΒΑΣΙΛΕΩΣ Eagle l. on thunderbolt, wings open.	
80	Wt. 26·9		to l., **A**.	Alexandria?
81	27·4		,, ,,	,,
			Silver.	
		Similar.	ΠΤΟΛΕΜΑΙΟΥ ΒΑΣΙΛΕΩΣ Eagle l. on thunderbolt.	
82	213·4		to l., **A**.	,,
83	228·		,, **A̸**	,,
84	219·5		,, **P̱A**	,,
85	230·3		,, **Δ·**	Daphnae?
86	216· worn.		,, **ΠΤ̱A̱** ; to r., ⊙	Ptolemais
87	220·5		,, **Π̱⊘** ; ,, ,,	,,
88	219·		,, **M̱N** ; ,, ,, [Pl. III. 8.]	,,
89	219·6		,, **ΣΤ K̸Æ ΓΤ** ; ,, ,	,,

No.	Wt. or Size.	Obverse.	Reverse.	Mint. — Date.
		\multicolumn{2}{c}{PTOLEMAEUS II., PHILADELPHUS. B.C. 284–247. Cyprus. A. SECOND COINAGE, *with monogram* Σ, Σ. (See also Ptolemaeus I. and II., p. 13.)}	
			Gold.	
1	Wt. 275·5	Head of Ptolemaeus I. r., diademed and wearing aegis.	ΠΤΟΛΕΜΑΙΟΥ ΒΑΣΙΛΕΩΣ Eagle l. on thunderbolt; to l., Σ. [Bank Coll.]	Uncert.
			Silver.	
2	216·5	Similar.	Similar. [Pl. IV. 1.]	,,
			Copper.	
3	Size. 1·15	Head of Zeus r., laur.	ΠΤΟΛΕΜΑΙΟΥ ΒΑΣΙΛΕΩΣ Eagle l. on thunderbolt, wings open; to l., Σ.	,,
			Gold.	
		Head of Ptolemaeus I.	ΠΤΟΛΕΜΑΙΟΥ ΒΑΣΙΛΕΩΣ Eagle l. on thunderbolt; to l., Σ.	
4	Wt. 275·5		between eagle's legs, E. [Bank Coll.]	,,
5	274·9		,, P.	,,
6	275·6		,, Y (Σ). [Pl. IV. 2.]	,,

No.	Wt. or Size.	Obverse.	Reverse.	Mint. Date.
			Silver.	
		Head of Ptolemaeus I.	ΠΤΟΛΕΜΑΙΟΥ ΒΑΣΙΛΕΩΣ Eagle l. on thunderbolt; to l., ⊠	
		[Countermark, ΣΑ (Salamis). See Ptolemaeus IV. Cyprus.]	[between eagle's legs, A].	Uncert.
		[Countermk., K (Citium?) See ibid.]	[,, ,, (*graffito*, αρχ /ϟ/).]	,,
7	Wt. 214·4		,, E.	,,
8	216·	Countermark, ✪.	,, ,,	,,
9	202·6		,, ,,	,,
10	worn. 215·7	Countermark, ,,	,, O.	,,
11	207·5		,, P.	,,
12	211·5	Countermark, Δ.	,, ,,	,,
13	worn. 217·7		,, Y.	,,
			Copper.	
		Head of Zeus r., laur.	ΠΤΟΛΕΜΑΙΟΥ ΒΑΣΙΛΕΩΣ Eagle l. on thunderbolt, wings open; to l., ⊠	
14	Size. 1·05		beneath shield, ΣΙ; between eagle's legs, Δ.	,,
15	1·05		between eagle's legs, I. [Pl. iv. 3.]	,,
16	1·1		,, ,,	,,
17	1·05		,, O.	,,
18	1·05		,, ,, ·	,,
19	1·15		,, P.	,,

No.	Wt. or Size.	Obverse.	Reverse.	Mint. — Date.
			B. SECOND COINAGE, *with* ◯.	
			Copper.	
			(*a*) *With buckler only.*	
		Head of Zeus r., laur.	ΓΤΟΛΕΜΑΙΟΥ ΒΑΣΙΛΕΩΣ Eagle l. on thunderbolt, wings open; to l., ◯.	
20	Size. 1·05		[Pl. IV. 4.]	Uncert
21	1·05			,,
22	1·			,,
			(β) *With letter or monogram to left, under buckler.*	
23	1·05		under buckler, A?	,,
24	1·1		,, NK.	,,
25	1·05		,, ,, [Pl. IV. 5.]	,,
26	1·05		,, Φ.	,,
			(γ) *With letter behind eagle.*	
27	1·05		behind eagle, A. [Pl. IV. 6.]	,,
28	1·		,, N.	,,
29	1·05		,, ,, [Bank Coll.]	,,
30	1·05		,, ,,	,,
31	1·05		,, Φ.	,,

PTOLEMAEUS II, PHILADELPHUS.   27

No.	Wt. or Size.	Obverse.	Reverse.	Mint. Date.
		Phœnicia.		
		A. First Coinage. ΠΤΟΛΕΜΑΙΟΥ ΒΑΣΙΛΕΩΣ.		
		(a) *Not dated.*		
		(*On one stater of Sidon engraver's mark,* Κ. See Introd., p. xxxiv.)		
		Silver.		
32	Wt. 215·7	Head of Ptolemaeus I. r., diademed and wearing aegis.	ΠΤΟΛΕΜΑΙΟΥ ΒΑΣΙΛΕΩΣ Eagle l. on thunderbolt; to l., ΣΙ. to l., ΣΙ. [Pl. iv. 7.]	Sidon.
33	213·7		,, ΣΙ M ·	,,
34	208·5		,, ΣΙ Ⓝ ·	,,
35	218·		,, ΣΙ ⓃΙ ·	,,
36	219·3		,, ΣΙ; to r., Ι.	,,
37	217·8	Similar.	Similar; to l., ⚱. [Pl. iv. 8.]	Tyre.
38	218·2	Similar.	Similar; to l., Α. to l., 🜉. A	Ace.
39	219·2		,, 🜉ᴾ. A [Pl. iv. 9.]	,,

No.	Wt. or Size.	Obverse.	Reverse.	Mint. — Date.
40	Wt. 213·2	Head of Ptolemaeus I.	ΓΤΟΛΕΜΑΙΟΥ ΒΑΣΙΛΕΩΣ Eagle l. on thunderbolt; to l., ᛘᛈ ⓜ	Ptolemais
41	216·			,,
42	215· worn.			,,
43	Size. 1·15	Head of Zeus r., laur.	*Copper.* Similar; between eagle's legs, A.	Ace?

(β) *Dated*, year 20—24=B.C. 266-5—262-1.

Silver.

No.	Wt. or Size.	Obverse.	Reverse.	Mint. — Date.
44	Wt. 218·7	Head of Ptolemaeus I.	Similar; to l., ⚱ ; to r., date. to r., K. [Pl. iv. 10.]	Tyre. B.C. 266-5.
45	220·4		,, Ҟ · [ΚΑ.]	265-4.
46	211·9		,, Ҟ	,,
47	218·1		,, Ḃ. [ΚΒ.]	264-3.
48	218·6		,, ,,	,,
49	217·8		,, Ҟ. [ΚΓ.]	263-2.
50	218·5		,, Ҟ. [ΚΔ.]	262-1.
51	213·8		,, ,,	,,
52	214·7		,, ,,	,,

PTOLEMAEUS II., PHILADELPHUS. 29

No.	Wt. or Size.	Obverse.	Reverse.	Mint. Date.
		B. SECOND COINAGE. ΠΤΟΛΕΜΑΙΟΥ ΣΩΤΗΡΟΣ.		
		Silver dated, year 25—39=B.C. 261-0—247.		
		Silver.		
53	Wt. 220·2	Head of Ptolemaeus I. r., diademed and wearing aegis.	ΠΤΟΛΕΜΑΙΟΥ ΣΩΤΗΡΟΣ Eagle l. on thunderbolt; to l., ΣΙ. to l., ΣΙ / ΑΚ ; to r., Κ. [ΚΕ.]	Sidon. B.C. 261-0.
54	217·	. .	” ” ” ” ”	”
55	213·		” ΣΙ / ΔΙ ” ”	”
56	220·1		” ΣΙ / Ⓝ ” ”	”
57	214·		” ΣΙ / Α ” Ε· [ΚΓ.] [Pl. v. 1.]	259-8.
58	213·		” ΣΙ / ΔΙ ” ΚΘ·	257-6.
59	213·5		” ΣΙ / ΜΤ ” ” [Pl. v. 2.]	”
60	215·4		” ” ” ”	”
61	219·		” ΣΙ / ΔΙ ” Λ·	256-5.
62	215·		” ΣΙ / ΑΔ ” ”	

30   THE PTOLEMAIC KINGS OF EGYPT.

No.	Wt. or Size.	Obverse.	Reverse.				Mint. – Date.
63	Wt. 211· worn.	Head of Ptolemaeus I.	ΠΤΟΛΕΜΑΙΟΥ ΣΩΤΗΡΟΣ Eagle l. on thunderbolt; to l., ΣΙ. to l., ΣΙ/ΔΙ; to r., ΛΑ.				Sidon. B.C. 255-4.
64	217·4		,,	,,	,,	,,	,,
65	207·4 worn.		,,	ΣΙ/ᴍ;	,,	ΛΑ.	,,
66	217·7		,,	,,	,,	,,	,,
67	216·8		,,	,,	,,	ΑΛ. [Pl. v. 3.]	,,
68	218·3		,,	,,	,,	ΛΒ. [Pl. v. 4.]	254-3.
69	213·4		,,	,,	,,	,,	,,
70	212·5		,,	ΣΙ/ΔΙ	,,	ΛΓ.	253-2.
71	217·5		,,	ΣΙ/ᴍ	,,	,,	,,
72	220·6		,,	,,	,,	,,	,,
73	201·9 plated.		,,	ΣΙ/ΔΙ	,,	ΛΔ.	252-1.
74	216·2		,,	ΣΙ/ᴍ	,,	,,	,,
75	218·8		,,	ΣΙ/ΔΙ	,,	ΛΕ.	250-49.
76	220·		,,	,,	,,	ΛΣ.	249-8.
77	218·		,,	,,	,,	ΛΗ/ᴍ. [Pl. v. 5.]	248-7.

PTOLEMAEUS II., PHILADELPHUS.

No.	Wt. or Size.	Obverse.	Reverse.			Mint. — Date.
		Head of Ptolemaeus I.	ΠΤΟΛΕΜΑΙΟΥ ΣΩΤΗΡΟΣ			
			Eagle l. on thunderbolt; to l., 𝄞 .			Tyre. B.C.
78	Wt. 221·1		to r., K̦. • [KE.]	[Pl. v. 6.]		261-0.
79	216·2		„ Ɛ. [KϚ.]			259-8.
80	219·5		„ H̲EI [KH]; between eagle's legs, A.			258-7.
81	210·3		„ Λ̂Ⓐ	„	„	256-5.
82	218·5		„ „	„	HP.	„
83	213·2		„ „	„	⊙.	„
84	217·2		„ „	„	M.	„
85	211·7		„ „	„	Ⓝ.	„
86	217·		„ ΛB ⋈	„	⊙.	254-3.
87	220·7		„ „	„	⊟.	„
88	213·8	(Double-struck).	„ „	„	M.	„
89	217·9		„ „	„	Ⓝ.	„
90	218·5		„ „	„	Ξ!	„
91	219·		„ ΛΓ ⋈	„	⊙.	253-2.
92	216·8		„ „	„	Ⓝ.	„
93	217·		„ ΛΔ ⋈	„	ΔΙ.	252-1.
94	214·3		„ „	„	⊙.	„

THE PTOLEMAIC KINGS OF EGYPT.

No.	Wt. or Size.	Obverse.	Reverse.	Mint. — Date.
95	Wt. 209·	Head of Ptolemaeus I.	ΠΤΟΛΕΜΑΙΟΥ ΣΩΤΗΡΟΣ Eagle l. on thunderbolt; to l., ⚹. to r., ΛΔ / ⋈ ; between eagle's legs, ⊙.	Tyre. B.C. 252-1.
96	216·5		,, ,, ,, ,, ⋈·	,,
97	215·		,, ,, ,, ,, altered in die from [IΨ . ΛΓ] [⋈ ⊙]	,, [Joppa. 253-2.]
98	211·3		,, ,, ,, Ⓝ.	,,
99	203·2 plated.		,, ΛΕ ; ⋈ ,, ΔΙ ·	251-0.
100	219·8		,, ΛΕ ; A ,, Ⓝ.	250-49.
101	219·3		,, ΛΙ · E ,, ,,	249-8.

Copper.

FIRST OR SECOND COINAGE.

No.	Wt. or Size.	Obverse.	Reverse.	Mint. — Date.
102	Size. 1·65	Head of Zeus Ammon r., wearing diadem, and globe.	ΠΤΟΛΕΜΑΙΟΥ ΒΑΣΙΛΕΩΣ Two eagles l. on thunderbolts; between legs of that in advance, ⚹. [Pl. v. 7.]	Tyre.
103	1·55			,,
104	1·4	Similar type.	Same inscr. Eagle l. on thunderbolt, wings open; between legs, same mon. [Pl. v. 8.]	,,
105	1·4		(Υ for ⚹.) ·	,,
106	1·2	Head of Zeus r., laur.	Same inscr. Eagle l. on thunderbolt; between legs, same mon.	,,
107	1·15		[Pl. v. 9.]	,,

PTOLEMAEUS II., PHILADELPHUS. 33

No.	Wt. or Size.	Obverse.	Reverse.	Mint.—Date.
			Silver.	
			SECOND COINAGE.	
		Head of Ptolemaeus I. r., diademed and wearing aegis.	ΠΤΟΛΕΜΑΙΟΥ ΣΩΤΗΡΟΣ Eagle l. on thunderbolt; to l., ⊕.	Ptolemais B.C.
108	Wt. 214·8		to r., 𐅽. [ΚΕ.]	261-0.
109	213·6		,, ,,	,,
110	209·6		to l., ⊕/ᖴ; to r., Ƕ/𐅉. [ΚΗ.]	258-7.
		Similar.	Similar; to l., ⋔.	
111	215·		to l., ΜΕ; to r., Λ/⊙.	256-5.
112	217·3		,, ,, ,, ΛΑ/⊙.	255-4.
113	216·		,, ,, ,, ΑΛ/⊙.	,,
114	198· worn.		,, ,, ,, [,,]/⊙.	,,
115	216·5		,, ,, ,, ΛΒ/⊙.	254-3.
116	191·8 worn.		,, ΝΕ ,, ΑΒ/⊙. (*sic*)	,,
117	216·9		,, ΜΕ to r., ΑΓ/⊙.	253-2.
118	218·		,, ,, ,, ,,	,,
119	218·5		,, ΛΕ ,, ,,	,,

F

No.	Wt. or Size.	Obverse.	Reverse.	Mint. Date.
		Head of Ptolemaeus I.	ΠΤΟΛΕΜΑΙΟΥ ΣΩΤΗΡΟΣ Eagle l. on thunderbolt.	
120	Wt. 214·5		to l., $\overset{m}{ME}$; to r., $\overset{\Lambda\Delta}{\odot}$.	Ptolemais B.C. 252-1.
121	214·6		,, ,, ,, $\overset{\Lambda E}{\odot}$.	251-0.
122	213·2		,, ,, ,, $\overset{\Lambda\digamma}{\odot}$.	250-49.
123	217·		,, ,, ,, $\overset{\Lambda Z}{\odot}$.	249-8.

Copper.

		Head of Zeus Ammon r., diademed.	ΠΤΟΛΕΜΑΙΟΥ ΒΑΣΙΛΕΩΣ Two eagles l. on thunderbolts.	Ptolemais
124	Size. 1·6		between eagles' legs, $\odot$, ME.	

Silver.

		Head of Ptolemaeus I.	ΠΤΟΛΕΜΑΙΟΥ ΣΩΤΗΡΟΣ Eagle l. on thunderbolt; to l., ⌐o⌐I.	
125	Wt. 214·3		to l., ⌐o⌐I ; to r., Κ. [ΚΕ.]	Joppa. 261-0.
126	216·5		,, ⁀ϥI ; ,, Ι. [ΚΙ.]	259-8.
127	212·2		,, ,, ,, ,,	,,
		Similar.	Similar ; to L, ΙϞΙ.	
128	215·9		to r., $\overset{\Lambda\Lambda}{\odot}$.	255-4.
129	216·		,, $\overset{\Lambda B}{\odot}$.	254-3.
130	213·		to l., $\overset{ΙϞΙ}{AA}$,, $\overset{\Lambda\Gamma}{\odot}$.	253-2.
131	212·7		,, $\overset{\Lambda\Delta}{\odot}$. ,, ,, ,,	252-1.
132	219·		,, $\overset{\Lambda E}{\odot}$. ,, ,, ,,	251-0.

PTOLEMAEUS II., PHILADELPHUS.

No.	Wt. or Size.	Obverse.	Reverse.	Mint.— Date.
		Head of Ptolemaeus I.	ΠΤΟΛΕΜΑΙΟΥ ΣΩΤΗΡΟΣ Eagle l. on thunderbolt; to l., ΙΨΠ.	Joppa.
133	Wt. 209·		to l., ΙΨΠ/ΑΑ; to r., ΛΕ/⊙.	B.C. 251-0.
134	217·5		,, ,, ,, ΛΖ/⊙.	249-8.
		Similar.	Similar; to l., Ⱶ or Ⱶ.	
135	214·6	Countermark, H (Σ?).	to l., Ⱶ; to r., Ϟ. [KE.]	Gaza. 261-0.
136	214·3		,, Ⱶ/Ⱶ; ,, ΚΘ.	257-6.
137	212·6		,, Ⱶ"; ,, ΛΛ/⚹. [ΑΛ or ΛΑ.]	255-4.
138	216·9		,, ,, ,, ΛΒ/⚹.	254-8.
139	217·3		,, ,, ,, ΛΓ/⚹.	253-2.
140	215·		,, ,, ,, ,,.	,,
141	218·3		,, ,, ,, ΛΞ/Ξ.	249-8.
		Similar.	Similar; to l., ΙΨΠ/Ⱶ or Ⱶ.	
142	208·4		to r., Λ/⊙.	Joppa and Gaza 256-5.
143	218·9		to l., Ⱶ; ,, ΛΕ/⊙.	250-49.
144	219·		,, Ⱶ; ,, ΛΞ/⊙.	249-8.

No.	Wt. or Size.	Obverse.	Reverse.	Mint. — Date.
			Egypt. *Gold.* See Gold, Arsinoë II.; and Ptolemaeus II. and Arsinoë II., with Ptolemaeus I. and Berenice I. *Silver.*	
145	Wt. 218·	Head of Ptolemaeus I. r., diademed and wearing aegis.	ΠΤΟΛΕΜΑΙΟΥ ΒΑΣΙΛΕΩΣ Eagle l. on thunderbolt; to l., A. [Pl. vi. 1.]	Alexandria.
146	214·5	Similar.	to l., ΓΤ; to r., ⊙. ΓΤ Ⓐ Ⓐ	Ptolemais
147	215·3		,, ,, ,, ,, [Pl. vi. 2.]	,,
148	212·5		,, Ⓐ Ⓜ	,,
149	217·5		,, Ⓐ Ⓜ [Bank Coll.]	,,
150	217·5		,, Ⓐ.	,,
151	215·5		,, Ⓐ.	,,
152	207·8 worn.	Similar.	Similar; to l., Π. Π to l., Ⓐ.	,,
153	208·5		,, ΚΛ.	,,
154	214·5		,, ,, ,,	,,
155	207· worn.		,, ΙΑ. (Ⓐ)	,,
156	216·9		,, Ⓐ. [Pl. vi. 3.]	,,

PTOLEMAEUS II., PHILADELPHUS. 37

No.	Wt. or Size.	Obverse.	Reverse.	Mint.—Date.
			Copper.	
		Head of Zeus Ammon r., diademed.	ΠΤΟΛΕΜΑΙΟΥ ΒΑΣΙΛΕΩΣ Eagle l. on thunderbolt, wings open, looking back.	
157	Size. 1·8		between eagle's legs, ⊙.	Uncert.
158	1·85		,, E.	,,
159	1·8			,,
160	1·75			,,
161	1·8			,,
162	1·8			,,
163	1·8		[Pl. vi. 4.]	,,

Cyrenaica.

LOCAL COINAGE.

Magas, Governor.

With monogram of Magas.

Copper.

No.	Wt. or Size.	Obverse.	Reverse.	Mint.—Date.
		Head of Ptolemaeus I. r., diademed and wearing aegis.	ΒΑΣΙΛ ΠΤΟ Fore-part of sea-horse r.	
1	·6		beneath 𝈣, crab. [Pl. vi. 5.]	Apollonia
		Similar.	ΒΑΣΙΛΕΩΣ ΠΤΟΛΕΜΑΙΟΥ Fore-part of sea-horse l.	
2	·6		beneath, 𝈣.	,,
		Similar.	ΠΤΟΛ Prow l. BAΣIΛ	
3	·75		to l., 𝈣.	,,

Restruck on earlier coin of Euesperides (cf. Müller, Num. Anc. Afr., vol. i., p. 89, nos. 335–8.)

No.	Wt. or Size.	Obverse.	Reverse.	Mint. — Date.
	Size.	Head of Ptolemaeus I. r., diademed and wearing aegis.	ΠΤΟΛΕΜΑΙΟΥ Winged thunder- ΒΑΣΙΛΕΩΣ bolt.	
4	·85		above, M. [Pl. vi. 6.]	Uncert.
5	·85		,, ,,	,,
6	·9		,, M.	,,
7	·85		,, ,,	,,
8	·9		,, ,,	,,
9	·9		,, (mon. effaced.)	,,
10	·55	Head of Ptolemaeus I. r., diademed and wearing aegis.	[ΒΑΣΙΛΕΩΣ ΠΤΟΛΕΜΑΙΟΥ?] Free horse galloping l. above, M.	,,

Magas, King, B.C. 280?–   ?

Copper.

| 11 | ·85 | Head of Ptolemaeus I. r., diademed and wearing aegis. | ΒΑΣΙΛΕΩΣ ΜΑΓΑ Head of Libya r., bound with tainia.
[Pl. vi. 7.] | ,, |
| 12 | ·95 | Head of Magas r., diademed and wearing aegis. | ΒΑΣΙΛΕΩΣ ΜΑΓΑ Head of Libya r., bound with tainia.
[Pl. vi. 8.] | ,, |

Ptolemaeus II., B.C.   ?–258.

Magas, Governor.

Copper.

13	·6	Head of Ptolemaeus I. r., diademed and wearing aegis.	ΒΑΣΙΛΕΩΣ ΠΤΟΛΕΜΑΙΟΥ Head of Libya r., bound with tainia; to r., cornucopiae.	,,
14	·55			,,
15	·55			,,
16	·5		[Pl. vi. 9.]	,,

PTOLEMAEUS II., PHILADELPHUS.

No.	Wt. or Size.	Obverse.	Reverse.	Mint. — Date.
	Size.	Head of Ptolemaeus I.	ΒΑΣΙΛΕΩΣ ΠΤΟΛΕΜΑΙΟΥ Head of Libya; to r., double cornucopiæ. [Pl. VI. 10.]	
17	·85			Uncert.
18	·85			,,
19	·55			,,
20	·55			,,
21	·5			,,
22	·4			,,
			Silver.	
23	Wt. 100·7	Head of Ptolemaeus I. r., diademed and wearing aegis.	ΠΤΟΛΕΜΑΙΟΥ ΒΑΣΙΛΕΩΣ Eagle r. on thunderbolt. to r., ⚚ (flaming race-torch?) (ΣΩΣΙΒΑΣ ΠΤΟΛΕΜΑΙΟΥ.)	,,
24	103·1	Similar.	Similar; eagle l. to l., ⚚.	,,
			With monogram of Magas. *Silver.*	
25	99·8	Similar.	ΒΑΣΙΛΕ ΠΤΟΛΕΜΑΙΟΥ Eagle r. on thunderbolt; to l., Ⲙ. to r., Χ.	,,
			Copper	
		Similar.	ΠΤΟΛΕΜΑΙΟΥ ΒΑΣΙΛΕΩΣ Eagle l. on thunderbolt, wings open; to l., Ⲙ.	
26	Size. ·85			,,
27	·75			,,
28	·7		[Pl. VI. 11.]	,,
29	·7		to l., Ⲙ. ΣΑ	,,
30	·75		,, ,, ,,	,,
			Cyrenaica? *Copper.*	
31	·5	Head of Ptolemaeus II. r., diademed.	ΠΤΟΛΕΜΑΙΟΥ ΒΑΣΙΛΕΩΣ Eagle l., wings open; in front, dolphin l. downwards. [Pl. VI. 12.]	,,

PTOLEMAEUS II. AND ARSINOË II., WITH PTOLEMAEUS I. AND BERENICE I.

Gold.

(α) Period of Ptolemaeus II., Philadelphus, and Ptolemaeus III., Euergetes.

Egypt?

No.	Wt. or Size.	Obverse.	Reverse.	Mint. Date.
1	wt. 215·4	ΑΔΕΛΦΩΝ Busts jugate r. of Ptolemaeus II., diademed and wearing chlamys, and Arsinoë II., diademed and veiled. to l., A ⊕; to r., double cornucopiae.	ΘΕΩΝ Busts jugate r. of Ptolemaeus I., diademed and wearing aegis, and Berenice I., diademed and veiled. [Pl. VII. 1.]	Alexandria?
2	427·8	„ ⊗.	[Pl. VII. 2.]	Uncert.
3	214·6	„ „ „ K (letter partly effaced).	[Pl. VII. 3.]	„
4	214·3	„ „		„
5	213·5	„ „		„
6	426·3	„ „	to l., ⚱.	„
7	428·6	„ „	„ ⚱. [Pl. VII. 4.]	„

(β) Struck by Ptolemaeus V., Epiphanes.

		Similar.	Similar.	
8	427·6	to l., ℞ (diadem of Philadelphus adorned with thunderbolt).	to l., ⚱ [Pl. VII. 5.]	„
9	429·	„ „ (diadem plain). [Bank Coll.]	„ ⚱. [Pl. VII. 6.]	„

No.	Wt. or Size.	Obverse.	Reverse.	Mint. Date.
		(γ) Struck by Ptolemaeus VI., Philometor?		
10	Wt. 428·5	ΑΔΕΛΦΩΝ Busts jugate. to L, ◊ .	ΘΕΩΝ Busts jugate. [Pl. vii. 7.]	Uncert.
		Silver.		
		Uncertain Period.		
11	23·7	Similar.	Similar.	,,

No.	Wt. or Size.	Obverse.	Reverse.	Mint. Date.
		ARSINOË II., PHILADELPHOS. (a) Struck by Ptolemaeus II. Egypt? *Gold.*		
1	wt. 429·	Head of Arsinoë r., with horn of Zeus Ammon, wearing diadem, stephane, and veil.	ΑΡΣΙΝΟΗΣ ΦΙΛΑΔΕΛΦΟΥ Double cornucopiæ bound with fillet. [Pl. VIII. 1.]	Uncert.
		(β) Struck by Ptolemaeus III., Euergetes I. Phœnicia. A. FIRST COINAGE. *Gold.*		
2	426·4	Head of Arsinoë r., with horn of Zeus Ammon, wearing diadem, stephane, and veil; behind head, sceptre.	Similar; beneath cornucopiæ, ΣΙ. in field, below, E ΣΙ/Η/Χ.	Sidon. B.C. 243-2.
3	428·3		Similar; beneath cornucopiæ, ⚹. in field, below, A $\frac{mon.}{\odot}$.	Tyre. 247-6.
4	427·4		,, Δ $\frac{mon.}{\odot}$. [Pl. VIII. 2.]	244-3.
5	428·4		Similar; beneath cornucopiæ, T. in field, below, B $\frac{mon.}{A}$. [Bank Coll.]	Ptolemais 246-5.
6	426·		Similar; beneath cornucopiæ, ΙϘϞ. in field, below, Γ $\frac{mon.}{\odot}$.	Joppa. 245-4.

ARSINOË II., PHILADELPHOS.

No.	Wt. or Size.	Obverse.	Reverse.	Mint.—Date.
			C. THIRD COINAGE.	
			Silver.	
7	Wt. 215·6	Head of Arsinoë, with sceptre.	ΑΡΣΙΝΟΗΣ ΦΙΛΑΔΕΛΦΟΥ Eagle l. on thunderbolt. between eagle's legs, X. [Pl. VIII. 3.	Uncert.
			(γ) Struck by Ptolemaeus II., and Ptolemaeus III.	
			Cyprus.	
			Gold.	
8	429·	Similar.	ΑΡΣΙΝΟΗΣ ΦΙΛΑΔΕΛΦΟΥ Double cornucopiae bound with fillet. beneath, thunderbolt and K.	Citium?
			Egypt.	
			Gold.	
		Similar.	Similar.	
9	429·2	Behind head, ☉ .		Uncert.
10	429·4	,, K .	[Pl. VIII. 4.]	,,
11	428·	,, Λ .		,,
12	428·5	No letter.		,,
			Silver.	
		Similar.	Similar.	
13	532·3	Behind head, Γ .		,,
14	543·8	,, E .		,,
15	542·	,, Λ .		,,

No.	Wt. or Size.	Obverse.	Reverse.	Mint. - Date.
		Head of Arsinoë.	ΑΡΣΙΝΟΗΣ ΦΙΛΑΔΕΛΦΟΥ Double cornucopiæ.	
16	Wt. 522· worn.	Behind head, Ξ.		Uncert.
17	521·	,, Ρ.		,,
18	534·	,, Υ.		,,
19	534·5	,, Ψ.		,,
20	546·2	,, ΒΒ.		,,
21	529·2	,, ΕΕ.		,,
22	514· worn.	,, ΗΗ.		,,
23	541·8	,, ΘΘ.	[Pl. VIII. 5.]	,,
24	518·5 worn.	,, ΙΙ.		,,
25	540·	,, ΚΚ.		,,
26	546·8	,, ΜΜ.		,,
27	527·4	,, ΝΝ.		,,
28	541·	,, ΞΞ.		,,
29	536·3	,, ΟΟ.		,,
30	540·3	,, ΠΠ.		,,
31	538·6	,, ΣΣ.		,,
32	538·8	,, ΤΤ.		,,
33	527·2	No letter.		,,

(δ) Struck by Ptolemaeus V., Epiphanes.

Cyprus.

Gold

		Similar.	Similar.	Citium. B.C. 190-189.
34	416·4 worn.		to l., ΚΙ ; to r., ΛΙΓ. [Pl. VIII. 6.]	

ARSINOË II., PHILADELPHOS.

No.	Wt. or Size.	Obverse.	Reverse.	Mint. — Date.
		(ε) Struck by Ptolemaeus VI., Philometor. *Egypt. Gold.*		
35	Wt. 428·3	Head of Arsinoë. Behind head, Λ.	ΑΡΣΙΝΟΗΣ ΦΙΛΑΔΕΛΦΟΥ Double cornucopiæ. [Pl. VIII. 7.]	Uncert.
		(ζ) Struck by Ptolemaeus IX., Euergetes II., or Ptolemaeus X., Soter II. *Egypt. Gold.*		
		Similar.	Similar.	
36	425·7	Behind head, K.	[Pl. VIII. 8.]	,,
37	429·	,, ,,		,,
38	426·5	,, ,,		,,
39	428·2	,, ,,	[Bank Coll. Pl. VIII. 9.]	,,
40	215·2	,, ,,	[Pl. VIII. 10.]	,,

PTOLEMAEUS III., EUERGETES I.

B.C. 247–222.

Cyprus.

A. First Coinage, *with* ⲙ̄.

Silver.

No.	Wt. or Size.	Obverse.	Reverse.	Mint. — Date.
1	Wt. 215·4	Head of Ptolemaeus I. r., diademed and wearing aegis.	ΠΤΟΛΕΜΑΙΟΥ ΒΑΣΙΛΕΩΣ Eagle l. on thunderbolt; to l., ⲙ̄. to r., ⋈. [Pl. ɪx. 1.]	Uncert.
2	215·7		,, ,,	,,
3	216·6		,, ⋏. [Pl. ɪx. 2.]	Idalium?
4	219·2		,, ,,	,,

Copper.

		Head of Zeus r., laur.	ΠΤΟΛΕΜΑΙΟΥ ΒΑΣΙΛΕΩΣ Eagle l. on thunderbolt, wings open; to l., ⲙ̄.	
5	Size. 1·05		between eagle's legs, ⋏. [Pl. ɪx. 3.]	,,
6	1·05		,, ,,	,,
7	1·05		to l. beneath buckler, ⋈; ,, A.	Uncert.
8	1·		,, ,, ,, ,, ,,	,,
9	1·05		,, ,, ,, ,, ,,	,,
10	1·		,, ,, ,, ,, K.	,,

No.	Wt. or Size.	Obverse.	Reverse.	Mint. — Date.
11	Size. ·8	Head of Alexander r., with horn of Zeus Ammon, clad in elephant's skin and aegis.	ΠΤΟΛΕΜΑΙΟΥ ΒΑΣΙΛΕΩΣ Eagle l. on thunderbolt, wings open. to l. beneath buckler, X.	Uncert.

B. SECOND COINAGE, *silver with portrait of Ptolemaeus III.*

Silver.

		Head of Ptolemaeus III. r., diademed and wearing lion's skin round neck.	ΠΤΟΛΕΜΑΙΟΥ ΒΑΣΙΛΕΩΣ Eagle l. on thunderbolt.	
12	Wt. 217·2		to l., ⚹ ; to r., K. [Pl. IX. 4.]	Idalium?
13	215·3		„ Ⓐ. [Pl. IX. 5.]	Uncert.
14	216·7		no mon. (restruck?). [Pl. IX. 6.]	,,

Copper.

		Head of Zeus r., laur.	ΠΤΟΛΕΜΑΙΟΥ ΒΑΣΙΛΕΩΣ Eagle l. on thunderbolt, wings open; in front, cornucopiæ.	
15	Size. 1·05		between eagle's legs, E. [Pl. IX. 7.]	,,
16	1·1		,, ,,	,,
17	·95		no mon.	,,

THE PTOLEMAIC KINGS OF EGYPT.

No.	Wt. or Size.	Obverse.	Reverse.	Mint. Date.
			Phœnicia.	
			A. First Coinage, *silver dated.*	
			Silver.	
18	Wt. 219·	Head of Ptolemaeus I. r., diademed and wearing aegis.	ΠΤΟΛΕΜΑΙΟΥ ΣΩΤΗΡΟΣ Eagle l. on thunderbolt; to l., ΣΙ. to l., ΣΙ/ΙΗ ; to r., Γ/Ν.	Sidon. B.C. 245-4.
19	218·8		,, ,, ,, ,, ,, ,,	,,
20	210·8 worn.		,, ,, ,, ,, Δ/Ν .	244-3.
21	216·		,, ,, ,, ,, ∪/Ν	242-1.
22	216·7	Similar.	Similar; to l., ⌶. to r., Γ/Ι ; between eagle's legs, ☉.	Tyre. 245-4.
23	189·2 broken.		,, Ε/Ι ; ,, Μ/☉·	243-2.
			Copper.	
24	Size. 1·55	Head of Zeus Ammon r., diademed.	ΠΤΟΛΕΜΑΙΟΥ ΒΑΣΙΛΕΩΣ Two eagles l. on thunderbolts. between legs of eagle in advance, Ι.	Tyre?

PTOLEMAEUS III., EUERGETES I. 49

No.	Wt. or Size.	Obverse.	Reverse.	Mint. – Date.
			Silver.	
		Head of Ptolemaeus I.	ΓΤΟΛΕΜΑΙΟΥ ΣΩΤΗΡΟΣ Eagle; to l., m	
25	Wt. 217·2		to l., m̲E̲; to r., B̲ A̲ . [Pl. x. 1.]	Ptolemais B.C. 246-5.
26	206·2 worn.		,, m̲ ΛE ; ,, ,,	,,
		Similar.	Similar; to l., ΙΟΓ .	
27	215·8		to l., ΙΟΓ HP ; to r., E̲ ⊙ .	Joppa. 243-2.
		Similar	Similar; to l., A̲ .	
28	211·3		to l., A̲ A̲ ; to r., B̲ I̲ .	Gaza. 246-5.
			Copper.	
		Head of Zeus Ammon.	ΓΤΟΛΕΜΑΙΟΥ ΒΑΣΙΛΕΩΣ Two eagles.	
29	Size. 1·6		between legs of eagle in advance, ⊙ . [Pl. x. 2.]	Central Mint?
30	1·7		,, ,, ,,	,,
		B. SECOND COINAGE; *silver generally with obv. dies of First Coinage.*		
			Silver.	
		Head of Ptolemaeus I.	ΓΤΟΛΕΜΑΙΟΥ ΣΩΤΗΡΟΣ Eagle; to l., ΠΤ, ΓΤ .	
31	Wt. 219·		to l., ΠΤ A̲ . A̲	Ptolemais

H

No.	Wt. or Size.	Obverse.	Reverse.	Mint.—Date.
		Head of Ptolemaeus I.	ΠΤΟΛΕΜΑΙΟΥ ΣΩΤΗΡΟΣ Eagle; to l., ΠΤ, ΓΤ.	
32	Wt. 218·		to l., ΠΤ ΑΣ·	Ptolemais
33	216·		" ΓΤ ΑΣ·	"
34	219·		" ΠΤ ΣΩ·	"
35	220·8		" ΠΤ ΣΩ· ΞΕ	"
36	219·8		" ΓΤ ΞΕ· (ΞΕ cut in die over ΣΩ.)	"
37	219·9		" " "	"
38	217·		" ΓΤ ΑΙ· ΒΙ [Pl. x. 3.]	"
39	214·2		" " " " "	"
40	213·8		" " ; between eagle's legs, ℞ .	"
41	220·		" " " " " ℞ . "	"
42	212·2		" ΓΤ ΑΙ· ΔΙ	"
43	220·		" ΠΤ ΑΙ· ΔΙ	"

PTOLEMAEUS III., EUERGETES I.   51

No.	Wt. or Size.	Obverse.	Reverse.	Mint. — Date.
		Head of Ptolemaeus I.	ΠΤΟΛΕΜΑΙΟΥ ΣΩΤΗΡΟΣ Eagle; to l., KΛ.	
44	Wt. 213·3		to l., KΛ 𐅝 Α'	Uncert.
45	213·		,, ⚹ (?) KΛ. ⊕	,,
46	221·2		,, KΛ ⊕· [Pl. x. 4.] ΦΙ	,,
		Similar.	Similar; between eagle's legs, X.	
47	217·6		[Pl. x. 5.]	Central Mint ?
48	205·5 worn.			,,
		Copper.		
		Head of Zeus Ammon.	ΠΤΟΛΕΜΑΙΟΥ ΒΑΣΙΛΕΩΣ Two eagles; between legs of eagle in advance, X.	
49	Size. 1·65			,,
		Similar.	Similar; between legs of eagle in advance, Δ.	
50	1·65		[Pl. x. 6.]	,,
		Head of Zeus r., laur.	ΠΤΟΛΕΜΑΙΟΥ ΒΑΣΙΛΕΩΣ Eagle l. on thunderbolt.	
51	1·15		between legs, Δ.	,,
52	1·25		,, ,, [Pl. x. 7.]	,,
53	1·15		,, ,,	,,

THE PTOLEMAIC KINGS OF EGYPT.

No.	Wt. or Size.	Obverse.	Reverse.	Mint.—Date.
54	Size. ·85	Head of Alexander r., with horn of Ammon, clad in elephant's skin and aegis.	ΠΤΟΛΕΜΑΙΟΥ ΒΑΣΙΛΕΩΣ Eagle l. on thunderbolt. ΔΙ to l., . [Pl. x. 8.]	Central Mint?
55	1·6	Head of Zeus Ammon r.	ΠΤΟΛΕΜΑΙΟΥ ΒΑΣΙΛΕΩΣ Two eagles l. on thunderbolts. (Barbarous imitation.)	,,

C. THIRD COINAGE.

Silver.

No.	Wt. or Size.	Obverse.	Reverse.	Mint.—Date.
56	Wt. 221·2	Head of Ptolemaeus I.	ΠΤΟΛΕΜΑΙΟΥ ΣΩΤΗΡΟΣ Eagle. ℞ in front, ΣΙ. ℞	Sidon.

Copper.

No.	Wt. or Size.	Obverse.	Reverse.	Mint.—Date.
57	Size. 1·15	Head of Zeus Ammon r., diademed.	ΠΤΟΛΕΜΑΙΟΥ ΒΑΣΙΛΕΩΣ City facing, wearing modius, right arm bent, left holding dress, on advancing prow.	Sidon?
58	1·15		[Bank Coll.]	,,
59	·9		[Pl. xi. 1.]	,,
60	·75			,,
61	·65		[Pl. xi. 2.]	,,
62	·6			,,

PTOLEMAEUS III., EUERGETES I.

No.	Wt. or Size.	Obverse.	Reverse.	Mint. — Date.
			Silver.	
		Head of Ptolemaeus I.	ΠΤΟΛΕΜΑΙΟΥ ΣΩΤΗΡΟΣ Eagle; to l., ⚹; to r., 𐅉.	
63	Wt. 217·7		[Pl. xi. 3.]	Tyre.
			Copper.	
		Head of Zeus Ammon.	ΠΤΟΛΕΜΑΙΟΥ ΒΑΣΙΛΕΩΣ Eagle l. on thunderbolt; to l., ⚹.	
64	Size. 1·65		between eagle's legs, ΔΙ.	,,
65	1·3		,, ,,	,,
66	1·35			,,
67	1·15		[Pl. xi. 4.]	,,
68	·95			,,
69	·9			,,
70	·8			,,
71	·75			,,
72	·65			,,
73	·6		[Pl. xi. 5.]	,,
			Silver.	
		Head of Ptolemaeus I.	ΠΤΟΛΕΜΑΙΟΥ ΣΩΤΗΡΟΣ Eagle; to l., 𐅉; to r., 𐅉.	
74	Wt. 218·6			Ptolemais

No.	Wt. or Size.	Obverse.	Reverse.	Mint. — Date.
75	Size. ·9	Head of Zeus Ammon.	*Copper.* ΠΤΟΛΕΜΑΙΟΥ ΒΑΣΙΛΕΩΣ Eagle; to l., tripod.	Ptolemais
76	·9		countermark, A.	,,
77	·8	Similar.	Similar; to l., ᛚ. [Pl. xi. 6.]	Joppa.
78	·6			,,
79	·65			,,
80	·6	Similar.	Similar; to l., ᛣ. [Pl. xi. 7.]	Berytus.
81	·5			,,
82	·5			,,
83	wt. 219·	Head of Ptolemaeus I.	*Silver.* ΠΤΟΛΕΜΑΙΟΥ ΣΩΤΗΡΟΣ Eagle; to l., cornucopiæ.	Uncert. ,,
84	Size. 1·5	Head of Zeus Ammon.	*Copper.* ΠΤΟΛΕΜΑΙΟΥ ΒΑΣΙΛΕΩΣ Eagle l., wings open; to l., double cornucopiæ bound with fillet. [Pl. xi. 8.]	,,

No.	Wt. or Size.	Obverse.	Reverse.	Mint. Date.
			Silver.	
		Head of Ptolemaeus I.	ΠΤΟΛΕΜΑΙΟΥ ΣΩΤΗΡΟΣ Eagle; to l., ◉.	
85	Wt. 212·			Uncert.
			Phoenicia or Syria? *Silver.*	
		Head of Ptolemaeus I.	ΠΤΟΛΕΜΑΙΟΥ ΒΑΣΙΛΕΩΣ Eagle.	
86	205·7		to l., 👤; to r., ⚭. [Pl. xi. 9.]	,,
			Egypt. A. First Coinage. *Copper.* (*a*) *Usual types.*	
		Head of Zeus Ammon r., wearing diadem and globe.	ΠΤΟΛΕΜΑΙΟΥ ΒΑΣΙΛΕΩΣ Eagle l. on thunderbolt; to l., cornucopiæ; between eagle's legs, ✳.	
87	Size. 1·65			Alexandria?
88	1·65			,,
89	1·4		[Pl. xii. 1.]	,,
90	1·4			,,
91	1·4	(This coin is very light, being mainly if not wholly patina.)		,,
92	1·2			,,
93	1·			,,
94	·6			,,
		Similar.	Similar; cornucopiæ rests on eagle's l. wing; same mon.	
95	·7			,

No.	Wt. or Size.	Obverse.	Reverse.	Mint. — Date.
96	Size. ·7	Head of Alexander the Great, with horn of Ammon, wearing elephant's skin and aegis.	ΠΤΟΛΕΜΑΙΟΥ ΒΑΣΙΛΕΩΣ Eagle l. on thunderbolt; to l, cornucopiæ; between eagle's legs, ⁂.	Alexandria?
97	·65			,,
98	·5			,,

(β) *With portrait of Ptolemaeus III., laureate.*

99	·9	Bust of Ptolemaeus III. r., laur., and wearing aegis.	ΠΤΟΛΕΜΑΙΟΥ ΒΑΣΙΛΕΩΣ Eagle l. on thunderbolt; to l., cornucopiæ.	Uncert.
100	1·	Similar.	Similar; to r., cornucopiæ.	,,
101	·8		[Pl. xii. 2.]	,,

B. SECOND COINAGE; *gold with portrait.*

Gold.

102	Wt. 429·1	Bust of Ptolemaeus III. r., wearing radiate diadem and aegis; behind shoulder, sceptre-trident.	ΠΤΟΛΕΜΑΙΟΥ ΒΑΣΙΛΕΩΣ Radiate cornucopiæ bound with fillet. beneath, **B**. [Bank Coll. Pl. xii. 3.]	,,
103	429·5		,, **ΔΙ**. [Pl. xii. 4.]	,,
104	429·4	(Same die.)	,, ,,	,,
105	214·4		,, ,, [Bank Coll. Pl. xii. 5.]	,,

Copper.

106	Size. 1·65	Head of Zeus Ammon.	ΠΤΟΛΕΜΑΙΟΥ ΒΑΣΙΛΕΩΣ Eagle l. on thunderbolt; to l., cornucopiæ bound with fillet (countermark, same symbol). between legs, **ΔΙ**.	,,

PTOLEMAEUS III., EUERGETES I.

No.	Wt. or Size.	Obverse.	Reverse.	Mint. Date.
		Head of Zeus Ammon.	ΠΤΟΛΕΜΑΙΟΥ ΒΑΣΙΛΕΩΣ Eagle l. on thunderbolt; to l., cornucopiæ bound with fillet.	
107	Size. 1·7		between legs, ΔΙ.	Uncert.
108	1·65		,, ,, [Pl. xii. 6.]	,,
109	1·4		,, ,,	,,
110	1·3		,, ,,	,,
		Head of Alexander the Great r., with horn of Ammon, clad in elephant's skin and aegis.	ΠΤΟΛΕΜΑΙΟΥ ΒΑΣΙΛΕΩΣ Eagle on thunderbolt l., wings open.	
111	·9		between eagle's legs, Δ.	,,
112	·9		,, ,, [Pl. xii. 7.]	,,
113	·9		,, ,,	,,
114	·85		,, E.	,,
115	·8		,, Є.	,,
116	·8		,, E. (E?)	,,
117	·75		,, E. (id. ?)	,,
118	·8			,,
119	·8			,,
120	·85			,,
			Cyrenaïca. *Copper.*	
		Head of Zeus Ammon r., diademed.	ΠΤΟΛΕΜΑΙΟΥ ΒΑΣΙΛΕΩΣ Eagle l. on thunderbolt, wings open.	
121	·85		to l., cornucopiæ. [Pl. xiii. 1.]	,,
122	·65		between eagle's legs, Δ.	,,

No.	Wt. or Size.	Obverse.	Reverse.	Mint. – Date.
		Head of Zeus Ammon.	ΠΤΟΛΕΜΑΙΟΥ ΒΑΣΙΛΕΩΣ Eagle.	
123	Size. ·75		between eagle's legs, E ?	Uncert.
124	·7			,,
125	·65			,,
126	·6			,,
127	·65			,,

BERENICE II.

i. Queen Regnant of Cyrenaïca, B.C. 258–247.

ii. Queen Consort of Egypt and Regnant of Cyrenaïca, B.C. 247–222.

A. *With name of Berenice only.*

Asia Minor.

Period II.

Gold.

No.	Wt. or Size.	Obverse.	Reverse.	Mint. Date.
1	wt. 427·9	Head of Berenice II. r., wearing diadem, veil, and necklace.	ΒΕΡΕΝΙΚΗΣ ΒΑΣΙΛΙΣΣΗΣ Cornucopiæ bound with fillet. to l., 🜨. [Pl. XIII. 2.] (Pierced.)	Ephesus.

Egypt.

Period II.

Silver.

| 2 | 493·6 | Similar bust. | Similar. [Pl. XIII. 3. Bank Coll.] (Much oxidized.) | Uncert. |

Cyrenaïca.

Period I. or II., or both.

Gold.

| 3 | 164·3 | Similar. | Similar; on either side of cornucopiæ, star of six rays. [Pl. XIV. 4.] | Cyrene. |
| 4 | 33·2 | | [Pl. XIV. 5.] | ,, |

No.	Wt. or Size.	Obverse.	Reverse.	Mint. — Date.
5	Wt. 16·6	Head of Berenice II.	ΒΕΡΕΝΙΚΗΣ ΒΑΣΙΛΙΣΣΗΣ Cornucopiæ and stars.	Cyrene.
6	16·5			,,
			Silver.	
		Similar.	Cornucopiæ bound with fillet; on either side, pileus of Dioscuri, wreathed.	
7	326·5		[Pl. XIII. 6.]	,,
8	313·		beneath, ✻. (Oxidized.)	,,
		Head of Berenice II. r., diademed.	ΒΕΡΕΝΙΚΗΣ Club; beneath, ΒΑΣΙΛΙΣΣΗΣ. ℳ; all in apple-wreath.	
9	103·6		to l., Γ; to r., ⲯ. [Pl. XIII. 7.]	Berenice. (Euesperides.)
10	107·4		,, ⲯ; ,, Γ.	,,
11	103·7		,, ☉.	,,
12	103·4		,, ✿. (silphium.)	,,
13	98·6 plated.		,, ℳ. (no mon. beneath.)	,,
			Copper.	
		Similar.	ΒΕΡΕΝΙΚΗΣ Oar-blade; beneath, ℳ; all in olive-wreath. ΒΑΣΙΛΙΣΣΗΣ.	
14	Size. ·8		[Pl. XIII. 8.]	Uncert. (Berenice?)
			Uncertain.	
			Gold.	
		Head of Berenice II. r., wearing stephane, diadem, and veil.	ΒΑΣΙΛΙΣΣΗΣ ΒΕΡΕΝΙΚΗΣ Cornucopiæ bound with fillet.	
15	Wt. 24· worn.			,,

BERENICE II., AND PTOLEMAEUS III.

Cyprus.

Copper.

No.	Wt. or Size.	Obverse.	Reverse.	Mint. — Date.
16	Size. ·8	ΒΕΡΕΝΙΚΗΣ ΒΑΣΙΛΙΣΣΗΣ Bust of Berenice II, r., diademed.	ΠΤΟΛΕΜΑΙΟΥ ΒΑΣΙΛΕΩΣ Cornucopiæ bound with fillet, between club and eagle l. [Pl. XIII. 9.]	Uncert. (Oitium?)
17	·8	Similar.	ΠΤΟΛΕΜΑΙΟΥ ΒΑΣΙΛΕΩΣ Eagle l. on thunderbolt.	Uncert.
18	·8			,,
		Uncertain.		
19	·7	Head of Berenice II. r., wearing stephane and veil.	ΠΤΟΛΕΜΑΙΟΥ ΒΑΣΙΕΛΩΣ Eagle l. on thunderbolt, wings open. to l., ✶ for ✶ ? ΑΙ ΠΙ	,,
20	·7	Head of Berenice II. r., wearing stephane, diadem, and veil.	Similar. to l., ✗. [Pl. XIII. 10.]	,,
21	·45	Similar.	ΠΤ .. ΒΑΣΙΛ Eagle l. [on thunderbolt?].	,,

THE PTOLEMAIC KINGS OF EGYPT.

No.	Wt. or Size.	Obverse.	Reverse.	Mint. Date.

PTOLEMAEUS IV., PHILOPATOR I.
B.C. 222–204.
Cyprus.
Silver.
Countermarked Series.

No.	Wt. or Size.	Obverse.	Reverse.	Mint. Date.
		Head of Ptolemaeus I.	ΠΤΟΛΕΜΑΙΟΥ ΒΑΣΙΛΕΩΣ Eagle. (Struck by Ptolemaeus II. Cyprus. See p. 25.)	
1	Wt. 214·8	Countermark, ΣΑ.	[Pl. XIV. 1.]	Salamis.
2	220·3	,, K.	(graffito, αροςΛ').	Citium.

Dated Series.
Silver.

No.	Wt. or Size.	Obverse.	Reverse.	Mint. Date.
3	209·4	Head of Ptolemaeus I. r., wearing diadem and aegis.	ΠΤΟΛΕΜΑΙΟΥ ΒΑΣΙΛΕΩΣ Eagle l. on thunderbolt. to l., owl; to r., LΔ/ΣΑ. [Pl. XIV. 2.]	Salamis. B.C. 219-18.

Copper.

No.	Wt. or Size.	Obverse.	Reverse.	Mint. Date.
		Head of Zeus Ammon r., diademed.	ΠΤΟΛΕΜΑΙΟΥ ΒΑΣΙΛΕΩΣ Eagle l. on thunderbolt; to l., ⚱.	
4	Size. 1·1	behind head, K.	to r., LΓ.	Uncert. 220-19.
5	1·05	,, K?	,, ,,	,,
6	1·05	,, ,, ?	,, ,, [Pl. XIV. 3.]	,,
7	1·1	,, ,, ?	,, LΔ.	219-18.
8	1·05	,, K.	,, ,,	,,
9	1·1	,, K.	,, ,, ? (Restruck at later time.)	,, ?

PTOLEMAEUS IV., PHILOPATOR I.

No.	Wt. or Size.	Obverse.	Reverse.	Mint. Date.
10	Size. ·9	Head of bearded Herakles r., clad in lion's skin. behind head, K.	ΠΤΟΛΕΜΑΙΟΥ ΒΑΣΙΛΕΩΣ Eagle l. on thunderbolt; to l., ⚥. to r., ᴸΓ.	Uncert. 220-19.
11	·85	,, ,,	,, ,, [Pl. XIV. 4.]	,,
12	·8	,, ,,	,, ,,	,,
13	·8	,, Ḳ.	,, ,,	,,
14	·75	Head of Pallas r., wearing crested Corinthian helmet.	Similar. to r., ᴸΔ.	219-18.
15	·7		,, ,, [Pl. XIV. 5.]	,,

DIONYSIAC COINAGE.

Probably struck by the Strategos of Cyprus as γραμματεύς τῶν περὶ τὸν Διόνυσον τεχνιτῶν.

Silver.

No.	Wt.	Obverse.	Reverse.	Mint.
16	Wt. 103·5	Bust of Ptolemaeus IV. r., as Dionysus, wearing diadem entwined with ivy-wreath, and nebris; behind shoulder, thyrsos.	ΠΤΟΛΕΜΑΙΟΥ ΒΑΣΙΛΕΩΣ Eagle l. on thunderbolt, wings open. [Pl. XIV. 6.]	Cyprus.
17	100·2			,,
18	100·9			,,
19	51·9	Similar.	Similar. [Pl. XIV. 7.]	,,
20	47·	Similar.	Similar.	,,

64 THE PTOLEMAIC KINGS OF EGYPT.

No.	Wt. or Size.	Obverse.	Reverse.	Mint. Date.
		Phoenicia.		
		FIRST COINAGE.		
		B.C. 222–219.		
		Silver.		
21	Wt. 221·	Head of Ptolemaeus I. r., diademed and wearing aegis.	ΠΤΟΛΕΜΑΙΟΥ ΒΑΣΙΛΕΩΣ Eagle l. on thunderbolt. to l., ⚒. [Pl. XIV. 8.] ΣΙ ΣΤΡ	Sidon ?
22	204·5 worn.	(Same die.)	,, ,, (Same die.)	,,
		SECOND COINAGE.		
		B.C. 217–204.		
		Silver.		
		α. With bust of Ptolemaeus Philopator, and $\overset{\Omega}{\Sigma}$, ΣΩ.		
23	216·5	Bust of Ptolemaeus Philopator r., diademed.	ΠΤΟΛΕΜΑΙΟΥ ΒΑΣΙΛΕΩΣ Eagle l. on thunderbolt. to l., ΣΩ; between legs, ΣΙ. [Pl. XIV. 9. Bank Coll.]	Sidon.
24	220·2	Similar.	ΠΤΟΛΕΜΑΙΟΥ Eagle l. on ΦΙΛΟΠΑΤΟΡΟΣ thunderbolt. to l., ☥; to r., $\overset{\Omega}{\Sigma}$; between eagle's legs, ⚱. [Pl. XIV. 10.]	Tyre.
		β. With head and title of Ptolemaeus I. Soter, and $\overset{\Omega}{\Sigma}$.		
25	220·	Head of Ptolemaeus I. r., diademed and wearing aegis.	ΠΤΟΛΕΜΑΙΟΥ ΣΩΤΗΡΟΣ Eagle l. on thunderbolt. to l., ☥; to r., $\overset{\Omega}{\Sigma}$.	,,

PTOLEMAEUS IV., PHILOPATOR I.

No.	Wt. or Size.	Obverse.	Reverse.	Mint. Date.
		γ. *With head and title of Ptolemaeus I. Soter.*		
		Uncertain magistrates or cities.		
		Silver.		
		Head of Ptolemaeus I. r., diademed and wearing aegis.	ΠΤΟΛΕΜΑΙΟΥ ΣΩΤΗΡΟΣ Eagle l. on thunderbolt.	
26	wt. 217·3		in front, ΔΙ.	Uncert.
27	219·		between legs, Π ?	,,
28	216·7		in front, cornucopiæ.	,,
		FIRST OR SECOND COINAGE. B.C. 222–219 or 217–204.		
		Copper.		
		Head of Zeus Ammon r., diademed.	ΠΤΟΛΕΜΑΙΟΥ ΒΑΣΙΛΕΩΣ Eagle l. on thunderbolt; in front, tripod; behind, ⚲.	
29	Size. ·8			Ptolemais
		Head of Zeus r., laur.	ΠΤΟΛΕΜΑΙΟΥ ΒΑΣΙΛΕΩΣ Eagle l. on thunderbolt; behind neck, cornucopiæ.	
30	·65			Uncert.
31	·7			,,
32	·6			,,
		Egypt.		
		Gold.		
		Head of Ptolemaeus Philopator r., diademed and wearing chlamys.	ΠΤΟΛΕΜΑΙΟΥ ΦΙΛΟΠΑΤΟΡΟΣ Eagle r. on thunderbolt.	
33	wt. 428·3		to r., ΜΕ. [Pl. xv. 1.]	,,
34	430·4		,, ,, [Pl. xv. 2. Bank Coll.]	,,

No.	Wt. or Size.	Obverse.	Reverse.	Mint. Date.
			Copper.	
		Head of Zeus Ammon r., diademed.	ΠΤΟΛΕΜΑΙΟΥ ΒΑΣΙΛΕΩΣ Eagle l. on thunderbolt, looking back; on l. wing, cornucopiæ.	
35	Size. 1·65		between eagle's legs, A.	Uncert.
36	1·55		,, ,, Λ (A?). [Pl. xv. 3.]	,,
37	1·65		,, ,, E.	,,
38	1·5		,, ,, E.	,,
		Head of Zeus r., laureate.	Similar.	
39	1·3		between eagle's legs, Λ (A?).	,,
		Head of Alexander the Great r., clad in elephant's skin and aegis.	Similar.	
40	·95		between eagle's legs, Λ (A?). [Pl. xv. 4.]	,,
41	1·		,, ,, E.	,,
42	1·		,, ,, E.	,,
		Head of Zeus Ammon.	ΠΤΟΛΕΜΑΙΟΥ ΒΑΣΙΛΕΩΣ Eagle l. on thunderbolt, wings open; on l. wing, cornucopiæ.	
43	1·4		between eagle's legs, Λ (A?). [Pl. xv. 5.]	,,
44	·75		,, ,, Δ.	,,
		Head of Alexander the Great.	Similar.	
45	·8		between eagle's legs, E?	,,
		Head of Zeus Ammon.	ΠΤΟΛΕΜΑΙΟΥ ΒΑΣΙΛΕΩΣ Eagle l. on thunderbolt, wings open; in front, cornucopiæ.	
46	·6		between eagle's legs, A.	,,

No.	Wt. or Size.	Obverse.	Reverse.	Mint. — Date.
		ARSINOË III., PHILOPATOR.		
		Egypt.		
		Gold.		
		Bust of Arsinoë III. r., wearing stephane, earring, and necklace; over l. shoulder, sceptre.	ΑΡΣΙΝΟΗΣ ΦΙΛΟΠΑΤΟΡΟΣ Cornucopiæ bound with fillet; above, star.	
1	Wt. 427·9		[Pl. xv. 6. Bank Coll.]	Uncert.
2	418·7			,,
		Arsinoë III. and Ptolemaeus IV. Philopator.		
		Cyprus.		
		Copper.		
		Head of Arsinoë III. r., wearing stephane and earring.	ΠΤΟΛΕΜΑΙΟΥ ΒΑΣΙΛΕΩΣ Double cornucopiæ, bound with fillet.	
3	Size. ·55		[Pl. xv. 7.]	,,
4	·5			,,
			Uncertain.	
		Similar, bust r.	ΠΤΟΛΕΜΑΙΟΥ ΒΑΣΙΛΕΩΣ Cornucopiæ bound with fillet.	
5	·5			,,

PTOLEMAEUS V., EPIPHANES. B.C. 204–181.

Cyprus.

Governors, Polycrates to B.C. cir. 196, from that time Ptolemaeus Makron to 181.

Silver.

A. *With portrait of Ptolemaeus V.; struck by Polycrates* (⊙).

No.	Wt. or Size.	Obverse.	Reverse.	Mint.—Date.
1	Wt. 217·	Bust of Ptolemaeus V. r., diademed and wearing chlamys.	ΠΤΟΛΕΜΑΙΟΥ ΒΑΣΙΛΕΩΣ Eagle l. on thunderbolt. to l., ⊙; to r., LЄ. [Pl. XVI. 1.]	Uncert. B.C. 201-0.

B. *With portrait of Ptolemaeus I.*

a. *Undated; struck by Polycrates* (ΓΘ).

2	219·	Head of Ptolemaeus I. r., diademed and wearing aegis.	ΠΤΟΛΕΜΑΙΟΥ ΒΑΣΙΛΕΩΣ Eagle l. on thunderbolt; to r. ΑΠ. to l., ΓΟ̣ ΑΡ	Paphos.

β. *Dated.*

		Similar.	Similar; to L or n, Γ·.	
3	219·5	(same die.)	to l., Γ·; to r., LB.	204-3.
4	219·6	(,,)	,, LB ,, Γ·. [Pl. XVI. 2.]	,,
5	219·4	(,,)	,, LЄ ,, ,,	201-0.
6	219·8	(,,)	,, LZ ,, ,,	199-8.

Copper.

7	Size. ·9	Head of bearded Herakles r., clad in lion's skin.	Similar. to l., ⊞. [Pl. XVI. 3.]	Paphos.

PTOLEMAEUS V., EPIPHANES.

No.	Wt. or Size.	Obverse.	Reverse.	Mint. — Date.
8	Size. 1·15	Head of bearded Herakles r., clad in lion's skin.	ΠΤΟΛΕΜΑΙΟΥ ΒΑΣΙΛΕΩΣ Eagle l. on thunderbolt. no letter.	Paphos ?
9	·95		,,	,,
10	·95		,,	,,
11	·7	Young male bust r., helmeted and wearing chlamys.	ΠΤΟΛΕΜΑΙΟΥ ΒΑΣΙΛΕΩΣ Eagle l. on thunderbolt; on l. wing, cornucopiæ.	,,
12	·6	Young male head r., wearing crested helmet.	ΠΤΟΛΕΜΑΙΟΥ ΒΑΣΙΛΕΩΣ Eagle l. on thunderbolt; to l., cornucopiæ.	,,
13	·55			,,
14	·55			,,
15	·5			,,

Silver.

No.	Wt. or Size.	Obverse.	Reverse.	Mint. — Date.
		Head of Ptolemaeus I. r., diademed and wearing aegis.	ΠΤΟΛΕΜΑΙΟΥ ΒΑΣΙΛΕΩΣ Eagle l. on thunderbolt; to r. or l., ΣΑ.	
16	Wt. 220·4		to l., LB ; to r., ΣA.	Salamis. B.C. 204-3.
17	219·2		,, LΔ ,, ,,	202-1.
18	219·		,, LE ,, ,,	201-0.
19	219·3	(Same die.)	,, ,, ,, ,, ,,	,,

THE PTOLEMAIC KINGS OF EGYPT.

No.	Wt. or Size.	Obverse.	Reverse.	Mint. — Date.
		Head of Ptolemaeus I. r., diademed and wearing aegis.	ΓΤΟΛΕΜΑΙΟΥ ΒΑΣΙΛΕΩΣ Eagle l. on thunderbolt; to r. or l., ΣΑ.	
20	Wt. 218·5		to l., LϹ; to r., [symbol]. ΣΑ [Pl. XVI. 4.]	Salamis. B.C. 200–199.
21	217·7		,, LΙ ,, ΣΑ. [Pl. XVI. 5.]	199–8.
22	209·2 worn.		,, [symbol] LH ,, ,,	198–7.
23	216·2		,, [symbol] LIA ,, ,, [Pl. XVI. 6.]	195–4.
24	219·3		,, LIE. ΣΑ		191–0.
25	199·2 worn.	(Same die.)	,, LIϚ ΣΑ ,, [lotus].	189–8.
26	213·3		,, LIΘ ,, ΣΑ. [Pl. XVI. 7.]	187–6.
27	218·		,, LK ΣΑ ,, [symbol]. [Pl. XVI. 8.]	186–5.
			Copper.	
		Head of Zeus Ammon r., diademed.	ΓΤΟΛΕΜΑΙΟΥ ΒΑΣΙΛΕΩΣ Eagle l. on thunderbolt; to l., [symbol] (lotus).	Salamis?
28	Size. 1·05		[Pl. XVI. 9.]	,,
29	1·			,,
30	·8			,,
		Head of Zeus r., laur.	Similar.	
31	·65			,,
32	·7			,,

PTOLEMAEUS V., EPIPHANES.

No.	Wt. or Size.	Obverse.	Reverse.	Mint. — Date.
33	Size. ·55	Head of Zeus r., laur.	ΠΤΟΛΕΜΑΙΟΥ ΒΑΣΙΛΕΩΣ Eagle l. on thunderbolt; to l., ⚱ (lotus).	Salamis?
34	·55			,,
35	·55			,,
36	·65	Similar.	Similar. to r., ✳.	,,
			Silver.	
37	Wt. 196·4 worn.	Head of Ptolemaeus I. r., diademed and wearing aegis.	ΠΤΟΛΕΜΑΙΟΥ ΒΑΣΙΛΕΩΣ Eagle l. on thunderbolt. to l., 𝚱; to r., ⚘? LA	Amathus? B.C. 204.
			Gold. [See Arsinoë II., no. 34; Citium, year 16].	[Citium. 190-189]
			Silver.	
38	218·3	Head of Ptolemaeus I. r., diademed and wearing aegis.	ΠΤΟΛΕΜΑΙΟΥ ΒΑΣΙΛΕΩΣ Eagle l. on thunderbolt; to r., KI. to l., LB .	Citium. B.C. 204-3.
39	217·4		,, LE .	201-0.
40	218·3	(Same die.)	,, ,,	,,
41	220·7	(,,)	,, LΓ .	200-199.
42	219·5		,, ,, (Same die.)	,,
43	220·5		,, LΔ.	199-8.

No.	Wt. or Size.	Obverse.	Reverse.	Mint. — Date.
			Copper.	
44	Size. ·95	Head of bearded Herakles r., wearing lion's skin.	ΠΤΟΛΕΜΑΙΟΥ ΒΑΣΙΛΕΩΣ Eagle l. on thunderbolt, looking back; across right wing, caduceus; between legs, Κ. [Pl. XVI. 10.]	Citium.
45	·95			,,
46	·9			,,
47	1·			,,
48	·7	Bust of Pallas r., wearing crested Corinthian helmet and aegis.	ΠΤΟΛΕΜΑΙΟΥ ΒΑΣΙΛΕΩΣ Eagle l. on thunderbolt; across r. wing, sceptre; between legs, Κ.	,,
			Phœnicia.	
			Silver.	
49	Wt. 219·	Bust of Ptolemaeus V. r., diademed and wearing chlamys.	ΠΤΟΛΕΜΑΙΟΥ ΒΑΣΙΛΕΩΣ Eagle l. on thunderbolt. to l., ⚱; between eagle's legs, ΝΙ.	Berytus.
			Gold.	
50	427·9	Bust of Ptolemaeus V. r., wearing radiate diadem and chlamys; over l. shoulder, spear.	ΠΤΟΛΕΜΑΙΟΥ ΒΑΣΙΛΕΩΣ Radiate cornucopiæ, bound with fillet, between two stars. beneath, ℞. [Pl. XVII. 1.] [Bank Coll.]	Tripolis?
51	428·6	(Rays of diadem varied.)	no mon. [Pl. XVII. 2.]	,,
			Silver.	
52	218·6	Bust of Ptolemaeus V. r., wearing diadem adorned with ear of corn and chlamys.	ΠΤΟΛΕΜΑΙΟΥ ΒΑΣΙΛΕΩΣ Eagle l. on thunderbolt. to l., ⚱; between eagle's legs, ΝΙ.	Tripolis.

No.	Wt. or Size.	Obverse.	Reverse.	Mint. Date.
53	Wt. 217·3	Head of Ptolemaeus I. r., diademed and wearing aegis.	ΠΤΟΛΕΜΑΙΟΥ ΣΩΤΗΡΟΣ Eagle l. on thunderbolt. to l., ⱥ ; to r., ⚱. [Pl. XVII. 3.]	Uncert.
54	201·4 worn.		,, ,, ,, ,,	,,
55	207·1 worn.	Similar.	ΠΤΟΛΕΜΑΙΟΥ ΒΑΣΙΛΕΩΣ Similar. to r., ⱥ.	,,

Copper.

No.	Wt. or Size.	Obverse.	Reverse.	Mint. Date.
56	Size. 1·45	Head of Zeus Ammon r., diademed.	ΠΤΟΛΕΜΑΙΟΥ ΒΑΣΙΛΕΩΣ Eagle l. on thunderbolt; on l. wing, cornucopiæ; to l., ⚱. between eagle's legs, ⱥ. [Pl. XVII. 4.]	Tyre.
57	1·4		,, ,,	,,
58	1·4		,, ,,	,,
59	1·4		,, Γ.	,,

Silver.

No.	Wt. or Size.	Obverse.	Reverse.	Mint. Date.
60	Wt. 220·5	Bust of Ptolemaeus V. r., wearing diadem adorned with ear of corn and chlamys.	ΠΤΟΛΕΜΑΙΟΥ ΒΑΣΙΛΕΩΣ Eagle l. on thunderbolt; to l., ⱥ.	Uncert.
61	215·3	Head of Ptolemaeus I.	Similar.	,,

THE PTOLEMAIC KINGS OF EGYPT.

No.	Wt. or Size.	Obverse.	Reverse.	Mint. — Date.
			Egypt.	
			Gold.	
62	Wt. 429·	Bust of Ptolemaeus V. r., wearing diadem adorned with ear of corn and chlamys.	ΠΤΟΛΕΜΑΙΟΥ ΒΑΣΙΛΕΩΣ Eagle l. on thunderbolt. to l., Θ; between eagle's legs, **NI**. [Pl. XVII. 5.]	Uncert. B.C. 197-6.
			Silver.	
		Similar.	Similar.	Uncert.
63	219·5		to l., **A**; between eagle's legs, **NI**.	204.
64	209· worn.		,, **B** ,,· ,,	204-3.
65	221·	Diadem plain.	,, **H** ,, ,, [Bank Coll.]	198-7.
66	218·5	Diadem adorned with ear of corn.	,,· ,, ,,	Uncert.
67	220·5		,, **ME**. [Bank Coll.]	,,
68	221·3		,, **Σ**.	,,
			Copper.	
			FIRST COINAGE. B.C. 204–193. Single cornucopiæ.	
		Head of Zeus Ammon r., diademed.	ΠΤΟΛΕΜΑΙΟΥ ΒΑΣΙΛΕΩΣ Eagle l. on thunderbolt; to l., cornucopiæ; between eagle's legs, **ΣE**.	
69	Size. 1·6		**ΣE**.	Uncert.
70	1·65		,,	,,
71	1·65		, **ΣE**. [Pl. XVII. 6.]	,,
72	1·3		,,	,,

PTOLEMAEUS V., EPIPHANES.

No.	Wt. or Size.	Obverse.	Reverse.	Mint. Date.
			SECOND COINAGE. B.C. 193-181. Reduced weight.	
		Head of Zeus Ammon r., diademed.	ΠΤΟΛΕΜΑΙΟΥ ΒΑΣΙΛΕΩΣ Eagle l. on thunderbolt, looking back, wings open; between legs, ΣΕ.	
73	Size. 1·5		ΣΕ. [Pl. XVIII. 1.]	Uncert.
74	1·45		,,	,,
75	1·45		Æ.	,,
76	1·45		,, (countermk., cornucopiæ.)	,,
			Double cornucopiæ.	
		Similar.	ΠΤΟΛΕΜΑΙΟΥ ΒΑΣΙΛΕΩΣ Eagle l. on thunderbolt; on left wing, double cornucopiæ; between legs, ΣΕ.	
77	1·25		ΣΕ.	,,
78	1·25		,, (countermk., cornucopiæ.)	,,
79	1·2		,, ?	,,
80	1·2		Æ. [Pl. XVIII. 2.]	,,
81	1·2		,,	,,
		Head of Nilus r., bound with lotus.	ΠΤΟΛΕΜΑΙΟΥ ΒΑΣΙΛΕΩΣ Eagle l. on thunderbolt, looking back, wings open.	
82	·7		between eagle's legs, K. [Pl. XVIII. 3.]	,,

No.	Wt. or Size.	Obverse.	Reverse.	Mint. — Date.
			Cyrenaica.	
			Copper.	
			FIRST COINAGE.	
			B.C. 204–193. Single cornucopiæ.	
		Head of Ptolemaeus I. r., diademed and wearing aegis.	ΒΑΣΙΛΕΩΣ ΠΤΟΛΕΜΑΙΟΥ Head of Libya r., with long curls, bound with tainia, wearing necklace.	
83	Size. ·8		to r., cornucopiæ. [Pl. XVIII. 4.]	Uncert.
84	·85		,, ,,	,,
85	·75		,, ,,	,,
86	·8		,, ,, ?	,,
87	·7		,, ,,	,,
88	·6		to l., ,,	,,
			SECOND COINAGE.	
			B.C. 193–181. Double cornucopiæ.	
		Head of Ptolemaeus I. r., diademed and wearing aegis.	ΠΤΟΛΕΜΑΙΟΥ ΒΑΣΙΛΕΩΣ Head of Libya r., with long curls, bound with tainia.	
89	1·		to l., ❦ (apple-branch); to r., double cornucopiæ; beneath, ΣΕ. [Pl. XVIII. 5.]	Euesperides.
90	1·		,, ,, ,, ,, ,, ,,	,,
91	1·		,, ,, ,, ,, ,, Σ.	,,
92	1·05		,, ,, ,, ,, ,, ΜΕ.	,,
93	1·		,, ,, ,, ,, ,, ΜΕ.	,,
94	1·15		,, ,, ,, ,, ,, ⋈?	,,

No.	Wt. or Size.	Obverse.	Reverse.	Mint. — Date.
95	Size. ·9	Head of Ptolemaeus I. r., diademed and wearing aegis. behind head, 🝆.	ΠΤΟΛΕΜΑΙΟΥ ΒΑΣΙΛΕΩΣ Head of Libya r., with long curls, bound with tainia. to r., double cornucopiæ.	Uncert.
96	·75	Similar; no symbol.	Similar. to r., double cornucopiæ. [Pl. XVIII. 6.]	,,
97	·7		,, ,,	,,
98	·75		,, ,,	,,
99	·7		,, ,,	,,

FIRST OR SECOND COINAGE.

100	·7	Similar.	Similar; no symbol. beneath head, **EY**.	Eues- perides.

PTOLEMAEUS VI., PHILOMETOR I.

B.C. 181–146.

PERIODS OF REIGN.

I. Cleopatra I., Regent . . . . B.C. 181–cir. 174.
II. Eulaeus and Lenaeus, Regents . . cir. 174–171.
III. Ptolemaeus VIII., Euergetes II., (Antiochus IV., Epiphanes, in Egypt) . . } 170–168.
IV. Ptolemaeus VI. and Ptolemaeus VIII. . 168–164-3.
V. Ptolemaeus VI. alone . . . . 164-3–146.
VI. Ptolemaeus VI. and Ptolemaeus VII., Eupator, 146.

Cleopatra I., Regent. B.C. 181–cir. 174.

Cyprus.

Copper.

No.	Wt. or Size.	Obverse.	Reverse.	Mint. Date.
1	Size. ·65	ΒΑΣΙΛΙΣΣΗΣ ΚΛΕΟΠΑΤΡΑΣ Head of Cleopatra r., as Isis, with long curls, bound with corn.	ΠΤΟΛΕΜΑΙΟΥ ΒΑΣΙΛΕΩΣ Eagle l. on thunderbolt, looking back; on l. wing, cornucopiæ bound with fillet. to l., ⌘ ? [Pl. XVIII. 7.]	Paphos?
2	·7	No inscr.; same type.	Similar.	,,
3	·7			,,
4	·7			,,
5	·55			,,
6	·55	Similar.	Same inscr.: Eagle l. on thunderbolt.	,,

No.	Wt. or Size.	Obverse.	Reverse.	Mint. — Date.
			Egypt ?	
			Silver.	
		Busts r., jugate, of Zeus Sarapis, wearing laurel-wreath, above which small cap of Osiris, and Cleopatra as Isis, wearing corn-wreath, above which globe and horns.	ΠΤΟΛΕΜΑΙΟΥ ΒΑΣΙΛΕΩΣ Eagle l. on thunderbolt, looking back; on r. wing, double cornucopiæ bound with fillet.	
7	Wt. 213·9		between legs, ΔΙ. [Pl. xviii. 8.]	Uncert.
8	211·9		,, ,,	,,
			Egypt.	
			Copper.	
		Head of Cleopatra r., as Isis, with long curls, bound with corn.	ΠΤΟΛΕΜΑΙΟΥ ΒΑΣΙΛΕΩΣ Eagle l. on thunderbolt, looking back; on r. wing, cornucopiæ bound with fillet.	
9	Size. ·9		[Pl. xviii. 9.]	,,
10	·9			,,
11	1·			,,
12	·9			,,
			Cyrenaica.	
			Copper.	
		Busts r., jugate, of Apollo, laur., wearing chlamys, and having bow behind shoulder, and Cleopatra as Artemis wearing stephane.	ΒΑΣΙΛΕΩΣ ΠΤΟΛΕΜΑΙΟΥ Bust of Ptolemaeus I. r., diademed and wearing aegis.	
13	1·1			,,

No.	Wt. or Size.	Obverse.	Reverse.	Mint. — Date.
		Eulaeus and Lenaeus, Regents. B.C. cir. 174–171.		
		Cyprus.		
		Silver.		
		Head of Ptolemaeus I. r., diademed and wearing aegis.	ΠΤΟΛΕΜΑΙΟΥ ΒΑΣΙΛΕΩΣ Eagle l. on winged thunderbolt.	Paphos. B.C.
14	Wt. 217·6		to l., **LZ**; to r., **ΠΑ**. [Pl. xix. 1.]	175-4.
15	219·		,, ,, ,, ,,	,,
		Egypt.		
		Copper.		
		Head of Zeus Ammon r., diademed.	ΠΤΟΛΕΜΑΙΟΥ ΒΑΣΙΛΕΩΣ Eagle l. on thunderbolt; under l. wing, sceptre; in front, ⚕ (lotus); between legs, **ΕΥΛ**.	
16	Size. 1·2		[Pl. xix. 2.]	Uncert.
17	1·15			,,
		Similar.	Similar, without sceptre; Υ (lotus).	
18	·95			,,
19	·95			,,
		(For this class, countermarked by Antiochus IV. in Egypt, see nos. 20–22 below).		

PTOLEMAEUS VI., PHILOMETOR I.

No.	Wt. or Size.	Obverse.	Reverse.	Mint. — Date.
		\[Antiochus IV., Epiphanes, in Cyprus and Egypt. B.C. 170–168.		
			Cyprus.	
			Silver.	
		Head of Antiochus r., diademed: fillet border.	ΒΑΣΙΛΕΩΣ Apollo seated l. on ΑΝΤΙΟΧΟΥ omphalos; holds arrow and bow. Size 1·05.	
	Wt. 262·4		to l., $\stackrel{A}{m}$ owl; to r., ΣΑ.	[Salamis]
		(See Catalogue of the Seleucid Kings of Syria, p. 111, no. 4a.)]		
			Egypt.	
			Copper.	
		Coinage of Ptolemaeus VI.: Eulaeus and Lenaeus, Regents, countermarked.		
		Head of Zeus Ammon r., diademed.	ΠΤΟΛΕΜΑΙΟΥ ΒΑΣΙΛΕΩΣ Eagle l. on thunderbolt; in front, ⚕; between legs, ΕΥΛ.	
20	Size. 1·		to r., countermark, anchor.	Uncert.
21	1·		on eagle, ,, ,,	,,
22	·9		to r., ,, ,,	,,
		[Coinage of Antiochus IV.		
		Copper.		
		Head of Zeus Sarapis r., wearing laurel-wreath ending above in cap of Osiris.	ΒΑΣΙΛΕΩΣ Eagle r., on thunderbolt. ΑΝΤΙΟΧΟΥ ΘΕΟΥ ΕΠΙΦΑΝΟΥΣ	Uncert.
		Head of Isis r., wearing corn-wreath ending above in head-dress of Isis.	Similar (thunderbolt wingless or winged).	,,
		Head of Antiochus r., radiate.	Similar (,, ,,).	,,
		(See Cat. of Sel. Kings of Syria, p. 38. Pl. XII., 11, 12, 13.)]		

No.	Wt. or Size.	Obverse.	Reverse.	Mint. Date.
		Ptolemaeus VIII., Euergetes II., alone. B.C. 170-168.		
		(Ptolemaeus Philometor, prisoner.)		
		No coins.		
		Ptolemaeus VI. Philometor and Ptolemaeus VIII. Euergetes II. B.C. 168-164-3.		
			Cyprus.	
			Copper.	
23	Size. 1·2	Head of Zeus Ammon r., diademed.	ΠΤΟΛΕΜΑΙΟΥ ΒΑΣΙΛΕΩΣ Eagle l. on thunderbolt; to l., helmet. to l., ⟨fig⟩.	Uncert.
24	1·1		,, . ⟨fig⟩ .	,,
			Egypt.	
			Copper.	
			First Coinage.	
25	1·2	Same type.	Similar; under eagle's l. wing, sceptre; to l., ⟨fig⟩.	,,
			Second Coinage.	
26	1·4	Same type.	Similar; to l., ⟨fig⟩ . [Pl. XIX. 3.]	,,
27	1·4			,,

No.	Wt. or Size.	Obverse.	Reverse.	Mint. Date.
			Cyrenaïca.	
			Struck after death of Cleopatra I., B.C. cir. 174, before sole reign in Cyrenaïca of Ptolemaeus Euergetes II. B.C. 164-3.	
			Copper.	
28	Size. 1·05	Head of Ptolemaeus I. r., diademed and wearing aegis.	ΒΑΣΙΛΕΩΣ ΠΤΟΛΕΜΑΙΟΥ Head of Libya r.; behind, cornucopiæ; beneath, ⚘ (part of silphium). [Pl. xix. 4.]	Uncert.
29	·95			,,
30	·95			,,
			Ptolemaeus Philometor I. B.C. 164-3–146.	
			Cyprus.	
			Silver.	
31	Wt. 218·1	Head of Ptolemaeus I. r., diademed and wearing aegis.	ΠΤΟΛΕΜΑΙΟΥ ΒΑΣΙΛΕΩΣ Eagle l. on thunderbolt; to r., ΠΑ. to l., LIΘ (thunderbolt winged.) [Pl. xix. 5.]	Paphos. B.C. 168-2.
32	218·3		,, ,, ,,	,,
33	162· plated.		,, ,,	,,
34	217·3		,, LK.	162-1.
35	197·7 worn.		,, LKΛ.	161-0.
36	216·6		,, LKB.	160-59.
37	218·		,, LKΓ. [Pl. xix. 6.]	159-8.

No.	Wt. or Size.	Obverse.	Reverse.	Mint. - Date.
			Silver.	
			(Ptolemaeus Philometor I., or Euergetes II.)	
38	Wt. 219.	Head of Ptolemaeus I. r., diademed and wearing aegis.	ΠΤΟΛΕΜΑΙΟΥ ΒΑΣΙΛΕΩΣ Eagle l. on thunderbolt; to r., ΠΑ. to l., LKH.	Paphos. B.C. {154-3. or 143-2.}
39	218·9		„ LKΘ.	{153-2. 142-1.}
40	219·2		„ LΛΛ.	{151-0. 140-39}
41	219·		„ LΛA. [Pl. xix. 7.]	{ „ „ }
42	208·5		„ LΛB.	{150-49 139-8.}
43	220·7		„ LΛΓ.	{149-8. 138-7.}
			(Ptolemaeus Philometor I.)	
		Similar.	Similar; to r., ΣA.	
44	213·9		to r., LKΛ.	Salamis. 161-0.
45	215·9		„ LKB.	160-59.
			(Ptolemaeus Philometor I., or Euergetes II.)	
46	218·3		to l., LΛB 𓅨. [Pl. xix. 8.]	{150-49 139-8.}
47	214·8		„ „	{ „ „ }
48	218·		„ 𓅨. „	{ „ „ }
49	210·8		„ LΛΔ. ✳	{148-7. 137-6.}
50	218·4		„ LΛΔ.	{ „ „ }

PTOLEMAEUS VI., PHILOMETOR I.

No.	Wt. or Size.	Obverse.	Reverse.	Mint.—Date.
			Silver.	
			(Ptolemaeus Philometor I., or Euergetes II.)	
		Head of Ptolemaeus I. r., diademed and wearing aegis.	ΠΤΟΛΕΜΑΙΟΥ ΒΑΣΙΛΕΩΣ Eagle l. on thunderbolt; to r., **KI**.	Citium.
51	Wt. 217·6		to l., **LKH**.	B.C. { 154-3. 148-2.
52	215·8		„ **LKΘ**. [Pl. xx. 1.]	{ 153-2. 142-1.
53	217·8		„ **LΛΑ**.	{ 151-0. 140-39
54	218·5		„ **LΛΓ** 🪶. [Pl. xx. 2.]	{ 149-8. 188-7.
55	218·8		„ „	{ „ „
56	217·8		„ **LΛΓ** 🪶	{ „ „
57	219·2		„ **LΛΔ** 🪶.	{ 148-7. 137-6.
			Copper.	
		Head of Zeus Ammon r., diademed.	ΠΤΟΛΕΜΑΙΟΥ ΒΑΣΙΛΕΩΣ Eagle l. on thunderbolt; to l., ✲ above date.	
58	Size. ·9		to l., **LKH**?	{ 154-3. 148-2.
		Same type.	Similar; to l., ☥.	
59	1·75		[Pl. xx. 3.]	
		Same type.	Similar; to l., ☥ below date.	
60	·95		to l., **LKC**.	{ 156-5. 145-4.
61	·9		„ **LKZ**. [Pl. xx. 4.]	{ 155-4. 144-3.
62	·9		„ „	{ „ „

THE PTOLEMAIC KINGS OF EGYPT.

No.	Wt. or Size.	Obverse.	Reverse.	Mint. Date.
		Head of Zeus Ammon r., diademed.	ΠΤΟΛΕΜΑΙΟΥ ΒΑΣΙΛΕΩΣ Eagle l. on thunderbolt; to l, ⚲ below date.	Citium.
63	Size. 1·		to l., LAΓ.	{ 149-8. 138-7.
64	·9		,, ,,	{ ,, ,,
65	·95		,, LAΔ. [Pl. xx. 5.]	{ 148-7. 137-6.
66	·95		,, ,,	{ ,, ,,
67	1·05		,, LAE.	{ 146-5. 135-4.

Dionysiac Series.

Silver.

		Head of Ptolemaeus IV. ? r., as Dionysus, wearing diadem entwined with ivy-wreath, and nebris.	ΠΤΟΛΕΜΑΙΟΥ ΒΑΣΙΛΕΩΣ Eagle l. on thunderbolt, wings open.	
68	Wt. 108·		to l., ⚹. [Pl. xx. 6.]	Uncert.
69	101·2		no symbol.	,,

Phoenicia.

(Phoenicia conquered, B.C. 146.)

[*Silver.*]

(See Tetradrachm of Ptolemaeus VI. as king of Syria. Mionnet, Suppl. IX. Pl. v. 1.)]   [Ptolemais. 146].

Copper.

| | | Head of Ptolemaeus VII. r., diademed. (Seleucid type.) | ΠΤΟΛΕΜΑΙΟΥ ΒΑΣΙΛΕΩΣ Eagle l. on thunderbolt, wings open; to l., dolphin, downwards. | |
| 70 | Size. ·75 | to r., countermark, ⱪ. | [Pl. xx. 7.] | Uncert. (146). |

PTOLEMAEUS VI., PHILOMETOR I.

No.	Wt. or Size.	Obverse.	Reverse.	Mint. — Date.
			Egypt.	
			Copper.	
		Head of Zeus Ammon r., diademed.	ΠΤΟΛΕΜΑΙΟΥ ΒΑΣΙΛΕΩΣ Eagle l. on thunderbolt; to l., ψ.	
71	Size. 1·8		between legs, uncertain letter. [Pl. xx. 8.]	Uncert.
72	1·45			,,
73	1·5		,, Ξ.	,,
74	1·45		,, ΔΙ (ΔΗ?)	,,

Ptolemaeus VI. Philometor I., and Ptolemaeus VII. Eupator.
B.C. 146.

Cyprus.

Silver.

(See Introduction.)

Paphos.
B.C.
146.

No.	Wt. or Size.	Obverse.	Reverse.	Mint. — Date.
		PTOLEMAEUS VIII., EUERGETES II. B.C. 170–117.		

PERIODS OF REIGN.

I. King of Egypt. B.C. 170–168. (no coins, p. 82).

II. With Ptolemaeus VI. B.C. 168–164-3. (p. 82,3).

III. King of Cyrene. B.C. 164-3–146.
  α. Before revolt. B.C. 164-3–cir. 156.
  β. After revolt. B.C. cir. 156–146.

IV. King of Egypt. B.C. 146–117.
  α. Alone. B.C. 146–127.
  β. With Cleopatra II. and III. B.C. 127–117.

  1. With Ptolemaeus IX. Philopator II., Cyprus only, year 50. B.C. 121-0.
  2. With Philopator II., whole kingdom, year 52–54. B.C. 119-8–117.

(III.) King of Cyrene.

Cyrenaïca.

(α.) Before revolt, B.C. 164-3–cir. 156.

Copper.

1	Size. 1·	Head of Zeus Ammon r., diademed.	ΒΑΣΙΛΕΩΣ ΠΤΟΛΕΜΑΙΟΥ ΕΥΕΡΓΕΤΟΥ Eagle l. on thunderbolt, looking back. to l., Φ. [Pl. XXII. 7.]	Uncert.

(See Ptolemaeus Euergetes II.? (p. 100), and later coins of Cyrenaïca, struck before B.C. 127 (p. 94), and in B.C. 127–117 (p. 98).

PTOLEMAEUS VIII., EUERGETES II.

No.	Wt. or Size.	Obverse.	Reverse.	Mint. Date.
		(IV.) King of Egypt. B.C. 146–117.		
		(a.) Alone. B.C. 146–127.		
		Cyprus.		
		(Ptolemaeus Euergetes II. or Philometor.)		
		Silver.		
		Head of Ptolemaeus I. r., diademed and wearing aegis.	ΓΤΟΛΕΜΑΙΟΥ ΒΑΣΙΛΕΩΣ Eagle l. on thunderbolt; to r., ΓΑ.	Paphos. B.C.
2	Wt. 217·6		to l., LKI.	{ 144-3. { 155-4.
3	218·5		„ LKH. [Pl. XXI. 1.]	{ 143-2. { 154-3.
4	218·7		„ LΛΑ. [Pl. XXI. 2.]	{ 140-39 { 151-0.
5	212·7		„ „	{ „ { „
		(4, 5, of fine style and work).		
		Copper.		
		Head of Cleopatra I. r., as Isis, with long curls, bound with corn.	ΓΤΟΛΕΜΑΙΟΥ ΒΑΣΙΛΕΩΣ Eagle l. on thunderbolt, wings open; to l., 🅰, 🅰.	Paphos.
6	Size. 1·1		[Pl. XXI. 3.]	„
7	1·15			„
8	1·15			„
9	1·05			„
10	1·			„
11	1·1			„
12	·8		(mon. obscure.)	„

No.	Wt. or Size.	Obverse.	Reverse.	Mint. Date.
		(Ptolemaeus Euergetes II. or Philometor.)		
		Silver.		
		Head of Ptolemaeus I. r., diademed and wearing aegis.	ΠΤΟΛΕΜΑΙΟΥ ΒΑΣΙΛΕΩΣ Eagle l. on thunderbolt; to r., ΣΑ.	
				Salamis. B.C.
13	Wt. 217·6		to l., LΚΕ. [Pl. xxi. 4.]	{146-5. 157-6.
14	218·7		„ LΚϜ.	{144-3. 155-4.
15	218·8		„ LΚΗ.	{143-2. 154-3.
16	205·3 worn.		„ LΚΘ.	{142-1. 153-2.
17	218·5		„ LΛ.	{141-0. 152-1.
18	219·		„ LΛΑ.	{140-39 151-0.
19	219·2		„ LΛΑ (?). [Pl. xxi. 5.]	{ „ ? „ ?
20	217·3	(Same die.)	„ LΛΒ ☥	{139-8. 150-49
21	212· worn.	(Same die.)	„ LΛΒ.	{ „ „
22	218·5		„ LΛΓ ⚱ (thyrsus.)	{138-7. 149-8.
23	218·8		„ LΛΓ.	{ „ „
24	219·	(Same die as no. 22.)	„ LΛΔ.	{137-6. 148-7.
25	218·5		„ LΛΕ.	{136-5. 147-6.

PTOLEMAEUS VIII., EUERGETES II.

No.	Wt. or Size.	Obverse.	Reverse.	Mint. Date.
			(Ptolemaeus Euergetes II.)	
		Head of Ptolemaeus I. r., diademed and wearing aegis.	ΠΤΟΛΕΜΑΙΟΥ ΒΑΣΙΛΕΩΣ Eagle l. on thunderbolt; to r., ΣΑ.	Salamis.
26	Wt. 211·5 worn.		to l., LΛϹ. Under l. wing of eagle, thyrsus bound with fillet.	B.C. 135-4.
27	219·		„ LΛZ. Under l. wing, sceptre.	134-3.
28	219·8		„ LΛH. ⛉ „ „	133-2.
29	209·3 worn.		„ LΛΘ. „ „	132-1.
30	218·		„ LMA. „ „	130-29.
			(Ptolemaeus Euergetes II. or Philometor.)	
		Similar.	Similar; to r., KI.	Citium.
31	218·3		to l., LKϹ (?). [Pl. XXI. 6.]	B.C. {145-4? 155-5?
32	219·		„ LKH.	{143-2. 154-3.
33	218·		„ LKΘ.	{142-1. 153-2.
34	199·5 worn.		„ LΛ.	{141-0. 152-1.
35	218·5		„ „	{ „ „
36	215·		„ LΛΑ.	{140-39 151-0.
37	217·5		„ LΛΑ (?).	{ „ ? „ ?
38	217·3	(Same die as no. 19, Salamis.)	„ LΛB ⛉ [Pl. XXI. 7.]	{139-8. 150-49
39	219·		„ LΛB ⛉ [Pl. XXI. 8.]	„
40	221·3		„ „ „	„

No.	Wt. or Size.	Obverse.	Reverse.	Mint. — Date.
41	Wt. 219·	Head of Ptolemaeus I. r., diademed and wearing aegis. (Same die as no. 39.)	ΠΤΟΛΕΜΑΙΟΥ ΒΑΣΙΛΕΩΣ Eagle l. on thunderbolt; to r., KI. to l., LΛB.	Citium. B.C. { 189-8. { 150-49
42	219·4	(Same die as no. 37.)	„ LΛB ⚱ [Pl. XXI. 9.]	„
43	217·3		„ LΛΓ.	{ 138-7. { 149-8.
44	216·1	(Same die as no. 37.)	„ LΛΓ ⚱	„
45	219·4	(Same die.)	„ LΛΓ.	„
46	218·7		„ ✹ LΛΔ.	{ 137-6. { 148-7.
47	218·8		„ LΛE..	{ 136-5. { 147-6.
48	211·7 worn.	(Same die as no. 37.)	„ „	„
49	218·5	(Same die.)	„ LΛC..	{ 135-4. { 146.
		(Ptolemaeus Euergetes II.)		
50	220·		to l., LΛZ. Under l. wing of eagle, thyrsus.	134-3.
51	219·3		„ 貝. LΛH Under l. wing, sceptre. [Pl. XXI. 10.]	133-2.
52	210·5 worn.		„ LM. „ „ [Pl. XXI. 11.]	131-0.
53	207·5 worn.		„ LMA. „ „	130-29.
54	218·		„ LMB.	129-8.

No.	Wt or Size.	Obverse.	Reverse.	Mint. Date.
			Egypt.	
			(Ptolemaeus Euergetes II. or Philometor.)	
			Silver.	
		Head of Ptolemaeus I. r., diademed and wearing aegis.	ΠΤΟΛΕΜΑΙΟΥ ΒΑΣΙΛΕΩΣ Eagle l. on thunderbolt; to r., ΠΑ.	Alexandria. B.C.
55	Wt. 218·5		to l., ᴸKE. [Pl. xxii. 1.]	{146-5. 157-6.
56	219·		,, LKH. [Bank Coll.]	{143-2. 154-8.
57	223·4		,, LKΘ. [Pl. xxii. 2.]	{142-1. 153-2.
58	217·		,, LΛ.	{141-0. 152-1.
59	218·8		,, ᴸΛB. [Pl. xxii. 3.]	{139-8. 150-49
60	219·		,, ᴸΛΓ.	{138-7. 149-8.
61	219·8		,, LΛE.	{136-5. 147-6.
62	217·		,, LΛϹ.	{135-4. 146.
			(Ptolemaeus Euergetes II.)	
63	218·8		,, LΛZ.	184-3.
64	221·3		,, LΛH.	183-2.
65	218·6		,, ,,	,,
66	222·		,, ᴸΛΘ. [Pl. xxii. 4.]	182-1.
			Copper.	
		Head of Cleopatra I. r., as Isis, with long curls, bound with corn.	ΠΤΟΛΕΜΑΙΟΥ ΒΑΣΙΛΕΩΣ Eagle l. on thunderbolt, wings open.	
67	Size. 1·3			Uncert.
68	1·25		[Pl. xxii. 5.]	,,
69	1·1			,,

No.	Wt. or Size.	Obverse.	Reverse.	Mint. — Date.
70	Size. 1·15	Head of Cleopatra I. r., as Isis, with long curls, bound with corn.	ΠΤΟΛΕΜΑΙΟΥ ΒΑΣΙΛΕΩΣ Eagle l. on thunderbolt, wings open.	Uncert.
71	1·1			,,
72	1·		[Pl. xxii. 6.]	,,
73	1·15	Similar; varied.	Similar.	,,
74	1·25	Similar; varied.	Similar.	,,
75	1·3			,,
76	1·35	Similar; varied.	Similar.	,,
77	1·3			,,

Cyrenaïca.

(III. β.) King of Cyrene, after revolt, B.C. cir. 156–146, and
(IV. α.) King of Egypt, alone, B.C. 146–127.

Copper.

		Head of Zeus Ammon r., diademed.	ΒΑΣΙΛΕΩΣ ΠΤΟΛΕΜΑΙΟΥ ΕΥΕΡΓΕΤΟΥ Eagle r. on thunderbolt, wings open.	
78	1·7		to r., Φ.	Uncert.
79	·95		,, ,,	,,
80	1·05	Similar.	Similar; type l. to l., Φ.	,,
81	1·15		,, ,,	,,

PTOLEMAEUS VIII., EUERGETES II.

No.	Wt. or Size.	Obverse.	Reverse.	Mint. Date.
		Head of Zeus Ammon r., diademed.	ΒΑΣΙΛΕΩΣ ΠΤΟΛΕΜΑΙΟΥ ΕΥΕΡΓΕΤΟΥ Eagle l. on thunderbolt, wings open.	
82	Size. ·8		to l., ΘΕ. [Pl. XXII. 8.]	Uncert.
83	·8		,, ,, .	,,
84	·55			,,
		Similar.	ΒΑΣ[ΙΛ] ΠΤΟΛΕ Similar type.	
85	·5			,,
		Similar.	ΒΑΣΙΛΕΩΣ ΠΤΟΛΕΜΑΙΟΥ ΕΥΕΡΓΕΤΟΥ Eagle r. on thunderbolt, wings open.	
86	1·3		to r., Κ. [Pl. XXII. 9.]	,,
87	1·3		,, ,, (Ε ΥΕΡΓΕΤΟΥ).	,,
88	1·35			,,

(IV. β.) Ptolemaeus VIII. Euergetes II., and Cleopatra II. and III. B.C. 127–117.

Cyprus

Silver.

		Head of Ptolemaeus I. r., diademed and wearing aegis.	ΠΤΟΛΕΜΑΙΟΥ ΒΑΣΙΛΕΩΣ Eagle l. on thunderbolt; to r., ΠΑ.	
89	Wt. 218·1		to l., LΜΓ. [Pl. XXIII. 1.]	Paphos. B.C. 128-7.
90	208· worn.		,, LΜΘ ♉ (modius.)	122-1.
91	213·5		,, LΝΑ.	120-19.
92	203·9 worn.		,, LΝΔ (thunderbolt winged.) ♀. [Pl. XXIII. 2.]	117.
93	212·8		,, LΝΔ. (thunderbolt winged.)	,,

No.	Wt. or Size.	Obverse.	Reverse.	Mint. Date.
			Copper.	
		ΒΑΣΙΛΙΣΣΗΣ ΚΛΕΟΠΑΤΡΑΣ Head of Cleopatra III. r., clad in elephant's skin.	ΠΤΟΛΕΜΑΙΟΥ ΒΑΣΙΛΕΩΣ Eagle l. on thunderbolt, wings open; to l., ⚑.	
94	Size. ·8		[Pl. xxiii. 3.]	Paphos.
95	·85			,,
96	·85			,,
		Similar type.	Similar.	
97	·85			,,
98	·65			,,

(IV. β. 1.) With Ptolemaeus IX. Philopator II., Cyprus only.

Silver.

| | | Head of Ptolemaeus I. r., diademed and wearing aegis. | ΠΤΟΛΕΜΑΙΟΥ ΒΑΣΙΛΕΩΣ Eagle l. on thunderbolt. | |
| 99 | Wt. 217·8 | | to l., LN ✱ ; to r., ΠΑ ✱. [Pl. xxiii. 4.] A | Paphos B.C. 121-0. |

(IV. β.) With Cleopatra II. and III.

Cyprus.

		Similar.	Similar; to r., ΣΑ.	
100	213·8		to l., LMΔ.	Salamis. 127·6.
101	216·3		,, ,, [Pl. xxiii. 5.]	,,
102	216·7		,, ,,	,,
103	205·6 worn.		,, LMH.	123-2.
104	182·2 worn.		,, LMΘ ℞.	122-1.
105	195·3 worn.		,, LNA.	120-19.

PTOLEMAEUS VIII., EUERGETES II.

No.	Wt. or Size.	Obverse.	Reverse.	Mint. — Date.
106	Wt. 215·	Head of Ptolemaeus I. r., diademed and wearing aegis.	ΠΤΟΛΕΜΑΙΟΥ ΒΑΣΙΛΕΩΣ Eagle l. on thunderbolt; to r., ΣΑ. to l., ∟ΝΒ.	Salamis. B.C. 119-8.
107	218·		„ ∟ΝΓ. ※ [Pl. XXIII. 6.]	118-7.
108	205·3		„ ∟ΝΓ. (thunderbolt with wing above).	„
109	207·8		„ ∟ΝΔ. ※	117.
110	209· worn.	Similar.	Similar; to r., ΚΙ. to l., ∟ΜΓ.	Citium. B.C. 128-7.
111	221·		„ ∟ΜΔ. [Bank Coll.]	127-6
112	215·4 worn.		„ „	„
113	219·		„ ∟ΜΗ.	123-2.
114	220·2		„ ∟ΜΘ. ☆	122-1.
115	212·2		„ ∟ΝΓ ※. (thunderbolt with wing above.) [Pl. XXIII. 7.]	118-7.
116	212·5		„ ∟ΝΔ. (thunderbolt with wing below).	117.

Copper.

		Head of Zeus Ammon r., diademed.	ΠΤΟΛΕΜΑΙΟΥ ΒΑΣΙΛΕΩΣ Eagle l. on thunderbolt, wings open; to l., star; between eagle's legs, Κ.	
117	Size. 1·15		to l., ※.	Citium.
118	1·15		„ ✶. [Pl. XXIII. 8.]	„
119	1·1		„ „ ; countermark, cornucopiæ.	„
120	1·2		„ „ ; „ „	„

o

No.	Wt. or Size.	Obverse.	Reverse.	Mint. Date.
	Wt.		Egypt. *Silver.*	
		Head of Ptolemaeus I. r., diademed and wearing aegis.	ΠΤΟΛΕΜΑΙΟΥ ΒΑΣΙΛΕΩΣ Eagle l. on thunderbolt; to r., ΠΑ.	Alexandria. B.C.
121	219·		to l., ᏞΜΘ. [Pl. XXIII. 9.]	122-1.
122	217·7		,, ,,	,,
123	206·3		,, ᏞΝΑ.	120-19.
124	206·3		,, ᏞΝΒ. ,,	119-8.
125	214·		,, ᏞΝΓ.	118-7.
126	214·7		,, ᏞΝΔ.	117.
	Size.		*Copper.*	
		Head of Cleopatra II. or III. r., clad in elephant's skin.	ΠΤΟΛΕΜΑΙΟΥ ΒΑΣΙΛΕΩΣ Eagle l. on thunderbolt, wings open.	
127	·85			Uncert.
128	·95		[Pl. XXIII. 10.]	,,
129	1·15			,,
130	1·05			,,
131	1·05			,,
		These coins may possibly be of Cleopatra II. and Ptolemaeus VI. Philometor. See Introduction.		
			Cyrenaïca. *Copper.*	
		Head of Zeus Ammon r., diademed.	ΒΑΣΙΛΕΩΣ ΠΤΟΛΕΜΑΙΟΥ ΕΥΕΡΓΕΤΟΥ Two cornuscopiæ, joined at the bottom, and bound with fillet. [Pl. XXIV. 1.]	
132	1·8			,,
133	1·8			,,

PTOLEMAEUS VIII., EUERGETES II. 99

No.	Wt. or Size.	Obverse.	Reverse.	Mint. Date.
			Cyprus, struck between B.C. 146 and 117.	
			DIONYSIAC COINAGE.	
			Silver.	
		Bust of Ptolemaeus IV. as Dionysus, r., wearing diadem entwined with ivy-wreath, and nebris; behind shoulder, thyrsus.	ΠΤΟΛΕΜΑΙΟΥ ΒΑΣΙΛΕΩΣ Eagle l. on thunderbolt, wings open.	
134	Wt. 105·4		to l., aplustre ? [Pl. XXIV. 2.]	Uncert.
135	104·3		„ 🝪 . [Pl. XXIV. 3.]	„
136	92·6 worn.		„ 🝪 .	„
137	101·2			„
138	105·8		„ 🝪 .	„
139	98·4 worn.			„
140	95·7			„

No.	Wt. or Size.	Obverse.	Reverse.	Mint. Date.
		PTOLEMAEUS VIII., EUERGETES II.?		
		Cyrenaïca ?		
		First Coinage.		
		Silver.		
		Head of Ptolemaeus I. r., diademed and wearing aegis.	ΠΤΟΛΕΜΑΙΟΥ ΒΑΣΙΛΕΩΣ Eagle l. on thunderbolt.	
1	Wt. 209·	(Fragment broken off.)	[Pl. xxiv. 4.]	Uncert.
2	218·4			,,
3	213·7		[Pl. xxiv. 5.]	,,
4	208·3			,,
5	102·3			,,
			Second Coinage.	
		Similar.	Similar.	
6	202·3		[Pl. xxiv. 6.]	,,
7	217·			,,
8	208·8			,,
9	219·		[Pl. xxiv. 7.]	,,
10	215·5		[Bank Coll.]	,,

No.	Wt. or Size.	Obverse.	Reverse.	Mint. Date.
		Coinage of the East, dated by an uncertain Era. See Introd., § 12, and Table IV.		
		Silver.		
		a. ΠΤΟΛΕΜΑΙΟΥ ΣΩΤΗΡΟΣ.		
1	Wt. 212·6 worn.	Head of Ptolemaeus I. r., diademed and wearing aegis.	ΠΤΟΛΕΜΑΙΟΥ ΣΩΤΗΡΟΣ Eagle l. on thunderbolt. between eagle's legs, MH. [Pl. xxv. 1.]	
2	180·3 plated.		,, N. [Pl. xxv. 2.]	
3	218·3		to l., OA. (ΣΩΤΗΡΟΣ).	
4	219·5		,, OB. [Pl. xxv. 3.]	
5	213·3 worn.		,, ,,	
6	219·	(Same die.)	,, ,,	
7	218·5	(Same die as no. 4.)	,, OΔ.	
8	221·3		,, OZ. [Pl. xxv. 4.]	
9	217·		in ex., OZ ?	
10	220·5		,, Γ.	
11	220·		,, ϡA.	
12	224·8		,, ϡB. [Pl. xxv. 5.]	
13	220·		,, ϡΓ. [Pl. xxv. 6.]	

No.	Wt. or Size.	Obverse.	Reverse.	Mint. Date.
		Head of Ptolemaeus I. r., diademed and wearing aegis.	ΠΤΟΛΕΜΑΙΟΥ ΣΩΤΗΡΟΣ Eagle l. on thunderbolt.	
14	Wt. 221·4		to l., ϡΔ.	
15	221·1		,, ,,	
16	211·4		,, ΠΗ. (thunderbolt doubly winged.) [Pl. xxv. 7.]	
17	185·1 worn.		,, ϙ̄.	
18	211·6		,, ϙ. (thunderbolt doubly winged.) [Pl. xxv. 8.]	
			β. ΠΤΟΛΕΜΑΙΟΥ ΒΑΣΙΛΕΩΣ.	
		Similar.	ΠΤΟΛΕΜΑΙΟΥ ΒΑΣΙΛΕΩΣ	
19	105·6		on thunderbolt, ϙ (9z.)	
20	106·2		,, PB. [Pl. xxv. 9.]	
21	103·5		,, PE.	
22	104·		,, PϚ. [Bank Coll.]	
23	108·3		,, PZ.	
24	106·7		in field, P Θ.	
25	109·		,, ,, Θ; on thunderbolt, ΕΙ.	
26	107·6		,, ,, Ι; ,, ,,	
27	108·		,, ,, ΙΑ.	
28	108·		,, ,, ΙΒ; thunderbolt winged	
29	105·1		,, Β ΙP; ,,	
30	106·3		,, P ΙΓ; ,,	
31	107·3		,, ,, ΙΔ; ,,	

PTOLEMAEUS VIII., EUERGETES II. ?

No.	Wt. or Size.	Obverse.	Reverse.	Mint. Date.
32	Wt. 109·	Head of Ptolemaeus I. r., diademed and wearing aegis.	ΠΤΟΛΕΜΑΙΟΥ ΒΑΣΙΛΕΩΣ in field, PI Δ; thunderbolt winged	
33	109·3		,, P IE; ,, above thunderbolt, Є.	
34	107·7		in field, P IϹ; thunderbolt winged	
35	103·4		,, ,, IZ; ,, [Pl. xxv. 10.]	

PTOLEMAEUS X. SOTER II. B.C. 117–81.

PERIODS OF REIGN.

I. With Cleopatra III. Philadelphos. B.C. 117–111.
  α. Ruling whole kingdom. B.C. 117–114.
  β. Ruling Egypt. B.C. 114–111.
II. Alone, king of Egypt. B.C. 111–107-6.
III. King of Cyprus. B.C. 107-6–88.
IV. King of Egypt and Cyprus. B.C. 88–81.

I. With Cleopatra III. B.C. 117–111.

α. Ruling whole kingdom. B.C. 117–114.

Cyprus.

Silver.

No.	Wt. or Size.	Obverse.	Reverse.	Mint. Date.
		Head of Ptolemaeus I. r., diademed and wearing aegis.	ΠΤΟΛΕΜΑΙΟΥ ΒΑΣΙΛΕΩΣ Eagle l. on thunderbolt; to r., ΠΑ.	Paphos. B.C.
1	Wt. 218·		LΓ to l., ⚴; to r., ⚴ beneath mint-letters. [Pl. XXVI. 1.]	115-4.
2	218·5		,, ,, no symbol.	,,
		Similar.	Similar; to r., KI.	
3	214·3		LB to l., ⚴. (thunderbolt winged.) [Pl. XXVI. 2.]	Citium. 116-5.
4	218·7	(Same die.)	,, LΓ.	115-4.

No.	Wt. or Size.	Obverse.	Reverse.	Mint. – Date.
			Copper.	
		Head of Zeus Ammon r., diademed.	ΠΤΟΛΕΜΑΙΟΥ ΒΑΣΙΛΕΩΣ Two eagles l. on thunderbolt; between legs of nearer eagle, **K**.	
5	Size. ·85		[Pl. xxvi. 3.]	Citium.
6	·8			
			Egypt.	
			I. With Cleopatra III. B.C. 117–111.	
			Silver.	
		Head of Ptolemaeus I. r., diademed and wearing aegis.	ΠΤΟΛΕΜΑΙΟΥ ΒΑΣΙΛΕΩΣ Eagle l. on thunderbolt; to r., **ΠΑ**.	Alexandria.
	Wt.			B.C.
7	221·4		to l., **LA**. [Pl. xxvi. 4.]	117-6.
8	216·		,, ,,	,,
9	220·8		,, **LB**.	116-5.
10	212·3		,, ,,	,,
11	54·		,, ,, [Pl. xxvi. 5.]	,,
12	28·7		,, ,, [Pl. xxvi. 6.]	,,
13	218·6		,, **LΓ**.	115-4.
14	217·5		,, **LΔ**.	114-3.
15	205·3 worn.		,, ,,	,,
16	222·		,, **LE**.	113-2.
17	221·7		,, **LϚ**.	112-1.
18	198· plated.		,, ,,	,,
19	206·8		,, **LZ**.	111.

P

No.	Wt. or Size.	Obverse.	Reverse.	Mint. Date.
			Copper.	
		ΒΑΣΙΛΙΣΣΗΣ ΚΛΕΟΠΑΤΡΑΣ Head of Zeus Ammon r., diademed.	ΠΤΟΛΕΜΑΙΟΥ ΒΑΣΙΛΕΩΣ Two eagles l. on thunderbolt; in front, double cornucopiæ; between legs of nearer eagle, 🜨.	
20	Size. 1·2		[Pl. xxvi. 7.]	Alexandria.
21	1·2			,,
22	1·15			,,
23	1·2			,,
		No inscr.; same type.	Similar; no monogram.	
24	1·35			Uncert.
25	1·35			,,
26	1·25			,,
27	1·15			,,
28	1·15			,,
29	1·15		[Pl. xxvi. 8.]	,,
30	1·15			,,
31	·8			,,
32	·8		cornucopiæ single.	,,
33	·9		(,,)	,,
34	·8		(,,)	,,
35	·7		(,,)	,,

Some of these coins may be of later periods up to the death of Ptolemy Soter II.

PTOLEMAEUS X., SOTER II.

No.	Wt. or Size.	Obverse.	Reverse.	Mint. — Date.
			Cyrenaica.	
			I. With Cleopatra III. B.C. 117–111?	
			Copper.	
		Head of Zeus Ammon r., diademed.	ΠΤΟΛΕΜΑΙΟΥ ΒΑΣΙΛΕΩΣ	
36	Size. 1·45		Two eagles l. on thunderbolt.	Uncert.
37	1·4		[Pl. xxvi. 9.]	,,
38	1·		to l., ⚹ (apple-branch.)	Berenice?
39	·85		,, ⚹ .	Uncert.
40	·85		,, ,,	,,
41	·8		,, ,,	,,
		Head of Zeus Ammon r., diademed.	ΠΤΟΛΕΜΑΙΟΥ ΒΑΣΙΛΕΩΣ Double cornucopiæ, bound with fillet, surmounted by two stars; on either side, $\frac{\Sigma}{\odot} \frac{\Omega}{E}$.	
42	·75			,,
43	·7			,,
44	·7		[Pl. xxvi. 10.]	,,
45	·75			,,
46	·7			,,
47	·8		(Π ΤΟΛΕΜΑΙΟΥ ΒΑΣΙΛΕΩΣ)	,,
		Similar.	Similar; on either side, Σ Ω.	
48	·7			,,
		Head of Zeus Ammon r., diademed.	ΒΑΣΙΛΕΩΣ ΠΤΟΛΕΜΑΙΟΥ (always incomplete). Headdress of Isis (globe, horns, plumes, and ears of corn, bound with fillet); beneath, ΣΩ.	
49	·55		[Pl. xxvi. 11.]	,,
50	·55			,,

108   THE PTOLEMAIC KINGS OF EGYPT.

No.	Wt. or Size.	Obverse.	Reverse.	Mint. — Date.
		Head of Zeus Ammon r., diademed.	ΒΑΣΙΛΕΩΣ ΠΤΟΛΕΜΑΙΟΥ (always incomplete). Headdress of Isis (globe, horns, plumes, and ears of corn, bound with fillet); beneath, ΣΩ.	
	Size.			
51	·55			Uncert.
52	·6			,,
		Similar.	Similar inscr. and type.	
53	·45			,,
54	·45			,,
55	·5			,,
56	·5			,,
		Head of Zeus Ammon r., diademed.	ΠΤΟΛΕΜΑΙΟΥ ΒΑΣΙΛΕΩΣ Two eagles l. on thunderbolt; to l., ⌁ (apple-branch).	
57	·8		[Pl. xxvi. 12.]	Berenice?
58	·7			,,

Egypt.

II. Alone, king of Egypt. B.C. 111–107-6.

Silver.

		Head of Ptolemaeus I. r., diademed and wearing aegis.	ΠΤΟΛΕΜΑΙΟΥ ΒΑΣΙΛΕΩΣ Eagle l. on thunderbolt; to r., ΠΑ.	Alexandria. B.C.
	Wt.			
59	216·		to l., ᛫H. [Pl. xxvii. 1.]	110-9.
60	212·		,, LH.	,,
61	221·6		,, LΘ.	109-8.
62	220·		,, ᛫Θ. [Pl. xxvii. 2.]	,,
63	219·		,, LI.	108-7.
64	215·8		,, ᛫I.	,,

No.	Wt. or Size.	Obverse.	Reverse.	Mint. — Date.
		\centering Cyprus. III. King of Cyprus. B.C. 107-6–88. *Silver.*		
65	Wt. 212·1	Head of Ptolemaeus I. r., diademed and wearing aegis.	ΠΤΟΛΕΜΑΙΟΥ ΒΑΣΙΛΕΩΣ Eagle l. on thunderbolt; to r., ΠΑ. to l., LIH. [Pl. xxvii. 3.]	Paphos. B.C. 100-99.
66	209·3 worn.	Similar.	Similar; to r., ΣΑ. to l., LKA.	Salamis. 97-6.
67	215·8	Similar.	Similar; to r., KI. to l., LK ⚡. [Pl. xxvii. 4.] (thunderbolt doubly winged.)	98-7.

(Later coins of Ptolemaeus Soter II., Period IV., as king of Egypt and Cyprus, B.C. 88–81, follow Ptolemaeus Alexander I.)

PTOLEMAEUS XI. ALEXANDER I. B.C. 114–88.

PERIODS OF REIGN.

I. King of Cyprus. B.C. 114-107-6.
II. King of Egypt. B.C. 107-6-88.
  a. With Cleopatra III. B.C. 107-6-99.
  β. Alone. B.C. 99-88.

I. King of Cyprus. B.C. 114–107-6.

Cyprus.

Silver.

No.	Wt. or Size.	Obverse.	Reverse.	Mint. Date.
		Head of Ptolemaeus I. r., diademed and wearing aegis.	ΠΤΟΛΕΜΑΙΟΥ ΒΑΣΙΛΕΩΣ Eagle l. on thunderbolt; to r., ΓΆ, ΓΑ.	Paphos. B.C.
1	Wt. 218·6		to l., LA; under r. wing, sceptre. [Pl. xxvii. 5.]	114-8.
2	198·		„ LΔ; „ „	111-0.
3	216·3		LZ „ ⚯·	108-7.
4	212·5		LH „ ✻; „ „	107-6.
5	215·5		„ „; „ „	„
6	214·3		„ LH; „ palm-branch. [Pl. xxvii. 6.]	„
7	186·		LH „ ⚯·	„
8	215·2		„ LΘ; „ „	106.
9	210·2		„ „ [Pl. xxvii. 7.]	„

PTOLEMAEUS XI., ALEXANDER I. 111

No.	Wt. or Size.	Obverse.	Reverse.	Mint. — Date.
	Wt.	Head of Ptolemaeus I. r., diademed and wearing aegis.	ΠΤΟΛΕΜΑΙΟΥ ΒΑΣΙΛΕΩΣ Eagle l. on thunderbolt; to r., ΣΑ.	
10	218·		to l., L E [Pl. xxvii. 8.]	Salamis. B.C. 110-9.
11	221·6		,, LΙ. [Pl. xxvii. 9.]	108-7.
		Similar.	Similar; to r., KI.	
12	220·2		to l., LΔ	Citium. 111-0.
13	220·6		,, LE	110-9. [Pl. xxvii. 10.]
14	203·		,, LϚ.	109-8.
15	218·6		,, LZ [Pl. xxvii. 11.]	108-7.
16	196·		,, LΘ.	106.

DIONYSIAC COINAGE.

		Bust of Ptolemaeus IV. as Dionysus r., wearing diadem entwined with ivy-wreath, and nebris; behind shoulder, thyrsus.	ΠΤΟΛΕΜΑΙΟΥ ΒΑΣΙΛΕΩΣ Eagle l. on thunderbolt, wings open.	
17	107·		[Pl. xxvii. 12.]	Uncert.
		(This coin is conjecturally here placed.)		

No.	Wt. or Size.	Obverse.	Reverse.	Mint.—Date.
			II. King of Egypt.	
			a. With Cleopatra III. B.C. 107-6–99.	
			1. Coins with dates of both sovereigns.	
			Silver.	
		Head of Ptolemaeus I. r., diademed and wearing aegis.	ΠΤΟΛΕΜΑΙΟΥ ΒΑΣΙΛΕΩΣ Eagle l. on thunderbolt; to r., ΠΑ.	
18	Wt. 223·		ᴸIA to l., H. [Pl. xxviii. 1.]	Alexandria. B.C. 107-6.
19	221·4		,, ,, ,,	,,
20	213·3		ᴸIB ,, Θ.	106-5.
21	224·2		,, ,, [Bank Coll.]	,,
22	218·8		,, ,, ,,	,,
23	217·3		,, ,, ,,	,,
24	212·7		ᴸIΓ ,, I. [Pl. xxviii. 2.]	105-4.
25	218·		,, ,, ,,	,,
26	211·		,, ,, ,,	,,
27	220·6		ᴸIE ,, IΓ.	102-1.
28	216·5	•	,, ,, ,,	,,

PTOLEMAEUS XI., ALEXANDER I.   113

No.	Wt. or Size.	Obverse.	Reverse.	Mint. Date.
		2. Coins with dates of Ptolemaeus XI. only.		
		Head of Ptolemaeus I. r., diademed and wearing aegis.	ΠΤΟΛΕΜΑΙΟΥ ΒΑΣΙΛΕΩΣ Eagle l. on thunderbolt; to r., ΠΑ.	Alexandria. B.C.
29	Wt. 218·8		to l., LIΔ.	101-0.
30	210·1		„ LIE.	100-99.
			β. Alone. B.C. 99–88.	
		Similar.	Similar.	
31	222·		to l., LIϚ.	99-8.
32	221·7		„ LIZ. [Pl. xxviii. 3.]	98-7.
33	220·		„ LIH.	97-6.
34	214·6		„ „	„
35	220·4		„ LIΘ.	96-5.
36	214·5		„ „	„
37	214·8		„ „ (ΠΑ).	„
38	219·3		„ „ „	„
39	215·		„ LK.	95-4.
40	221·4		„ „	„
41	218·3		„ LKA.	94-3.
42	221·		„ „ [Pl. xxviii. 4.]	„
43	226·5		„ „ [Pl. xxviii. 5.]	„
44	205· plated.		„ „	„
45	227·6		„ „ (KA).	„
46	217·6		„ LKB.	93-2.
47	223·3		„ „	„
48	201·8 worn.		„ LKΓ.	92-1.

Q

114   THE PTOLEMAIC KINGS OF EGYPT.

No.	Wt. or Size.	Obverse.	Reverse.	Mint. Date.
		Ptolemaeus X. Soter II. ?		
		Cyprus ?		
		Copper.		
68	Size. 1·35	.... Head of Zeus Ammon r., diademed.	ΠΤΟΛΕΜΑΙΟΥ ΒΑΣΙΛΕΩΣ Two eagles l. on thunderbolt; in front, winged thunderbolt, upright. [Pl. xxviii. 6.]	Uncert.
69	1·3	Similar type.	Same inscr.; similar type; in front, eagle l. on thunderbolt. [Pl. xxviii. 7.]	,,
		Ptolemaeus X. Soter II.		
		Period IV. King of Egypt and Cyprus. B.C. 88–81.		
		Egypt.		
		Silver.		
70	Wt. 219·5	Head of Ptolemaeus I. r., diademed and wearing aegis.	ΠΤΟΛΕΜΑΙΟΥ ΒΑΣΙΛΕΩΣ Eagle l. on thunderbolt; to r., ΠΑ. to l., ᒪΚΘ. [Pl. xxviii. 8.]	Alexandria. B.C. 88.
		Ptolemaeus (Apion), King of Cyrene ? B.C. 114 ?–96.		
		Cyrenaica.		
		Copper.		
1	Size. ·45	Head of Zeus Ammon r., diademed.	B A Eagle l. on thunderbolt. [Pl. xxviii. 9.]	Uncert.
2	·5			,,
3	·5			,,
4	·45			,,

PTOLEMAEUS XIII., NEUS DIONYSUS. B.C. 81–52.

I. First Reign. B.C. 81–58.

Egypt.

Silver.

No.	Wt. or Size.	Obverse.	Reverse.	Mint. — Date.
		Head of Ptolemaeus I. r., diademed and wearing aegis.	ΠΤΟΛΕΜΑΙΟΥ ΒΑΣΙΛΕΩΣ Eagle l. on thunderbolt; under r. wing, palm; to l., ⚓ ; to r., ΠΑ.	Alexandria. B.C.
1	Wt. 205·3 worn.		to l., ∟A̲*.	81-0.
2	214·5		,, ∟B. [Pl. xxix. 1.]	80·79.
3	221·		,, ,,	,,
4	176· worn.		,, ∟Γ.	79-8.
5	199·8 worn.		,, ∟Δ̲*.	78-7.
6	211·8		,, ∟Δ.	,,
7	201·6 worn.		,, ∟H.	. 74-3.
8	206·8 worn.		,, ∟Θ.	73-2.
9	213·6		,, ,, [Pl. xxix. 2.]	,,
10	181·5		,, ∟I.	72-1.
11	201·		,, ,,	,,
12	203·7 worn.		,, ∟IA.	71-0.
13	202·		,, ∟IB.	70-69.
14	210·9		,, ∟IΓ.	69-8.
15	202·1		,, ,,	,,
16	197·5		,, ∟IΔ.	68-7.

THE PTOLEMAIC KINGS OF EGYPT.

No.	Wt. or Size.	Obverse.	Reverse.	Mint. — Date.
17	Wt. 208·2	Head of Ptolemaeus I. r., diademed and wearing aegis.	ΠΤΟΛΕΜΑΙΟΥ ΒΑΣΙΛΕΩΣ Eagle l. on thunderbolt; under r. wing, palm; to l., ⚵; to r., ΠΑ. to l., ⌐IE.	Alexandria. B.C. 67-6.
18	199·5		„ ⌐IϚ.	66-5.
19	211·6		„ ⌐IZ.	65-4.
20	213·7		„ ⌐IH.	64-3.
21	213·8		„ „	„
22	207·5		„ „	„
23	202·5		„ ⌐IΘ.	63-2.
24	197·5		„ „	„
25	204·5		„ ⌐K.	62-1.
26	211·		„ ⌐KB.	60-59.

II. SECOND REIGN. B.C. 55-52.

Silver.

No.	Wt. or Size.	Obverse.	Reverse.	Mint. — Date.
27	216·6	Head of Ptolemaeus I. r., diademed and wearing aegis.	ΠΤΟΛΕΜΑΙΟΥ ΒΑΣΙΛΕΩΣ Eagle l. on thunderbolt; under r. wing, palm; to l., ⚵; to r., ΠΑ. to l., ⌐KZ. [Pl. XXIX. 3.]	55-4.
28	216·4		„ „	„
29	212·8		„ „	„
30	219·		„ „	„
31	182·8		„ „	„
32	212·5		„ ⌐KH.	54-3.
33	219·5		„ „	„

PTOLEMAEUS XIII., NEUS DIONYSUS.   117

No.	Wt. or Size.	Obverse.	Reverse.	Mint. — Date.
34	Wt. 42·3 worn.	Head of Ptolemaeus I. r., diademed and wearing aegis.	ΠΤΟΛΕΜΑΙΟΥ ΒΑΣΙΛΕΩΣ Eagle l. on thunderbolt; under r. wing, palm; to l., ⚱ ; to r., ΠΑ. to l., ∟ΚΗ .	Alexandria. B.C. 54-3.
35	222·6		„ ∟ΚΘ .	53-2.
36	206·9		„ „	„
37	147·6		„ ∟Λ .	52.

PTOLEMAEUS, KING OF CYPRUS. B.C. 81-58.

Cyprus.

Silver.

No.	Wt. or Size.	Obverse.	Reverse.	Mint. Date.
1	Wt. 219·2	Head of Ptolemaeus I. r., diademed and wearing aegis.	ΠΤΟΛΕΜΑΙΟΥ ΒΑΣΙΛΕΩΣ Eagle l. on thunderbolt; to r., ΠΑ. to l., LA. [Pl. xxix. 4.]	Paphos. B.C. 81-0.
2	214·8		,, LB.	80-79.
3	219·		,, ,, [Bank Coll.]	,,
4	219·1		,, ,,	,,
5	214·7		,, LΓ.	79-8.
6	218·3		,, ,,	,,
7	212·5		,, ,,	,,
8	221·8		,, LΔ.	78-7.
9	219·5		,, LE.	77-6.
10	193·2		,, LϚ.	76-5.
11	216·1		,, LZ.	75-4.
12	233·6		,, ,, (beneath, L., Θ; die altered?)	,,
13	213·7		,, LH.	74-3.
14	213·		,, ,, [Pl. xxix. 5.]	,,
15	214·6		,, LΘ.	73-2.
16	202·5		,, ,,	,,
17	218·6		,, LI.	72-1.
18	211·2		,, ,,	,,

No.	Wt. or Size.	Obverse.	Reverse.	Mint. — Date.
19	Wt. 220·3	Head of Ptolemaeus I. r., diademed and wearing aegis. (Same die.)	ΠΤΟΛΕΜΑΙΟΥ ΒΑΣΙΛΕΩΣ Eagle l. on thunderbolt; to r., ΠΑ. to l, ⌐IA .	Paphos. B.C. 71-0.
20	193·		,, ,, (Same die.)	,,
21	223·2		,, ⌐IB .	70-69.
22	219·3		,, LIΓ . [Pl. xxix. 6.]	69-8.
23	222·3		,, ,,	,,
24	217·		,, ⌐IΔ .	68-7.
25	206·7		,, ,,	,,
26	209·5		,, ,,	,,
27	221·2		,, ,,	,,
28	221·2		,, ,,	,,.
29	190·5		,, ⌐IE .	67-6.
30	208·		,, ⌐IᏟ .	66-5.
31	182·8		,, ,,	,,
32	223·1		,, ,,	,,
33	202·5		,, ⌐IZ .	65-4.
34	192·6		,, ,,	,,
35	216·8		,, ,, [Pl. xxix. 7.]	,,
36	181 8		,, ⌐IH .	64-3.
37	207·3		,, ,,	,,
38	187·8		,, ⌐IΘ .	63-2.
39	159·		,, ⌐K .	62-1.
40	189·5		,, ,,	,,

No.	Wt. or Size.	Obverse.	Reverse.	Mint. — Date.
41	Wt. 188·7	Head of Ptolemaeus I. r., diademed and wearing aegis.	ΠΤΟΛΕΜΑΙΟΥ ΒΑΣΙΛΕΩΣ Eagle l. on thunderbolt; to r., ΠΑ. to l., ᴸΚΑ.	Paphos. B.C. 61-0.
42	171·5		,, ,,	,,
43	166·		,, ᴸΚΒ. [Pl. xxix. 8.]	60-59.
44	157·5		,, ,,	,,
45	124·8		,, ᴸΚΓ.	59-58.
46	174·		,, ,,	,,

Copper.

No.	Size.	Obverse.	Reverse.	Mint. Date.
47	1·05	Head of Zeus Ammon r., diademed.	ΠΤΟΛΕΜΑΙΟΥ ΒΑΣΙΛΕΩΣ Eagle l. on thunderbolt; in front, Δ, surmounted by star of eight rays. [Pl. xxx. 1.]	Uncert.
48	1·05	Similar.	Similar; in front, aplustre. [Pl. xxx. 2.]	,,
49	1·05			,,
50	1·			,,
51	1·05			,,
52	1·05	Similar.	Similar; under eagle's r. wing, palm; to r., ⸙. [Pl. xxx. 3.]	,,
53	1·			,,

Roman Rule.
B.C. 58–47.
No Coins.

No.	Wt. or Size.	Obverse.	Reverse.	Mint. Date.
		_____ PTOLEMAEUS XV. AND ARSINOË IV. ? B.C. 47. Cyprus. *Copper.*		
1	Size. ·95	Head of Zeus Ammon r., diademed.	ΠΤΟΛΕΜΑΙΟΥ ΒΑΣΙΛΕΩΣ Two eagles l. on thunderbolt; in front, head-dress of Isis, horns, globe, and plumes, on stand. [Pl. xxx. 4.]	Uncert. B.C. 47.
2	·9			,,
3	·95		head-dress of Isis, without stand.	,,
4	1·		no symbol.	,,
5	·95		,,	,,

R

No.	Wt. or Size.	Obverse.	Reverse.	Mint. – Date.

CLEOPATRA VII. PHILOPATOR. B.C. 52–30.

I. Cleopatra VII. and Ptolemaeus XIV. B.C. 52–49.
II. Ptolemaeus XIV. B.C. 49–48.
III. Cleopatra VII. B.C. 48–47.
IV. Cleopatra VII. and Ptolemaeus XV. B.C. 47–44.
V. Cleopatra VII. and Ptolemaeus XVI. Cæsar. B.C. 45–30.

III. Cleopatra VII. B.C. 48–47.

Egypt.

Silver.

No.	Wt.	Obverse	Reverse	Mint. Date.
1	Wt. 45·9	Head of Cleopatra VII. r., diademed.	ΚΛΕΟΠΑΤΡΑΣ ΒΑΣΙΛΙΣΣΗΣ Eagle l. on thunderbolt; under r. wing, palm; to r., ΠΑ; to l., ⚹ to l., L⌐. [Pl. xxx. 5.]	Alexandria. B C. 47.

V. Cleopatra VII. and Ptolemaeus XVI. Cæsar. B.C. 45–30.

Cyprus.

Copper.

| 2 | Size. 1·15 | Bust of Cleopatra VII. r., as Aphrodite, wearing stephane, and Ptolemaeus XVI. Cæsar l., as Eros, in her arms; behind her shoulder, sceptre. | ΚΛΕΟΠΑΤΡΑΣ ΒΑΣΙΛΙΣΣΗΣ Two cornuacopiæ, joined at the bottom and bound with fillet; to r., below, ⚹. [Pl. xxx. 6.] | Uncert. |
| 3 | 1·15 | | | ,, |

Egypt

Copper.

No.	Wt. or Size.	Obverse.	Reverse.	Mint. — Date.
			Bust of Cleopatra VII. r., diademed.	ΚΛΕΟΠΑΤΡΑΣ ΒΑΣΙΛΙΣΣΗΣ Eagle l. on thunderbolt; to l., double cornucopiæ; to r., Π .	
4	Size. 1·05			Alexandria.
5	1·05		[Pl. xxx. 7.]	,,
		Similar type.	Similar; to r., M .	
6	·85		[Bank Coll.]	Uncert.
7	·8			,,
8	·8			,,
9	·9		[Pl. xxx. 8.]	,,
10	·8			,,
11	·85		(M)	,,

124 THE PTOLEMAIC KINGS OF EGYPT.

No.	Wt. or Size.	Obverse.	Reverse.	Mint.—Date.
		PTOLEMAEUS XVI. CÆSAR. Cyprus? *Copper.*		
1	Size. ·95	Bearded head r., laur. ?	ΠΤΟΛΕΜΑΙΟΥ ΦΙΛΟΜΗΤ ΘΕΟ ⊥Δ . . . . . . ? Eagle r. on thunderbolt, wings open; on breast, countermark, ✣ . [Pl. xxx. 9.]	Uncert.

(This coin has been tooled in the inscription.)

INDEX I.

GEOGRAPHICAL.

A.

Ace, 27.
Ace? 28.
Alexandria, 36, 93, 98, 105, 106, 108, 112–117, 122, 123.
Alexandria? 10, 23, 40, 55, 56.
Amathus? 71.
Apollonia (Cyrenaïcae), 11, 37.
Apollonia? 11.

B.

Berenice (Euesperides), 60, 76, 77.
Berenice? 60, 107, 108.
Berytus, 54, 72.

C.

Citium, 16, 44, 62, 71, 72, 85, 86, 91, 92, 97, 104, 105, 111.
Citium? 5, 43, 61.
Cos? 9, 16.
Cyrene, 11, 59, 60.

D.

Daphnae (Aegypti)? 23.

E.

Ephesus, 59.
Euesperides. (*See* Berenice.)

G.

Gaza, 35, 39.
Gaza and Joppa. (*See* Joppa and Gaza.)

I.

Idalium? 46, 47.
Joppa, 32, 34, 35, 42, 49, 54.
Joppa and Gaza, 35.

M.

Miletus? 20.
Mint, Central, of Phoenicia? 49, 51, 52.
Mylasa? 19

P.

Paphos, 3, 7, 15, 68, 80, 83, 84, 87, 89, 95, 96, 104, 109, 110, 118-120.
Paphos ? 2, 3, 5, 69, 78.
Ptolemaïs (Phoen.), 28, 33, 34, 42, 49, 50, 53, 54, 65, 86.
Ptolemaïs (Aegypti), 10, 23, 36.

S.

Salamis (Cypri), 16, 62, 69, 70, 81, 84, 90, 91, 96, 97, 109, 111.

Salamis ? 7, 70, 71.
Sidon, 27, 29, 30, 42, 48, 52, 64.
Sidon ? 52, 64.

T.

Tripolis (Phoeniciae), 72.
Tripolis ? 72.
Tyre, 27, 28, 31, 32, 42, 48, 53, 64, 73.
Tyre ? 48.

INDEX II.

TYPES.

A.

Alexander the Great, Head of, with horn of Zeus Ammon, 3, 5, 6.
—hair long, 8, 9, 10.—in elephant's skin and aegis, 1–6, 14, 16, 18, 19, 21, 47, 52, 56, 57, 66.
Antiochus IV., Head of, 81.
Apple-wreath. (*See* Club in.)
Apollo, Head of, 11.
Apollo, Bust of, with Cleopatra I. as Artemis, 79.
Apollo seated, 81.
Aphrodite, Head of, 7.— ? 7.
Arsinoë II., Head of, with horn of Ammon, veiled, 42.—with sceptre, 42 – 45. (*See* also Ptolemaeus II. and Arsinoë II.)
Arsinoë III., Bust of, with sceptre, 67.—Head of, 67.
Artemis, Cleopatra I. as. (*See* Apollo.)

B.

Berenice I., Bust of. (*See* Ptolemaeus I.)
Berenice II., Bust of, 61.—veiled, 59, 60.—Head of, 60.—veiled, 60, 61.

C.

City (Sidon ?) on advancing Prow, 52.
Cleopatra I., Head of, as Isis, 78, 79, 89, 93, 94.
Cleopatra I. with Zeus Sarapis. (*See* Zeus Sarapis.)
Cleopatra II. or III., Head of, in elephant's skin, 96, 98.
Cleopatra VII., Bust of, as Aphrodite, with Ptolemaeus XVI. Caesar as Eros in her arms, 122.
Club and Eagle. (*See* Cornucopiae, Club and Eagle.)
Club in apple-wreath, 60.
Cornucopiae, 59, 60, 67.—and Pilei of Dioscuri, 60.—and star, 67. —and two stars, 59, 60.
Cornucopiae, Double, 42–45, 67, 98, 122.—and two stars, 107.
Cornucopiae, Radiate, 56.—and two stars, 72.
Cornucopiae, Club, and Eagle, 61.

E.

Eagle and Club. (*See* Cornucopiae, Club, and Eagle.)

Eagle on Thunderbolt, 7, 9, 10, 13-25, 27-36, 39, 43, 46-57, 61-65, 68-74, 78, 80-87, 89-93, 95-98, 100-105, 108-114, 118-120, 123.—on r. wing, cornucopiae, 65.—on l. wing, cornucopiae, 55, 69, 73.—on l. wing, double cornucopiae, 75. — under r. wing, palm, 110, 115-117, 120, 122.—under r. wing, sceptre, 72, 110.—under l. wing, sceptre, 80, 82, 91, 92.—under l. wing, thyrsus, 91, 92.

Eagle on Thunderbolt, looking back, 88.—on right wing, cornucopiae, 79.—on l. wing, cornucopiae, 68, 78.—on r. wing, double cornucopiae, 79.—under r. wing, caduceus, 72.

Eagle on Thunderbolt, wings open, 3, 5, 7, 8, 10-12, 14-26, 39, 46, 47, 57, 58, 61, 63, 66, 86, 89, 93-99, 111, 124.—on left wing, cornucopiae, 66.

Eagle on Thunderbolt, wings open, looking back, 37, 75.

Eagles, Two, on Thunderbolts, 32, 34, 48, 49, 51, 52, 105-108, 114, 121.

H.

Head, bearded, 124.
Headdress of Isis. (*See* Isis, Headdress of.)
Herakles, bearded, Head of, 63, 69, 72.
Horse, Free, galloping, 38.

I.

Isis, Head of, 81. (*See* Zeus Sarapis with Cleopatra I. as Isis.)
Isis, Headdress of, 107, 108.

L.

Libya, Head of, 38, 39, 76, 77, 83.

M.

Magas, Head of, 38.
Male bust, Young, helmeted, 69.
Male head, Young, helmeted, 69.

N.

Nike, bearing wreath and palm, 11.
Nilus, Head of, 75.

O.

Oar-blade in olive-wreath, 60.
Olive-wreath. (*See* Oar-blade.)

P.

Pallas, Bust of, 72.
Pallas, Head of, 63.
Pallas Promachos, 2-5.
Prow, 37. (*See* City on Prow.)
Ptolemaeus I., Head of, 9-11, 13-25, 27-39, 46, 48-55, 62, 64, 65, 68-71, 73, 76, 77, 79, 80, 83-85, 89-93, 95-98, 100-105, 108-120.
Ptolemaeus I. and Berenice I., Busts of, jugate, 40, 41.
Ptolemaeus II., Head of, 39.

Ptolemaeus II. and Arsinoë II., Busts of, jugate, 40, 41.
Ptolemaeus III., Bust of, laureate, 56.
Ptolemaeus III., Bust of, wearing radiate diadem, with sceptre-trident, 56.
Ptolemaeus III., Head of, lion's skin round neck, 47.
Ptolemaeus IV., Bust of, 64.
Ptolemaeus IV., Bust of, as Dionysus, with thyrsus, 63, 86, 99, 111.
Ptolemaeus IV., Head of, 65.
Ptolemaeus V., Bust of, 68, 72, 74.
Ptolemaeus VI., Head of, 86.
Ptolemaeus XVI., Caesar. (*See* Cleopatra VII.)

Q.

Quadriga of Elephants, in which Alexander as young Ammon? 11.

S.

Sea-horse, Fore-part of, 37.
Sidon? Figure of. (*See* City.)

T.

Thunderbolt, Winged, 38.

Z.

Zeus, Head of, 12, 14, 15, 17–22, 24–26, 28, 46, 47, 51, 65, 66, 70, 71.
Zeus Aetophoros, seated, 1, 2.
Zeus Ammon, Head of, 32, 34, 37, 48, 49, 51–58, 62, 65, 66, 70, 73–75, 80–82, 85–88, 94, 95, 97, 98, 105–108, 114, 121.
Zeus Sarapis, Head of, 81.
Zeus Sarapis, Bust of, with Cleopatra I. as Isis, 79.

INDEX III.

SYMBOLS.

A.

Agalma. —— Uncert. Phoenicia or Syria, 55.
Apple-branch. — Euesperides-Berenice, 76. Berenice? 107, 108.
Aplustre.——Cyprus, 4, 8, 85, 91, 104, 111.

B.

Bee.—Uncert., 5; Ephesus, 59.
Buckler.—Ptolemaïs Aegypt., 10, 23, 36; Cypr. 24-26, 46, 47; Alexandria? Uncert. Aegypt.? 40, 41; Phoen., 55.

C.

Caduceus.—Cypr., 111.
Cap of Osiris.—Salamis, 70; Amathus, 71.
Club.—Cypr., 5; Citium, 104, 111; Salamis, 109; Cos? 9, 16; Tyre, 27, 28, 31, 32, 48, 53, 64, 73; Cyrenaïca, 77.
Corn, Ear of.—Phoen., 52; Citium, 85.

Cornucopiae.—Cypr., 47, 57; Paphos? 69; Phoen., 54, 65; Alex.? 55, 56; Aegypt., 56, 57, 66, 74; Cyrenaïca, 57.
Cornucopiae, Double.—Phoen. 54; Alex., 123; Uncert. Aegypt., 123; Euesperides-Berenice, 76; Cyrenaïca 77.
Crab.—Apollonia Cyr., 11, 37.

D.

Dioscuri, Pilei of. (*See* Pilei.)
Dolphin.—Phoen., 86; Cyrenaïca? 39.

E.

Eagle on Thunderbolt.—Cypr., 3; Cypr.? 2, 3; Cyrenaïca 6; Uncert. 5, 6. 114.
Ear of Corn. (*See* Corn, Ear of).

F.

Flower.—Cyrenaïca, 107.

H.

Harpa.—Joppa, 54.

Headdress of Isis. (*See* Isis, Headdress of.)
Helmet, Crested.—Cypr., 82, 86; Citium, 85; Salamis, 84.
Helmet, without crest.—Cypr. 4, 8.

I.

Isis, Headdress of. — Cypr. 121; Alex., 115–117, 122.

L.

Lotus.—Citium, 85, 86; Paphos, 104; Salamis, 70; Salamis ? 71; Aegypt., 80–82.

M.

Modius.—Citium, 92; Paphos, 95; Salamis, 91.

O.

Osiris. (*See* Cap of Osiris.)

P.

Palm.—Tripolis, Phoen., 72.
Petasus.—Citium, 91, 92, 97; Salamis, 69, 70, 90, 96; Cypr., 99.
Pilei of Dioscuri.—Salamis, 69, 70.
Pileus of Dioscuri.—Salamis, 70.

R.

Race-torch ? (*See* Torch.)

S.

Sceptre.—Citium, 92.
Silphium.—Cyrene, 11; Euesperides-Berenice, 60; Cyrenaica, 83.
Spear-head.—Phoen., 73; Aegypt.? 40.
Star.—Citium, 85, 92, 97; Paphos, 110; Salamis, 84; Salamis ? 71; Cypr., 4, 5, 86; Alex., 115.
Stars, Two.—Paphos, 96.

T.

Thunderbolt.—Uncert., 1, 2, 114.
Thyrsus.—Salamis, 90.
Torch ? Race-, Cyrenaica, 39.
Trident.—Berytus, 54, 72; Euesperides-Berenice, 60.
Tripod.—Ptolemaïs, Phoen., 65.

W.

Wheel.—Euesperides-Berenice, 60.
Wreath.—Paphos, 7, 95, 110; Salamis ? 7; Cypr., 99.

INDEX IV.

KINGS AND GOVERNORS.

A.

Alexander IV., 1–6.
Antiochus IV., Epiphanes, 81.
Arsinoë II., Philadelphos, 42–45.
Arsinoë III., Philopator, 67.
Arsinoë III. and Ptolemaeus IV., 67.
Arsinoë IV. and Ptolemaeus XV. ? 121.

B.

Berenice I. and Ptolemaeus I., 40, 41.
Berenice II., 59–61.
Berenice II. and Ptolemaeus III. ? 61.

C.

Cleopatra I., 78, 79.
Cleopatra II. and Ptolemaeus VI. ? 98.
Cleopatra II. or III. and Ptolemaeus VIII., 95, 96.
Cleopatra III. and Ptolemaeus X., 104–108.
Cleopatra III. and Ptolemaeus XI., 112, 113.

Cleopatra VII., 122, 123.
Cleopatra VII. and Ptolemaeus XVI. Caesar, 122, 123.

E.

Eulaeus and Lenaeus, 80, 81.

M.

Magas, 6, 11, 12, 37–39.

P.

Polycrates, 68.
Ptolemaeus (Apion), King of Cyrene ? 114.
Ptolemaeus, King of Cyprus, 118–120.
Ptolemaeus I. (Soter I.), 1–12.
Ptolemaeus I. and Berenice I., 40, 41.
Ptolemaeus I. and II., 13–23.
Ptolemaeus II. (Philadelphus), 24–39.

KINGS AND GOVERNORS.

Ptolemaeus II. and Arsinoë II., with Ptolemaeus I. and Berenice I., 40, 41.
Ptolemaeus II., 43, 44.
Ptolemaeus III. (Euergetes I.), 46–58.
Ptolemaeus III. and Berenice II., 61.
Ptolemaeus IV. (Philopator I.), 62–66. —? 86, 99, 111.
Ptolemaeus IV. and Arsinoë III., 67.
Ptolemaeus V. (Epiphanes), 68. (*See* also 40, 44.)
Ptolemaeus VI. (Philometor I.), 78–87, 89, 90, 91, 93. (*See* also —? 41—45.)
Ptolemaeus VI. and Ptolemaeus VII., Introd. lxvii, lxviii.
Ptolemaeus VI. and Ptolemaeus VIII., 82, 83.
Ptolemaeus VII. (Eupator), and Ptolemaeus VI. Introd. lxvii, lxviii.
Ptolemaeus VIII. (Euergetes II.), 82, 83, 84–86, 88, 89. —? 100. (*See* also 45.)
Ptolemaeus VIII. and Cleopatra II. or III., 95, 96.
Ptolemaeus VIII. and Ptolemaeus IX., 96.
Ptolemaeus IX. (Philopator II.), 96.
Ptolemaeus VIII. or X., 45.
Ptolemaeus X. (Soter II.) 104–109, 114.
Ptolemaeus X. and Cleopatra III., 104–108.
Ptolemaeus XI. (Alexander I.), 110–113.
Ptolemaeus XI. and Cleopatra III., 112, 113.
Ptolemaeus XV. and Arsinoë IV. ? 121.
Ptolemaeus XVI. (Caesar), 124.
Ptolemaeus XVI. and Cleopatra VII., 122, 123.

T.

Theodotus ? 64, Introd. li.

TABLE
OF
THE RELATIVE WEIGHTS OF ENGLISH GRAINS AND FRENCH GRAMMES.

Grains.	Grammes.	Grains.	Grammes.	Grains	Grammes.	Grains.	Grammes.
1	·064	41	2·656	81	5·248	121	7·840
2	·129	42	2·720	82	5·312	122	7·905
3	·194	43	2·785	83	5·378	123	7·970
4	·259	44	2·850	84	5·442	124	8·035
5	·324	45	2·915	85	5·508	125	8·100
6	·388	46	2·980	86	5 572	126	8·164
7	·453	47	3·045	87	5·637	127	8·229
8	·518	48	3·110	88	5·702	128	8·294
9	·583	49	3·175	89	5·767	129	8·359
10	·648	50	3·240	90	5·832	130	8·424
11	·712	51	3·304	91	5·896	131	8·488
12	·777	52	3·368	92	5·961	132	8·553
13	·842	53	3·434	93	6·026	133	8·618
14	·907	54	3·498	94	6·091	134	8·682
15	·972	55	3·564	95	6 156	135	8·747
16	1·036	56	3·628	96	6·220	136	8·812
17	1·101	57	3·693	97	6·285	137	8·877
18	1·166	58	3·758	98	6·350	138	8·942
19	1·231	59	3·823	99	6·415	139	9·007
20	1·296	60	3·888	100	6·480	140	9·072
21	1·360	61	3·952	101	6·544	141	9·136
22	1·425	62	4·017	102	6·609	142	9·200
23	1·490	63	4·082	103	6·674	143	9·265
24	1·555	64	4·146	104	6·739	144	9·330
25	1·620	65	4·211	105	6·804	145	9·395
26	1·684	66	4·276	106	6·868	146	9·460
27	1·749	67	4·341	107	6·933	147	9·525
28	1·814	68	4·406	108	6·998	148	9·590
29	1·879	69	4·471	109	7·063	149	9·655
30	1·944	70	4·536	110	7·128	150	9·720
31	2·008	71	4·600	111	7·192	151	9·784
32	2·073	72	4·665	112	7·257	152	9·848
33	2·138	73	4·729	113	7·322	153	9·914
34	2·202	74	4·794	114	7·387	154	9·978
35	2·267	75	4·859	115	7·452	155	10·044
36	2·332	76	4·924	116	7·516	156	10·108
37	2 397	77	4·989	117	7·581	157	10·173
38	2·462	78	5·054	118	7·646	158	10·238
39	2·527	79	5·119	119	7·711	159	10·303
40	2·592	80	5·184	120	7·776	160	10·368

TABLE
OF
THE RELATIVE WEIGHTS OF ENGLISH GRAINS AND FRENCH GRAMMES.

Grains	Grammes.	Grains	Grammes.	Grains	Grammes.	Grains.	Grammes.
161	10·432	201	13·024	241	15·616	290	18·79
162	10·497	202	13·089	242	15·680	300	19·44
163	10·562	203	13·154	243	15·745	310	20·08
164	10·626	204	13·219	244	15 810	320	20·73
165	10·691	205	13·284	245	15·875	330	21 38
166	10·756	206	13·348	246	15·940	340	22·02
167	10·821	207	13·413	247	16·005	350	22·67
168	10·886	208	13·478	248	16 070	360	23·32
169	10·951	209	13·543	249	16·135	370	23·97
170	11·016	210	13·608	250	16·200	380	24·62
171	11·080	211	13·672	251	16·264	390	25·27
172	11·145	212	13·737	252	16·328	400	25 92
173	11·209	213	13·802	253	16·394	410	26·56
174	11·274	214	13·867	254	16·458	420	27·20
175	11·339	215	13·932	255	16·524	430	27·85
176	11·404	216	13 996	256	16·588	440	28·50
177	11·469	217	14·061	257	16 653	450	29·15
178	11·534	218	14·126	258	16·718	460	29·80
179	11·599	219	14·191	259	16·783	470	30 45
180	11·664	220	14·256	260	16·848	480	31·10
181	11·728	221	14·320	261	16·912	490	31·75
182	11·792	222	14 385	262	16 977	500	32·40
183	11·858	223	14·450	263	17 042	510	33·04
184	11·922	224	14·515	264	17·106	520	33·68
185	11·988	225	14·580	265	17·171	530	34·34
186	12·052	226	14 644	266	17·236	540	34·98
187	12·117	227	14 709	267	17·301	550	35·64
188	12·182	228	14·774	268	17·366	560	36·28
189	12·247	229	14·839	269	17·431	570	36·93
190	12·312	230	14·904	270	17·496	580	37·58
191	12·376	231	14·968	271	17·560	590	38·23
192	12·441	232	15·033	272	17·625	600	38 88
193	12·506	233	15·098	273	17·689	700	45·36
194	12·571	234	15·162	274	17·754	800	51·84
195	12·636	235	15·227	275	17·819	900	58·32
196	12·700	236	15·292	276	17·884	1000	64·80
197	12·765	237	15·357	277	17·949	2000	129 00
198	12·830	238	15·422	278	18·014	3000	194·40
199	12·895	239	15·487	279	18·079	4000	259·20
200	12·960	240	15·552	280	18·144	5000	324 00

TABLE

FOR

CONVERTING ENGLISH INCHES INTO MILLIMÈTRES AND THE MEASURES OF MIONNET'S SCALE.

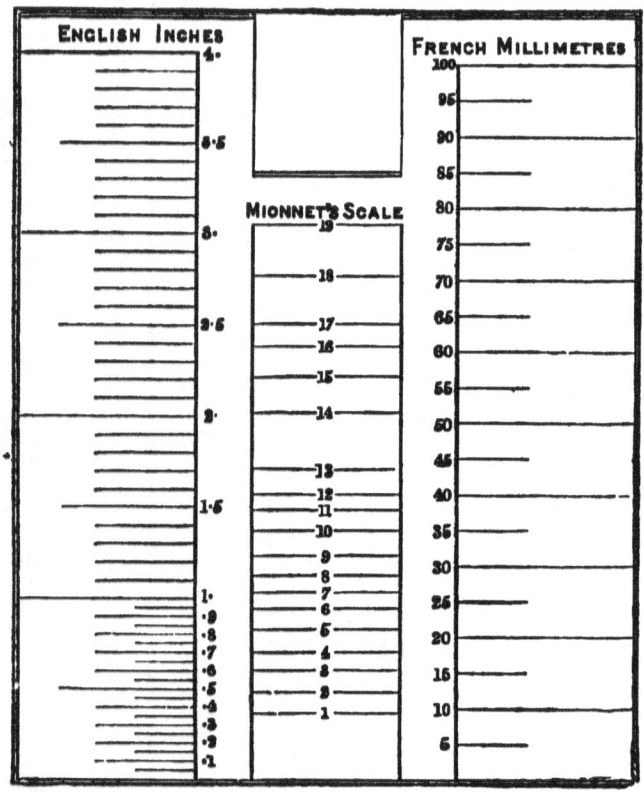

Lagidae I.

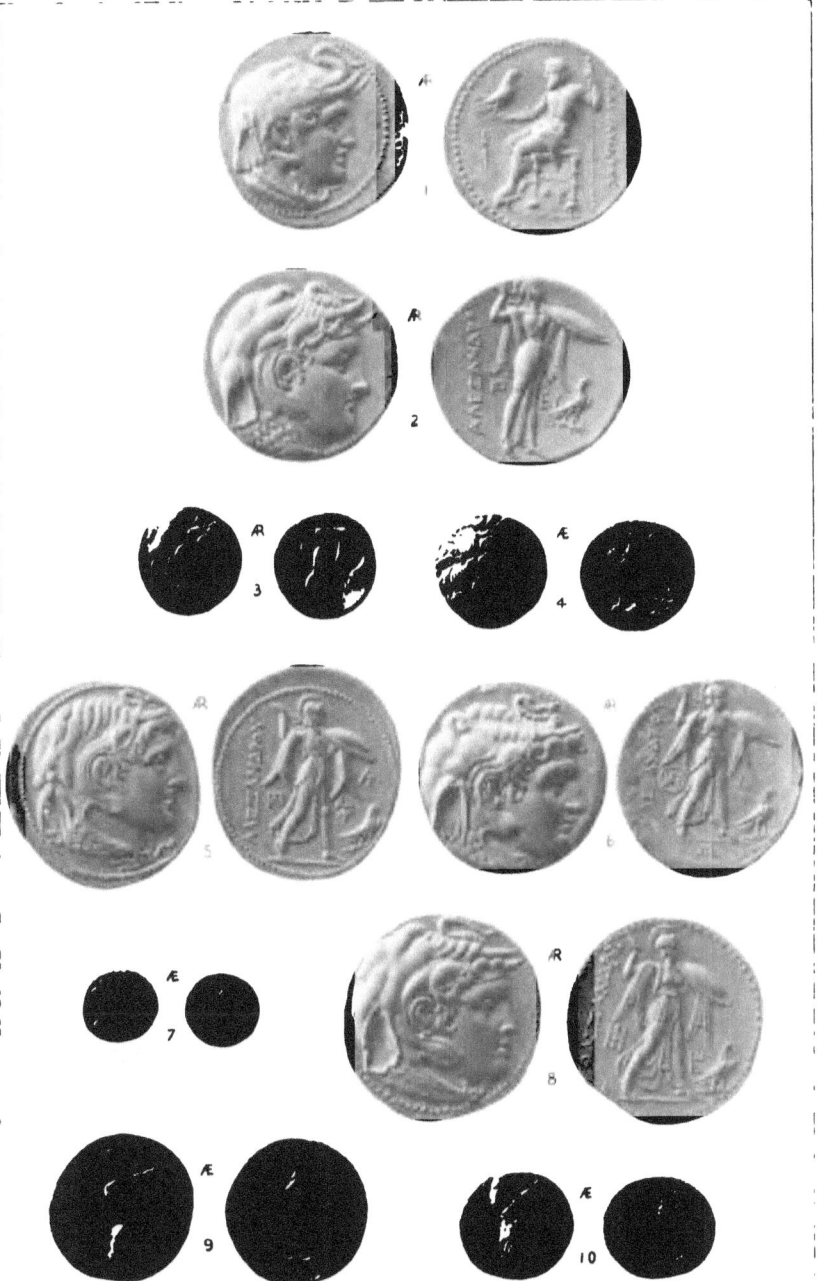

PTOLEMAEUS SOTER AS GOVERNOR

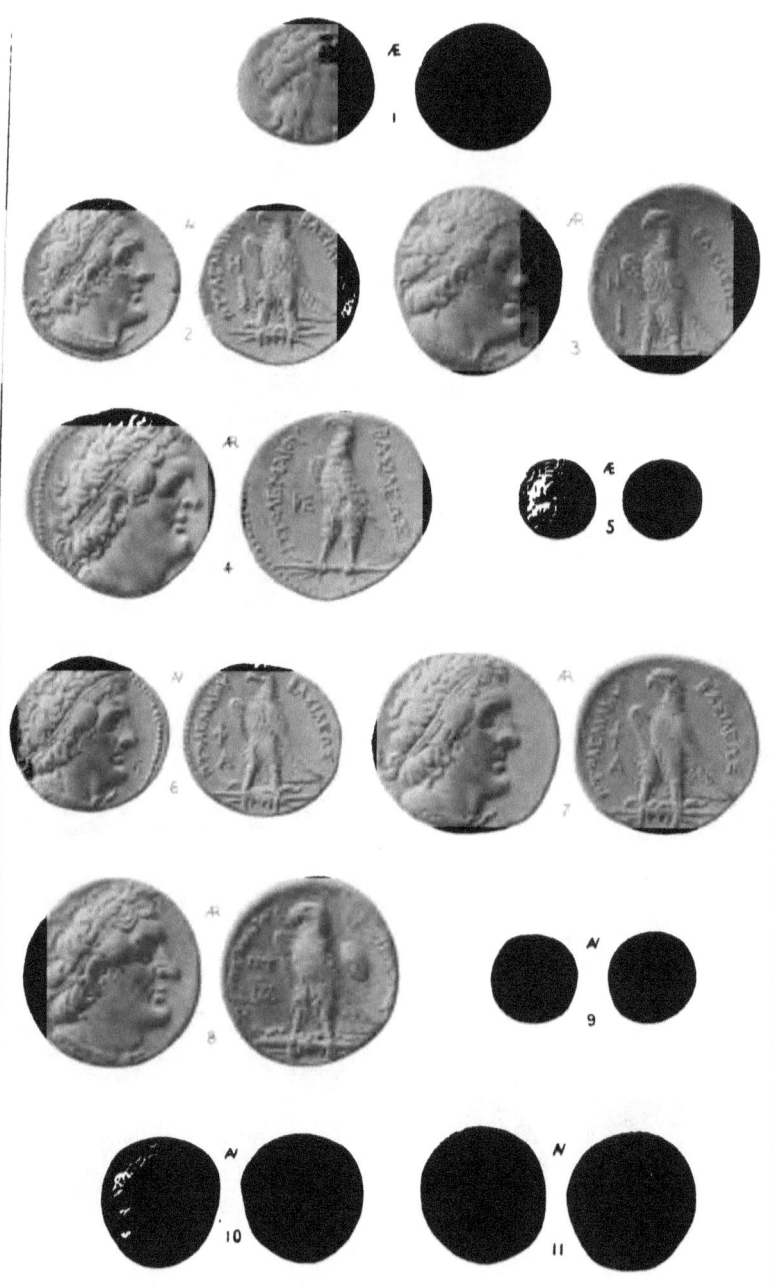

PTOLEMAEUS SOTER.

PTOL. SOTER AND PTOL. PHILADELPHUS.

Lagidae IV.

PTOLEMAEUS PHILADELPHUS.

Lagidae V.

PTOLEMAEUS PHILADELPHUS.

Lagidae VI.

PTOLEMAEUS PHILADELPHUS, MAGAS.

Lagidae VII.

PTOLEMAEUS PHILADELPHUS AND FAMILY.

Lagidae VIII.

ARSINOE PHILADELPHOS.

Lagidae IX.

PTOLEMAEUS EUERGETES.

Lagidae XI.

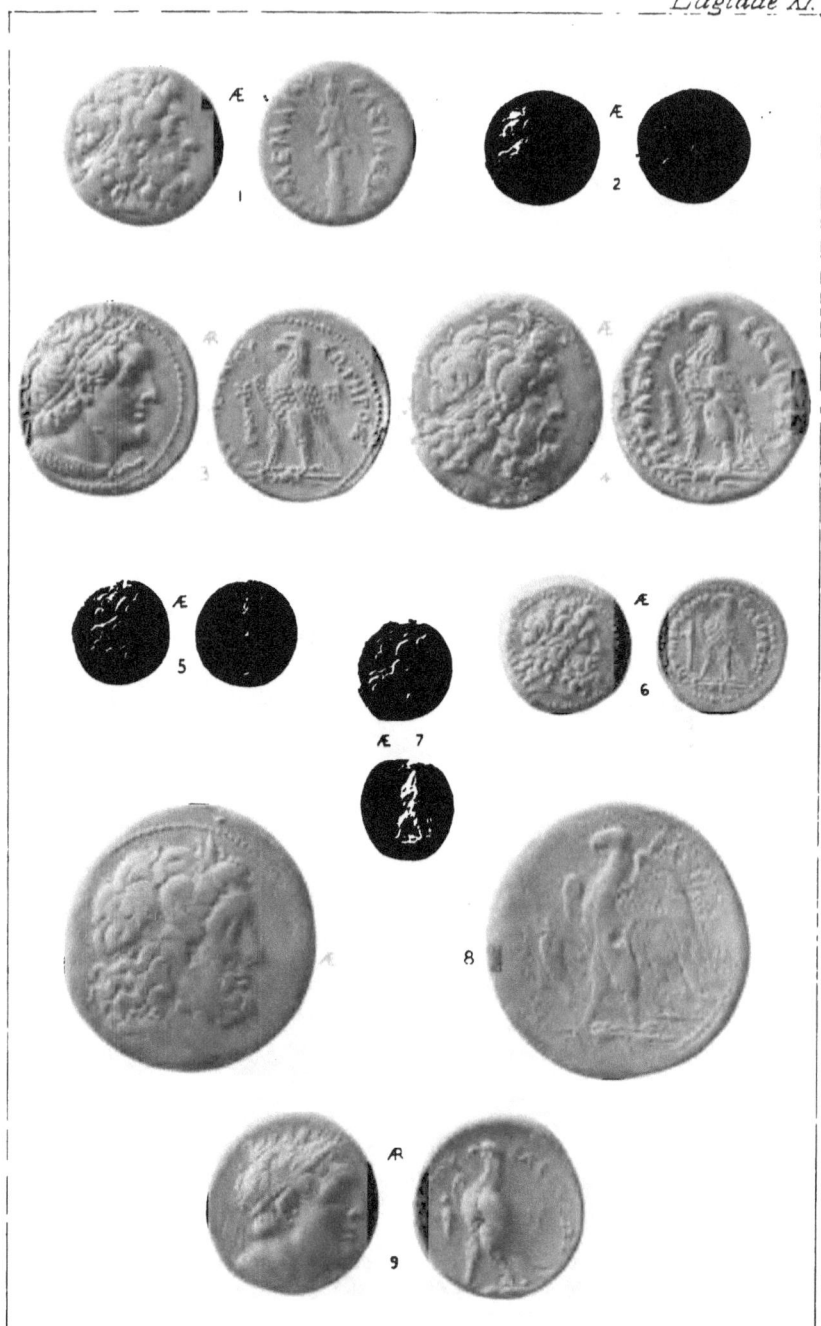

PTOLEMAEUS EUERCETES.

Lagidae XII.

PTOLEMAEUS EUERCETES.

Lagidae XIII.

PTOL. EUERCETES, BERENICE II.

Lagidae XIV.

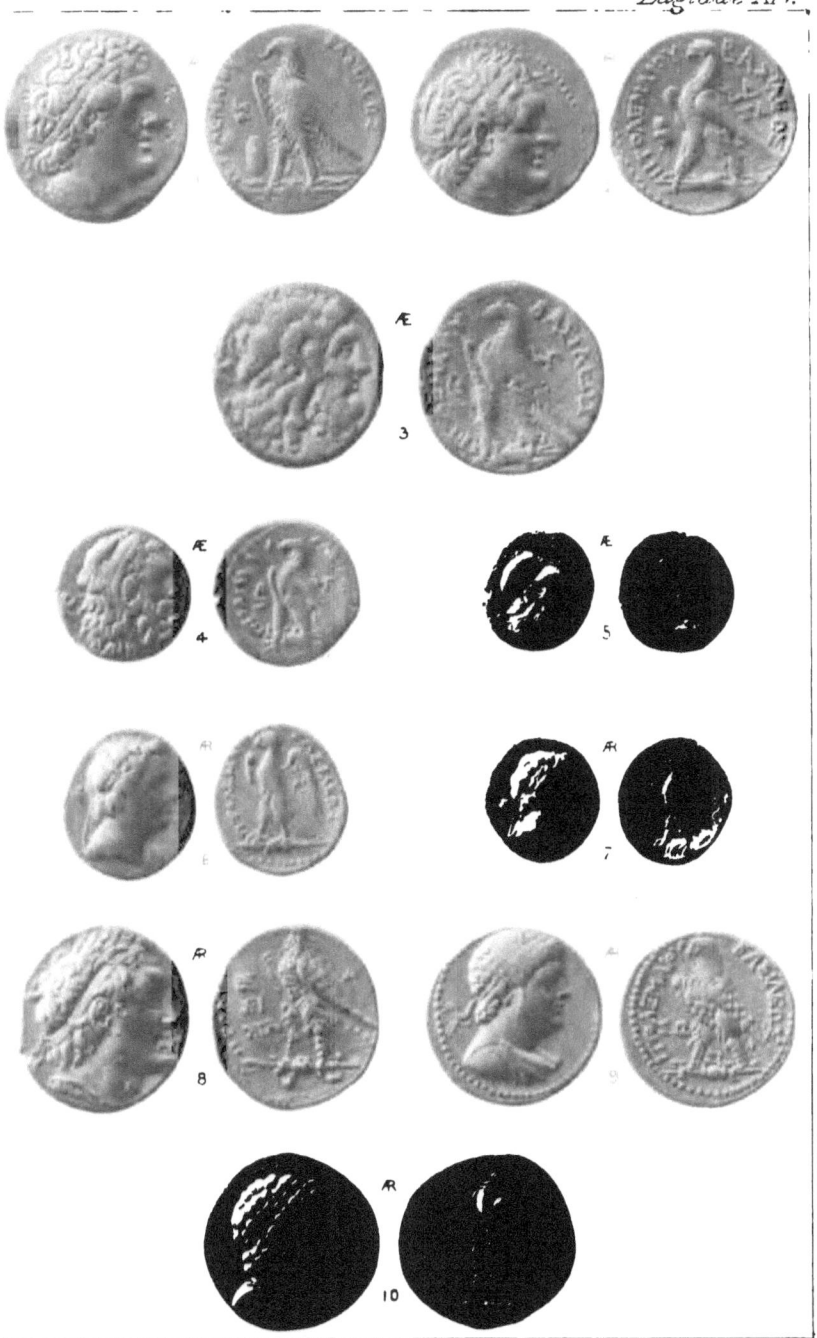

PTOLEMAEUS PHILOPATOR.

Lagidae XVI.

PTOLEMAEUS EPIPHANES.

Lagidae XVII.

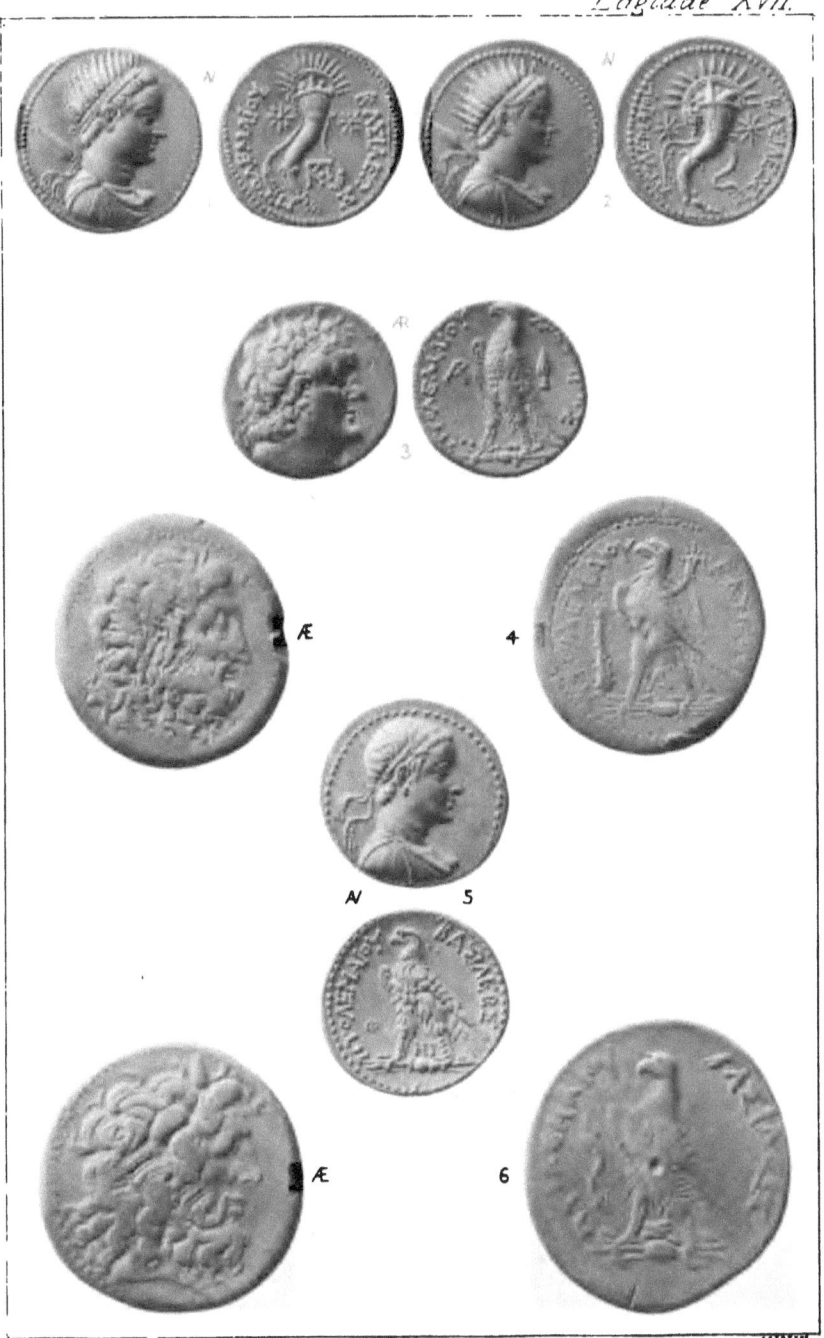

PTOLEMAEUS EPIPHANES.

Lagidae XIX.

PTOLEMAEUS PHILOMETOR.

Lagidae XX.

PTOLEMAEUS PHILOMETOR.

PTOLEMAEUS EUERCETES II.

PTOLEMAEUS EUERCETES II, ETC.

COINS OF AN ERA.

Lagidae XXVI.

PTOLEMAEUS SOTER II AND CLEOPATRA III.

Lagidae XXVII.

PTOL. SOTER II.   PTOL. ALEXANDER I.

Lagidae XXVIII.

PTOL. ALEXANDER I AND CLEOPATRA III,

Lagidae XXX.

PTOL. KING OF CYPRUS, CLEOPATRA VII,

Lagidae XXXI.

COINS WITH PORTRAITS, NOT EGYPTIAN CURRENCY.

Lagidae XXXII.

ILLUSTRATIVE COINS (2-10 NOT IN BRIT. MUS.)

Lagidae XXIX.

PTOL. NEUS DIONYSUS, PTOL. KING OF CYPRUS.

Lagidae XXX.

PTOL. KING OF CYPRUS, CLEOPATRA VII,

Lagidae XXXI.

COINS WITH PORTRAITS, NOT EGYPTIAN CURRENCY.

Lagidae XXXII.

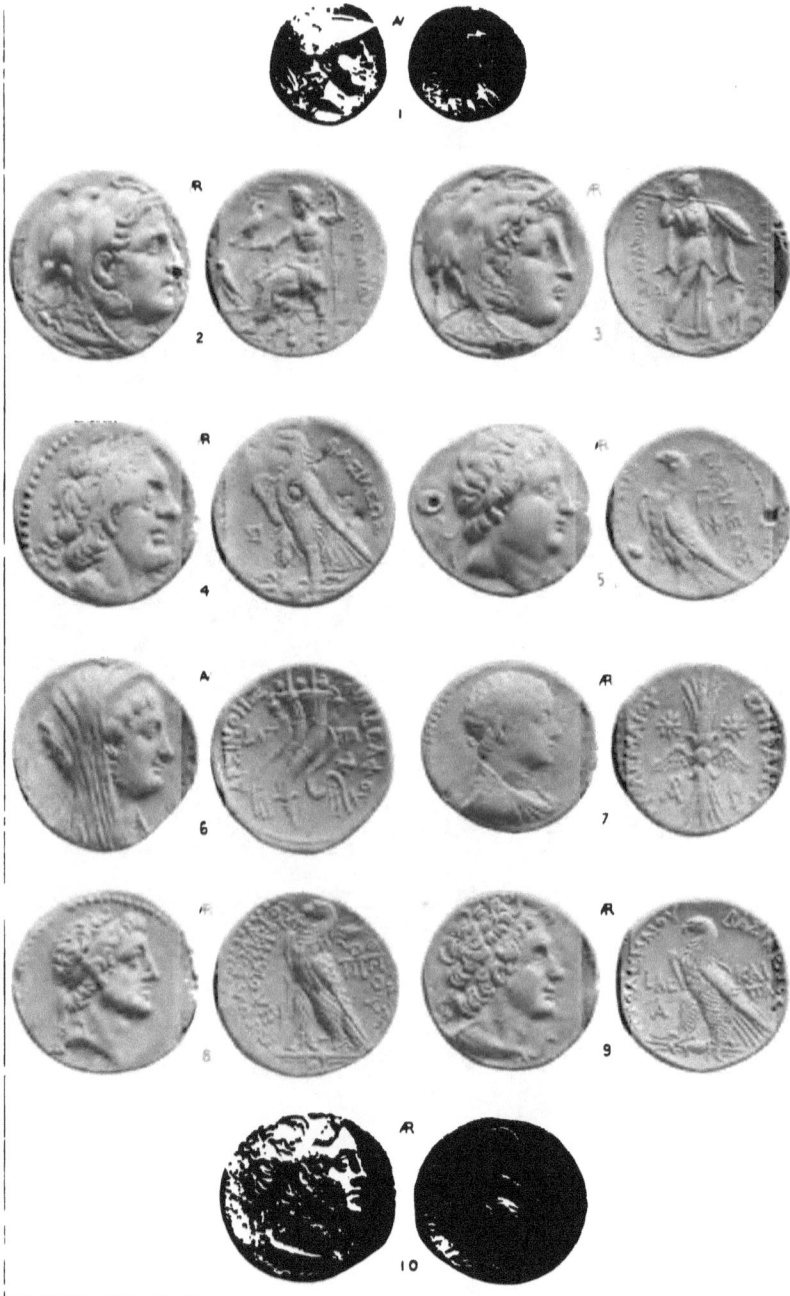

ILLUSTRATIVE COINS (2-10 NOT IN BRIT. MUS.)

www.ingramcontent.com/pod-product-compliance
Lightning Source LLC
Chambersburg PA
CBHW020327170426
43200CB00006B/293